RILLINGTON PLACE

uncovered editions

Titles in the series

uncovered editions

RILLINGTON PLACE

∞◦◊◊◦∞

London: The Stationery Office

First published 1966 Cmmd. 3101
© Crown Copyright

This abridged edition
© The Stationery Office 1999
Reprinted with permission.

ISBN 0 11 702417 1

A CIP catalogue record for this book is available from the
British Library.

Printed in the UK by Biddles Limited, Guildford, Surrey
J93523   C50   11/99

Uncovered Editions are historic official papers which have not previously been available in a popular form. The series has been created directly from the archive of The Stationery Office in London, and the books have been chosen for the quality of their story telling. Some subjects are familiar, but others are less well known. Each is a moment of history.

Since 1949 there have been two government enquiries into these matters, this one of 1965 and the Scott Henderson inquiry of 1953. There have also been a number of private enquiries which are referred to here.

(By) The warrant under which I was appointed to hold this Inquiry . . . I am called upon to report such conclusions as I may find it possible to form. If the evidence permits me to come to a conclusion on the balance of probability, I must do so.

DANIEL BRABIN

August 1966

‹‹❦››

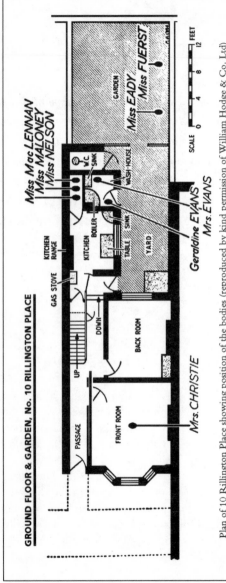

Plan of 10 Rillington Place showing position of the bodies (reproduced by kind permission of William Hodge & Co. Ltd)

Timothy Evans was 25 years of age on 20th November 1949. He had spent much of his boyhood in Merthyr Vale where he was born. In about 1935 his family moved to London but Evans later returned to Merthyr Vale for about two years. Beryl Evans was aged 18 at the time of their marriage on 20th September 1947. She was then employed at a telephonist at Grosvenor House, Park Lane, London. After living with the Evans family for about seven months the young couple went to live at 10 Rillington Place. On 10th October 1948 their daughter Geraldine was born. Evans was last employed as a van driver by a firm of confectioners in Lancaster Road, London, W.11. Save for writing digits, single letters and his signature or reading a few simple words Evans could neither read nor write, having missed much schooling due to an injury to his foot when he was about eight years of age.

At 3.10 p.m. on Wednesday 30th November 1949, Timothy Evans entered the Enquiry Office at the Central Police Station, Merthyr Tydfil. He was seen by Detective Sergeant, then Detective Constable, G. H. Evans. Evans wished to see a Sergeant or an Inspector. He was told that this was not possible, and he then said: "I want to give myself up. I have disposed of my wife." "What do you mean?" said the Constable. Evans replied "I put her down the drain." The officer told Evans to think again before he said any more, and Evans said "I know what I am saying. I cannot sleep and I want to get it off my chest." The officer then cautioned Evans and asked him whether he wished to make a statement in writing about this. Evans replied "I will tell you all about it and you can write it down. I am not very well educated and cannot read or write." Constable Evans fetched Detective Sergeant Gough and then invited Evans to tell them in his own way what had happened and told him that it would all be written down afterwards. Evans then made an oral statement which on completion was dictated to Constable Evans. The writing began at 3.20 p.m. The dictation was slow and there were long pauses so that the officer at times had to tell Evans to continue. Although unaware of the facts disclosed in the statement Constable Evans thought that it was taking a very long time in the telling, longer than a statement of such length would normally take, and it appeared to the police officer that Evans was not remembering events that had happened, but trying to remember what he had said earlier. The police officer did not take long to form the opinion that Evans was a "terrible liar" and was "telling a cock and bull story."

The statement was finished at 5.10 p.m. It read:

"About the beginning of October, my wife, Beryl Susan Evans, told me that she was expecting a baby. She told me that she was about three months gone. I said, 'If you are having a baby, well you've had one, another one won't make any difference.' She then told me she was going to try and get rid of it. I turned round and told her not to be silly that she'd make herself ill. Then she bought herself a syringe and started syringing herself. Then she said that didn't work and I said, 'I'm glad it won't work.' Then she said she was going to buy some tablets. I don't know what tablets she bought because she was always hiding them from me. She started to look very ill and I told her to go and see a doctor and she said she'd go when I was in work but when I'd come home and ask her if she'd been she'd always say that she hadn't. On the Sunday morning that would be the sixth of November she told me that if she couldn't get rid of the baby she'd kill herself and our baby Geraldine. I told her she was talking silly.

She never said no more about it then, but when I got up Monday morning to go to work she said she was going to see some woman to see if she could help her. Who the woman was she didn't tell me and that if she wasn't in when I came home she'd be up her grandmother's. Then I went to work. I loaded up my van and went on my journey.

About 9 o'clock that morning I pulled up at a Transport cafe between Ipswich and Colchester. I can't say exactly where it is, that's the nearest I can give. I went up to the counter and ordered a cup of tea and breakfast and I sat down by the table with my cup of tea waiting for my breakfast to come up and there was a man sitting by the table opposite me. He asked me if I had a cigarette I could give him. I gave him one and he started talking about married life. He said to me, 'You are looking pretty worried, is there anything on your mind?' Then I told him all about it. So he said, 'Don't let that worry you I can give you something that can fix it.' So he said, 'Wait there a minute, I'll be back,' and he went outside. When he came back he handed me a little bottle that was wrapped up in brown paper. He said, 'Tell your wife to take it first thing in the morning before she has any tea, and then to lay down on the bed for a couple of hours and that should do the job.' He never asked no money for it. I went up to the counter and paid my bill and carried on with my journey.

After I finished my work I went home, that would be between seven and eight. When I got in the house I took off my overcoat and hung it on the peg behind the kitchen door. My wife asked me for a cigarette and I told her there was one in my pocket, then she found this bottle in my pocket and I told her all about it. Then I had my tea and sat down and read the papers and listened to the wireless. We went to bed at ten o'clock. I got up in the morning as usual at six o'clock to go to work. I made myself a cup of tea and made a feed for the baby. I told her then not to take that stuff when I went in and said 'Good morning' to her and I went to work, that would be about half past six. I finished work and got home about half past six in the evening. I then noticed that there was no lights in the place. I lit the gas and it started to go out and I went in the bedroom to get a penny and I noticed my baby in the cot. I put the penny in the gas and went back in the bedroom and lit the gas in the bedroom. Then I saw my wife laying in the bed. I spoke to her but she never answered me, so I went over and shook her, then I could see she wasn't breathing. Then I went and made some food for my baby. I fed my baby and I sat up all night. Between about one and two in the morning I got my wife downstairs through the front door. I opened the drain outside my front door that is No. 10 Rillington Place, and pushed her body head first into the drain. I closed the drain then I went back in the house. I sat down by the fire smoking a cigarette.

I never went to work the following day. I went and got my baby looked after. Then I went and told my governor where I worked that I was leaving. He asked me the reason and I told him I had a better job elsewhere. I had my cards and money that afternoon then I went to see a man about selling my furniture. The man came down and had a look at my furniture and he offered me £40 for it. So I accepted the £40. He told me he wouldn't be able to collect the furniture until Monday morning. In the meanwhile I went and told my mother that my wife and baby had gone for a holiday. I stopped in the flat till Monday. The van come Monday afternoon and cleared the stuff out. He paid me the money. Then I caught the five to one train from Paddington and I come down to Merthyr Vale and I've been down here ever since. That's the lot.

(Signed) T. J. EVANS."

Constable Evans was anxious about the baby referred to in the statement and he thought that Evans was unconcerned about her and said so. The officer became annoyed with Evans and asked to be told the whereabouts of the child. The answer was evasive. He said that she was somewhere in London with friends. When pressed for fuller details Evans said that he had told his aunt, Mrs. Lynch, with whom he had been staying, that the baby was with some friends from Newport, and it was the police officer's view that he was expected to believe this also. The officer said that Evans did not want to talk about the child at all. Eventually Evans said that the child had been handed over to Reginald Christie who also lived at 10 Rillington Place.

At 6 p.m. Evans was put under arrest on reasonable suspicion of having committed a felony. This discussion about the child had taken about an hour, and at 6.08 p.m. Constable Evans telephoned Scotland Yard and immediately afterwards Notting Hill Police Station. He thinks that it was to Detective Sergeant Corfield that he spoke when he outlined the story and asked for the drain to be examined. Scotland Yard passed on a Metropolitan Police telegram. It read as follows:

METROPOLITAN POLICE TELEGRAM

"To (CH) SUPT.FH FROM IR.
30-11-49

The following telephone message received from Police Merthyr Tydfil (TELE 541) begins:

A man named Timothy John Evans has come to this Station this afternoon and stated that on 8–11–49 at 10 Rillington Place, W.11, his wife had a miscarriage at that address, after which she apparently drank some liquid which he obtained from a lorry driver some time previous at a cafe between Chelmsford and Ipswich. During the night of 9-11-49 between 1 a.m. and 2 a.m. he disposed of his wife's body down a manhole or drain outside that address. He handed his 14 month old child to a man named Reginald Christie at the same address who stated he could have the child taken care of. He also sold the furniture and left the address. Will you please cause enquiries to be made. A written statement has been taken from Evans. Ends.

Forwarded for necessary action on directions of CH/SUPT.

This message was forwarded at 6.46 p.m. but would have been telephoned through to Notting Hill on its receipt at Scotland Yard. It contains two mistakes in transmission in that it refers to the wife taking liquid after her miscarriage and Chelmsford has been substituted for Colchester.

From Notting Hill police station various officers went to 10 Rillington Place. They now disagree amongst themselves about the identity of all their fellow officers, but Sergeant Corfield, Detective Inspector then Detective Constable Byers, and Detective Sergeant then Detective Constable McCann were there. At 10 Rillington Place there was a drain in front of the ground floor bay window and another in the back garden. There was a manhole cover in the middle of the road. The officers had difficulty in removing the front drain cover, and the noise they made brought Christie to the door. According to Sergeant Corfield Christie was asked about Beryl Evans and her child. He said that they had both left some time ago. Constable McCann's recollection is that the period spoken about was a few days and that Christie gave the police the address where Evans' mother could be found.

It is Constable Evans' recollection that he received a message from London that the drain cover could not be removed and a request to confirm the genuineness of the information, whereupon he asked the Metropolitan Police to persevere with their efforts. Eventually with the aid of tyre levers the drains were opened. There was no sign of a body. This information was telephoned to Wales, and also that the front drain cover had obviously not been off for many years.

At 9 p.m. as appears in the Merthyr Tydfil police Occurrence Book which Constable Evans fortunately preserved from destruction, Evans was again seen by Constable Evans. He was told that the drain had been examined and was empty and that it was as much as three men could do to move it. He insisted that he had put the body there and when asked who helped him to remove the lid he claimed to have done it himself. Eventually the officer told Evans that he did not think that his wife's body had ever been in the drain, whereupon Evans replied "I said that to protect a man named Christie. It's not true about the man in the cafe either. I will tell you the truth now."

Thereupon Evans, at his own request, made a second statement. This statement took a long time to dictate, being completed at 11.50 p.m. There was still some hesitation in the making of it and at times Constable Evans had to say "Carry on, tell me what happened." Comparing the manner in which these two statements were given, Constable Evans thought that, in the second, Evans seemed more sure of his facts. He spoke with greater fluency and more spontaneously, although on this occasion the officer said that he did not have a prior oral statement with which to compare it as he had when the first statement had been given. The officer said that Evans appeared to be recalling events as they happened, but he would go no further than to say that the second statement was given in a more impressive manner than the first. He thought that the pauses were long, as can be seen from the time the statement took, for though not in his view a very long statement it had taken 2 hours and 40 minutes to dictate.

That second statement reads as follows:—

"The only thing that is not true in the statement I made to you this afternoon is the part about meeting the man in the cafe and about disposing of my wife's body. All the rest is true. As I was coming home from work one night, that would be about a week before my wife died, Reg Christie who lived on the ground floor below us approached me and said, 'I'd like to have a chat with you about your wife taking these tablets. I know what she's taking them for she's trying to get rid of the baby. If you or your wife had come to me in the first place I could have done it for you without any risk.' I turned around and said, 'Well I didn't think you knew anything about medical stuff.' So he told me then that he was training for a doctor before the war. Then he started showing me books and things on medical. I was just as wise because I couldn't understand one word of it because I couldn't read. Then he told me that the stuff that he used one out of every ten would die with it. I told him that I wasn't interested so I said goodnight to him and I went upstairs.

When I got in my wife started talking to me about it. She said that she had been speaking to Mr. Christie and asked me if he had spoken to me. I said 'Yes' and I told her what he had spoke to me about. I turned round and told her that I told him I didn't want nothing to do with it and I told her she wasn't to have anything to do with it either. She turned round and told me to mind my own business and that she intended to get rid of it and that she trusted Mr. Christie. She said he could do the job without any trouble at all.

On the Monday evening, that was the seventh of November when I came home from work my wife said that

Mr. Christie had made the arrangements for first thing Tuesday morning. I didn't argue with her, I just washed and changed and went to the pub until 10 o'clock. I came home and had supper and went to bed. She wanted to start an argument but I just took no notice. Just after six I got up the following morning to go to work. My wife got up with me. I had a cup of tea and a smoke and she told me, 'On your way down tell Mr. Christie that everything is alright. If you don't tell him I'll go down and tell him myself.' So as I went down the stairs he came out to meet me and I said, 'Everything is alright.' Then I went to work

When I came home in the evening he was waiting for me at the bottom of the staircase. He said, 'Go on upstairs I'll come behind you.' When I lit the gas in the kitchen he said, 'It's bad news. It didn't work.' I asked him where was she. He said, 'Laying on the bed in the bedroom.' Then I asked him where was the baby. So he said, 'The baby's in the cot.' So I went in the bedroom I lit the gas then I saw the curtains had been drawn. I looked at my wife and saw that she was covered over with the eiderdown. I pulled the eiderdown back to have a look at her. I could see that she was dead and that she had been bleeding from the mouth and nose and that she had been bleeding from the bottom part. She had a black skirt on and a check blouse and kind of a light blue jacket on. Christie was in the kitchen. I went over and picked my baby up. I wrapped the baby in a blanket and took her in the kitchen. In the meanwhile Mr. Christie had lit the fire in the kitchen. He said, 'I'll speak to you after you feed the baby.' So I made the baby some tea and boiled an egg for her, then I changed the baby and put her to sit in front of the fire.

Then I asked him how long my wife had been dead. He said, 'Since about three o'clock.' Then he told me that my wife's stomach was septic poisoned. He said, 'Another day and she'd have to have gone to hospital.' I asked him what he had done but he wouldn't tell me. He then told me to stop in the kitchen and he closed the door and went out. He came back about a quarter of an hour later and told me that he had forced the door of Mr. Kitchener's flat and had put my wife's body in there. I asked him what he intended to do and he said, 'I'll dispose of it down one of the drains.' He then said, 'You'd better go to bed and leave the rest to me.' He said, 'Get up and go to work in the morning as usual' and that he'd see about getting someone to look after my baby. I told him that it was foolish to try to dispose of the body and he said, 'Well that's the only thing I can do or otherwise I'll get in trouble with the Police.' He then left me.

Before I went to bed I took the eiderdown and one blanket off the bed and put them in a cupboard in the bedroom. I got up next morning about six o'clock. I made myself a cup of tea and made the baby some breakfast and fed her and changed her and put her back into her cot. Christie had told me that he was going to look after the baby that day so I went to work. I saw Christie before I went and he told me that he would slip up and feed the baby during the day. I had wanted to take the baby to my mother the night before but he said not to as it would cause suspicion straight away. He also told me in the morning that he knew a young couple over in East Acton who would look after the baby and he'd go over and see them. When I came home from work on that Wednesday night at five or six Christie told me that the young couple from East Action would be in Thursday to take the baby. I fed the baby that night and was playing with her by the fire when Christie came in. He said, 'In the morning when you get up feed the baby and dress her then put her back in the cot, the people will be here just after nine in the morning to fetch her.' He said, 'I've told them to knock three knocks and I'll let them in.' He also told me to pack some clothes for the baby. I did all that in the morning before I went to work. I saw him as I was going out that morning about half past six and told what I had done.

About half past five that evening I came home. I went upstairs and as I got in the kitchen, he came up behind me. He told me that the people had called and took the baby with them and to pack the rest of her things and he had a case and would take them over to East Acton with the pram and her chair later in the week. I then asked him how did he dispose of my wife's body. He said he put it down one of the drains. That's all he said to me then he went downstairs. Later that evening I went around to see my mother, Mrs. Thomasina Probert, at No. 11, St. Marks Road, London, W.11. She asked me where Beryl and the baby was. I told her they had gone away on a holiday. When I left my mother's place that night I went up to the pub to have a drink. I didn't go to work on the Friday as I had finished there on Thursday. On that Thursday evening Christie said, 'Now the best thing you can do is to sell your furniture and get out of London somewhere.' I just said, 'All right.'

On the Friday I went up to see a man in Portobello Road about selling my furniture. He came down on the Friday afternoon and said it was worth £40. He told me he would pick it up on the following Monday. On the Friday I went to the pictures and the pub then went home to sleep. On the Saturday I did the same thing. On Sunday afternoon I went to see a rag dealer. I met him outside a cafe in Ladbrook Grove, that's where he lives. I told him that if he came down to my place on the Monday there was quite a lot of rags he could have. I got up about six o'clock on the Monday morning and ripped up all my wife's clothes and the eiderdown and cut up the blanket. The man came around just after nine o'clock and he took about two sack fulls and I didn't take nothing off him for them. About three o'clock the furniture van came. They cleared all the furniture out and the bed clothes and lino and the furniture man paid me £40 which I signed for. The only things left in the house then was the vases, a clock, some dishes, saucepans and a bucket and the case with the baby's clothes, her pram and small chair. Christie had all that stuff. He asked me where I was going to go and I told him I didn't know. Then I got my case I took it up to Paddington, left it in the luggage department until half past twelve that evening. I went to the pictures and a pub and then I went to Paddington again and picked up my case about half past twelve that evening and caught the five to one train to Cardiff. I got into Merthyr Vale about twenty to seven in the morning, then went to 93, Mount Pleasant and I've been there ever since.

(Signed) T.J. EVANS.

This statement was made to me between 9.10 p.m. and 11.50 p.m. on Wednesday 30th November 1949, at the Criminal Investigation Department, Central Police Station, Merthyr Tydfil. It was read over to Evans in the presence of Detective Sergeant Gough before he signed it as being true.

(Signed) G. H. EVANS. D/Cons. 53
(Signed) G. H. GOUGH. D/Sgt."

Sergeant Gough has a limited recollection of the Evans incident, no doubt because his subordinate Constable Evans in the main carried out the police inquiries and investigations. Sergeant Gough does remember that on hearing that Beryl Evans' body had been put down the drain he examined a copy of the Police Gazette for 29th November 1949 and found within it reference to the unidentified body of a woman wearing a wedding ring which had been washed up at Seaford. The Sergeant asked Evans whether his wife had been wearing a wedding ring when he last saw her and Evans said that she had. Sergeant Gough went no further in his inquiry. After the second statement had been signed and witnessed Constable Evans again pressed for more information about the child, for she was now said to be with friends of Christie's in East Action, and Christie was now declared to be the abortionist whose acts had killed the child's mother.

It was not until further questions had been put to him that Evans asked Constable Evans to communicate with the police in London so that they might tell Evans' mother about the child. The message was passed to London. Constable Evans said that he was satisfied that there was something very wrong going on. He thought that Evans was incapable of telling the truth, and there came a time when he wanted the Metropolitan Police to come and take Evans away.

At Notting Hill enquiries were conducted by Detective Inspector Black, who in 1963 retired as Detective Superintendent after 36 years service. He is the holder of the Queen's Police Medal. He was stationed at Kensington Police Station but at this time was temporarily in charge at Notting Hill also. Inspector Black went to 10 Rillington Place. This was a small squalid dwelling house in a seedy neighbourhood. It consisted of three floors each occupied as a flat. None was self-contained. There was a communal staircase. The ground floor flat was occupied by Christie and Mrs. Christie. It consisted of a sitting room in the front, a bedroom and a kitchen in the rear. There was a yard and a small plot called the garden. Beyond the kitchen, with its entrance in the yard, there was a wash house, and next to that a lavatory. There was no other lavatory in the house. The first floor was occupied by a Mr. Kitchener. His eyesight was failing and he had been in hospital. He used the front room as a living room and bedroom. The back room next to it was empty. There was also a kitchen on this floor, situated above the Christies' kitchen. The second floor was occupied by Evans and Beryl Evans and their 13 months old daughter Geraldine. It consisted of two rooms, a bedroom in the front and a kitchen in the rear. The garden and wash house were solely occupied by the Christies. The lavatory was for the use of all.

Inspector Black examined the drains and using a torch searched the garden for signs of recently disturbed earth. In the darkness nothing suspicious was visible. Inspector Black posted officers outside Evans' flat, in the garden and at the front door. During the night the police interviewed Christie and Mrs. Christie and took statements from each of them. The evidence of the taking of Mrs. Christie's statement is reasonably clear; but as regards the timing of Christie's statement the recollections of the police officers who gave evidence presented at first a confusing picture. It is established that Mrs. Christie was interviewed in her kitchen by Inspector Black, who later ordered Detective Inspector then Detective Sergeant Fensome to take a statement from her. But where was Christie meanwhile? It appears that he was taken that night to Notting Hill Police Station, from where he returned about 5 a.m., having given a statement to Sergeant Corfield. Inspector Black had some difficulty in explaining the whereabouts of Christie at this time.

At first he was quite sure that he did not see Christie

that night at all, for he thought that Christie was at the police station. One of the records that cast doubt upon this was a copy of an original statement taken from Christie on 1st December 1949, endorsed as having been written, read over and its signature witnessed by Detective Sergeant Corfield in the presence of Inspector Black. Moreover a police report written in 1955 by Detective Superintendent Jennings was to record that while Sergeant Fensome was engaged at 10 Rillington Place in taking a statement from Mrs. Christie from 1 a.m. to 5 a.m., Inspector Black was engaged at Notting Hill Police Station taking a statement from Christie until 5 a.m. when he returned to 10 Rillington Place with Christie and checked the statement of Mrs. Christie.

Sergeant Fensome agreed that he took Mrs. Christie's statement in the early morning when Christie was not present, but disputed that he was engaged in taking it until 5 a.m. as appears in the 1955 Report. An examination of the original statement taken from Christie on 1st December 1949 does not contain the endorsement placed upon the copy which showed Inspector Black to be at Notting Hill Police Station. Sergeant Corfield explained that he took that statement from Christie and that Inspector Black was not present at the time. The inaccuracy of the endorsement was due, so Sergeant Corfield said, to a mistake by a civilian typist then employed at Notting Hill who made a wrong assumption.

During the Inquiry and before he had finished his lengthy period in the witness box, Inspector Black was able to confirm his earlier evidence that he was at 10 Rillington Place whilst Detective Sergeant Fensome was taking the statement from Mrs. Christie. At one time Inspector Black had been under the impression that it was he who had taken a statement from Mrs. Christie, but before the Inquiry started he realised that this was not so but that he had questioned her before Sergeant Fensome took her statement. The Inspector during his evidence remembered Christie coming back to 10 Rillington Place with Sergeant Corfield, who handed over to him the statement that Christie had made at Notting Hill police station. Inspector Black was then in possession of the statements made by Christie and Mrs. Christie. This matter was further complicated by the evidence given by Sergeant Corfield. He maintained that Christie's statement was made to him in the afternoon and not the early hours of the 1st December 1949, and that it was made not at the police station but in the kitchen at 10 Rillington Place with Mrs. Christie present at the time. He remembered too, that the kitchen was overheated by an enormous fire, and that at the time Christie claimed to be crippled with arthritis. Another witness, Police Constable Davies, claimed that from midnight to 6 a.m. he had Christie and Mrs. Christie together under his observation in their flat with no one else present. It is clear that he has confused his movements on this night with some other night.

It would be odd if the police, occupying this small house in this way and taking a statement from Mrs. Christie during the night, should have failed to take a statement from Christie himself when his name had been given as the abortionist with knowledge of the child's whereabouts. Sergeant Corfield's recollection of these days is often unreliable and I have no doubt that Inspector Black is right in his final recollection on this matter. The error in the 1955 police report made six years after the events to which it refers, was in part based upon a document which included an inaccurate endorsement. Sergeant Corfield did take a statement from Christie in his overheated kitchen but this must have been on 8th December when he took another statement from Christie. He has forgotten taking Christie's first statement at

Notting Hill Police Station in the early hours of 1st December.

During this night the Evans flat was searched. A brief case with the initials J.N. was found there. This was part of the property stolen from a flat at 164 Westbourne Park, W.2 when the premises were broken into during the period of 19th-23rd August 1949. Some newspaper cuttings referring to a murder which had recently taken place and was known as the Setty murder were also found. The police took from Christie clothing which belonged to Geraldine and which had been left with him by Evans. The pram and the baby's chair which Christie said had also been left with him were seen by the police but they did not take possession of them.

Some confusion arose over the time when the police first saw this clothing. This was due in the main to Sergeant Corfield's mistaken recollection of the time when Christie had been interviewed. It arose also because the entry of the receipt of the articles so possessed was not made in the appropriate property receipt book at Notting Hill Police Station until almost a month later when Chief Inspector Jennings discovered the omission.

When searching the garden for signs of disturbed soil and earth, Inspector Black did not search the wash house. The reason for this was, I think, that Mrs. Christie had said that the wash house was their property and it did not occur to him to search it. Constable McCann who searched the garden by torch light did not search the wash house because he thought that the outhouses were part of the adjoining property. Sergeant Fensome's recollection is that the wash house was not inspected by him during a search made in early daylight on 1st December, because he was told that it had already been searched and he did not himself suspect that Evans had any connection with it. Sergeant Fensome maintains that he was ordered to search the garden only. The result was that no one searched the wash house that night and somehow in the misunderstanding the impression was created that it had been searched by someone.

Constable McCann remembered that during the night Sergeant Corfield went to 11 St. Marks Road, to interview Evans' mother. The distance between this address and 10 Rillington Place is about 300 yards. At that time she lived with her husband Mr. Probert and her two daughters Eileen (Eleanor) now Mrs. Ashby, who was older than Evans, and his younger half-sister Maureen (Mary Josephine) now Mrs. Westlake. Save that the address sounds familiar to him, Sergeant Corfield has no recollection of this visit.

In 1953 at the Scott Henderson Inquiry he did remember seeing Mrs. Evans and had a less clear recollection of seeing one of her daughters from whom he thought that he had taken a statement. Reading now what he said in 1953 does not help to recall the visit to his mind. He did not take any statement on that occasion, but, according to Mrs. Ashby, made notes in his notebook of the matters told to him. Mrs. Westlake remained in the room with her mother for a short time only. Mrs. Ashby's recollection is that the police came in the early hours of the morning.

In 1953 Mrs. Ashby's memory of this night was that two police officers had called and that one of them told her mother that he had a message from her son that she should see Christie and find out from him the address in East Acton where the baby could be found. Mrs. Ashby says that she thinks that the police officer said that there was no point in going round to see Christie as he had already said that he did not know where the baby was. This officer was in all probability Sergeant Corfield repeating what Christie had said. The identity of Sergeant Corfield's fellow police officer has not been established.

It would seem probable that Sergeant Corfield, having seen Christie earlier, did call at 11 St. Marks Road after Christie had been taken to Notting Hill police station. Having learned what he could from the Evans family Sergeant Corfield then went to the police station and took a statement from Christie, which later was handed to Inspector Black.

On 1st December Chief Inspector Jennings took charge of the investigation. He retired from the Metropolitan Police Force in 1963 with the rank of Detective Superintendent. At the start of his evidence he was under the impression that he went to 10 Rillington Place after seeing Inspector Black at 9 a.m. He was not alone in thinking this. Later he was quite sure that he did not go to 10 Rillington Place until the afternoon of the 1st December. He fixes the time of this visit by means of his report of 22nd October 1955, which he said was made when his 1949 diary was in existence. His recollection is that after a telephone call he saw

Inspector Black at Hammersmith at 9 a.m. and that he there learned what he called "the strength of the job." He said that he was himself occupied that morning in Court on a manslaughter inquiry. Inspector Black thinks that he saw his senior officer at Hammersmith on 1st December and that he was himself engaged dealing with other matters during the morning but that he met Chief Inspector Jennings by appointment at 10 Rillington Place in the afternoon.

Chief Inspector Jennings searched the house. In the Christies' flat he made a search, looking for instruments of abortion, but found only an old and perished Higginson's syringe which Mrs. Christie said was hers. Visual examination of it by Mr. Montgomery, then the principal Scientific Officer for the Metropolitan Police Laboratory confirmed that there was no sign of its recent use. The Chief Inspector noticed that new floor boards had been laid and he ordered the removal of one to see what had been done beneath it. He is, I think, right when he says that he asked Christie about the pram and was told that it had been left there when Evans had gone. By this time Chief Inspector Jennings had read Christie's statement and knew that he was a War Reserve Policeman. The Chief Inspector was told that the wash house had been searched. Inspector Black must have thought that it had been whereas in fact it had not.

Acting on the order of Detective Chief Superintendent Barratt who is now dead and who had taken charge of the inquiry, Inspector Black and Sergeant Corfield were ordered to Wales to bring Evans back to London. Ostensibly the lawful reason was for further enquiries to be made about the stolen brief case, but the real reason for bringing him back was to question him about the disappearance of his wife and child. I think also that the Metropolitan Police were being urged by those in

Merthyr Tydfil to take Evans off their hands. During the rest of the day various people were questioned and more information about Evans was being collected. The two police officers travelled overnight to Wales.

∞◦◦◦

On the 1st December, Mrs. Evans made a lengthy statement to the police which in the main she does not
dispute. From it and other statements later obtained and
from the evidence which has been given, some of the
events in the lives of Evans and his wife leading up to her
death can be traced. In July 1949 Beryl Evans had a job. It
is not known with whom Geraldine was left during working hours. Whilst at work, Beryl Evans had, or pretended
that she had had, a mild flirtation with a painter. Mrs.
Evans said that her son brought her round to the flat to
speak to his wife about her conduct. When she spoke to

her mother-in-law Beryl Evans explained that she was only teasing her husband about having a laugh with the painter or about having kissed the painter and that as a result Evans had slapped her face. Mrs. Evans told her daughter-in-law that she was stupid even to mention such a thing to her husband. He however was not content to forget the matter, for he went round to his wife's place of work, made a scene and she lost her job.

By August 1949, Beryl Evans was again pregnant. In that month she brought a friend named Lucy, then approaching her 17th birthday, to stay at the flat. The conditions were very cramped. It would seem probable that at that time Beryl Evans was under the impression that her husband was going to take employment abroad, and she wanting companionship invited her friend to stay with her. According to Lucy, Evans' proposed plans of foreign employment were checked with his would-be employers and found to be non-existent.

In a statement which she made to the police on the 7th December 1949, Lucy, who was unable to give evidence before me, alleged that she witnessed rows between Evans and his wife. She spoke of an occasion when Evans struck his wife across the face and body because she had gone to the cinema leaving Geraldine alone in the flat. At the time Evans was in a furious temper and Beryl Evans took hold of a breadknife. When in a further argument Evans said to his wife "I'll push you through the bloody window" Lucy tripped him up as he made towards his wife. Evans, according to the statement, had a violent temper and on several occasions when Lucy was there had said to his wife, "I'll do you in." It may be that it is this or a similar incident which is mentioned by a neighbour, Mrs. Swan, in a statement which she made on the 8th

December 1949. She said that at about 11 p.m., hearing shouting, she saw the shadows of two persons, a man and a woman, struggling violently in the back room of Evans' flat. She assumed that the two persons were Evans and his wife. Mrs. Swan also heard a woman shouting as if pleading, and thought that after about four or five minutes she heard a woman running downstairs but no one came out of the house.

On the 28th August there was another row, this time over Lucy. Mrs. Evans was present and sent her daughter-in-law to fetch a policeman. Inspector Parks arrived and according to his statement Beryl Evans was accusing Lucy of carrying on with her husband. Lucy vehemently denied this. The complaint to the Inspector was that when ordered to leave, Lucy had struck Beryl Evans in the face. The Inspector advised Beryl Evans to seek help at the Magistrates Court, and according to Mrs. Evans her daughter-in-law saw the Probation Officer. It was probably around this time that another neighbour, Mrs. Hide, spoke of a quarrel when she heard Beryl Evans repeating the phrase "she's got to go." Lucy left the house on the 28th August and Evans went with her. They spent two nights together, after which Lucy left a note for Evans and returned to her mother's home. According to a statement made by Mr. Vincent, who with his wife Joan was a friend of the Evans', Lucy's departure angered Evans, for he brought Lucy's note for Mr. Vincent to see and said that he would smash Lucy up or run her over with his lorry. Mr. Vincent warned Lucy to be careful. It would seem that in order to smooth things over Lucy met Evans on a few occasions at the Vincents' home. Nothing untoward happened and Evans returned to his wife.

Lucy's present recollection is contained in a statement which she gave to the Treasury Solicitor. She now only remembers the threat "I'll do you in" being used by Evans once, and that was during the fight to which I have referred. She says that when she made her first statement to the police one of the officers told her that there was no doubt that Evans was guilty and it was then that she learned of Beryl Evans' pregnancy. She insists that until then she was unaware of the pregnancy, and denies the suggestion made by Mr. Peter Baker that she told him in 1953 that Beryl Evans had said that Christie would perform an abortion on her.

Mr. Baker was then a newspaper reporter employed by the Daily Mirror who, in the course of his work, started enquiries about the Evans case in 1953. He interviewed a number of people including the members of the Evans family and thereafter gave assistance to those interested in establishing Evans' innocence. Lucy's denial is one of two instances where Mr. Baker has recorded evidence about Christie being the person who was to perform an abortion on Beryl Evans which is challenged by the person said to have been his informant. The second arises out of a chain of hearsay evidence, as unreliable as it is lengthy, in which Mr. Baker recorded that he was told by Beryl Evans' brother, Mr. Basil Thorley, that he had learned from Mrs. Collins who had it from Beryl Evans that Christie was going to abort her. Mr. Thorley denied telling this to Mr. Baker or that he knew anything about it. Mrs. Collins indignantly denied passing on this information to Mr. Thorley. She said that she knew nothing of it.

Lucy did not see Beryl Evans after 28th August 1949. It is, I think, unlikely that she knew before that date that Christie was to perform an abortion on Beryl Evans, since the attempted abortion, if it took place at all, did not take place until the 8th November, when Beryl Evans was four months pregnant.

On the 5th November, Mrs. Evans went with her son and

daughter-in-law to Hammersmith to buy a pram for their unborn child and a small chair for Geraldine. The chair was carried home; the pram was to be delivered later. This pram has often been associated with Geraldine. No doubt when convenient she could have been put into it when the younger baby was also in it. But the pram was not bought for Geraldine. These purchases are typical of the generosity shown by Mrs. Evans to her son and daughter-in-law. Beryl Evans it seems was always short of money. One reason was no doubt that she was a poor manager in everything connected with the running of a home. Mrs. Evans who was herself working, would on occasions give her daughter-in-law small sums of money to help her out, and her sisters-in-law would similarly and with loans, help her, and they were all loyal enough to her not to tell Evans what they had done.

When the pram was purchased nothing could have been said to Mrs. Evans about an abortion otherwise it would not have been bought. Mrs. Evans said that she learnt of Beryl Evans' pregnancy from her son at a time variously put at about August or October, when he, knowing that his mother disapproved of abortion, asked if he might take, and took, some Bile Beans which were in her flat. Although Mrs. Evans says that her daughter-in-law did not mention anything to her at any time about an abortion, she was aware that Beryl Evans had mentioned the matter to Mrs. Westlake, who had warned Beryl Evans not to say anything to her mother-in-law about it.

As far as one can be certain Beryl Evans was killed on 8th November. Christie and his wife gave their accounts of this day in the various statements which they made and the evidence which they gave. In his statements made on the 1st and 5th December 1949, Christie said that he last saw Beryl Evans on about this date going out into the street at about 1 p.m. with Geraldine. Mrs. Christie said much the same in her statement of 1st December. As will be seen later a Mr. Jones said that he saw Beryl Evans at 10 a.m. on this day. Christie had said in both his statements that he had seen Evans at about 7 p.m. and although off work and at home he had not seen Beryl Evans return. He said that he left the house himself at 5.30 p.m. to visit the doctor, and returned at 6.45 p.m. Shortly afterwards he saw Evans and told him that Beryl Evans was not in yet whereupon Evans said that his wife had gone to friends in Bristol for a short holiday and that he was joining them later in the week. Christie said that he heard Evans go out about half an hour later.

In his deposition he gave a different account of this day's events. He said that he had made a mistake and corrected his earlier account of seeing Evans on this day, saying that he did not recollect seeing Evans. In his evidence at Evans' trial, Christie enlarged upon his sickness, his milk diet and his visit to the doctor and the public library on this day. During the night Christie claimed that he was awakened by a heavy thud from somewhere above and that the noise, which also awakened Mrs. Christie, sounded like heavy furniture being moved upstairs. He said he looked out of the window of the bedroom but saw nothing. This window overlooks the yard and small garden and is very close to the wash house. If a heavy bundle had been brought downstairs and placed in the wash house it would be unlikely that both Christie and Mrs. Christie would sleep through the unfamiliar noise. If Christie had been awake and had looked out of the window he could not have failed to have been aware of any movement in the yard. Mrs. Christie in her second statement and in her evidence also said that she heard this noise in the night which she could not place as she was half asleep. She did not pay much attention to it, thinking that Evans and his wife were preparing to leave quickly because of their mounting debts. In evidence she described hearing the movement as of furniture. In her deposition Mrs. Christie did not think that she had seen Beryl Evans on this day.

On Wednesday evenings, Evans and his wife usually took Geraldine to 11 St. Marks Road and left her with Mrs. Evans for a few hours whilst they went to the cinema. On Wednesday 9th November 1949, according to his mother, Evans arrived alone at her home and told her that Beryl Evans and the child had gone on holiday to Brighton, where they were staying with her father, and that they would not be back for a week or two. Mrs. Evans felt hurt because of her daughter-in-law's failure to bring Geraldine round before leaving. Evans apologised for his wife saying that she did not have time to do so but that she would be writing. Mrs. Evans accepted what her son told her. She knew better than anyone else, although others knew it too, that Evans was a liar. Mrs. Evans thought that she could tell when her son was lying, both from the manner of his speech and the things he said. The ability to recognise his lies has been exaggerated by both Mrs. Evans and Mrs. Ashby, for the mother said that Evans prefaced his lies with the expression "I bet you", while the sister remembered this phrase as an introduction to the truth. On this day Evans showed no signs of being upset for in her second statement to the police Mrs. Evans said that her son at this time seemed quite calm and normal.

Mrs. Christie's account of the events of the 9th November is mainly contained in her statement made on the 1st December, which was repeated in precis form in her deposition and in her evidence. Evans, she said, came in at about 10.30 p.m. and as there were floor boards up in the passage she shone a light to prevent an accident. I think she was wrong about the floorboards being up. She asked where Beryl Evans was and was told by Evans that his wife and child had gone to stay with friends in Bristol. Mrs. Christie immediately remarked that Beryl Evans had not said anything about going, and Evans said that his wife would be writing. Mrs. Christie did not believe Evans. the reasons for her disbelief were first, that Evans had often said that his wife was going on holiday to different places and she had not gone, but more so because Mrs. Christie thought that at last Beryl Evans had left her husband. She had frequently, so Mrs. Christie said, spoken of her intention to do so, saying that she could no longer stand her husband's behaviour.

Christie dealt with this in his deposition taken on 15th December 1949. In his statement made ten days before, he had confined his account of this day to Evans' earlier arrivals and departure, but in his deposition and in evidence he claimed that from beside his bedroom door he heard the conversation between his wife and Evans on the latter's return that night. With slight variations, his recollection accorded with that of his wife, and he added that Evans had said that Beryl Evans had not told his mother that she was going away. Mrs. Christie included this remark in her evidence at Evans' trial. It was not challenged for when Evans himself gave evidence he said that he had lied to Mrs. Christie about his wife being away. He was thereby underlining that he had not lied to Christie, who on Evans' story knew the full facts. This would seem to leave little room for doubt that Mrs. Christie's account of the events of this night is a true one. Whether Evans was lying to Christie also or whether he was acting by arrangement with or, as he claimed, on the direction of Christie, the indications are that Mrs. Christie certainly knew nothing about the death of Beryl Evans on the previous day. The suggestion was made that Mrs. Christie knew that Beryl Evans was dead but feigned ignorance by agreement with Christie, so that Evans, thinking he was deceiving Mrs. Christie, was himself deceived because she knew the truth all the time. I do not think that this is right.

The 10th November 1949 was probably the day on which Geraldine was murdered. On this day Evans was driving his employer's van in the Brighton area. Since the 15th August 1949, there had been an arrangement between Evans and his employer, Mr. Adler, that Beryl Evans should collect her husband's wages of £5 10s. from the employer each Friday. This arrangement was made because Evans worked overtime and might not return in time to be paid on Friday night. With Beryl Evans dead, Evans would need to collect the money himself. Why Evans wanted the money on the Thursday night is not at all clear. He did not wait until Friday but on his return after making his deliveries on Thursday 10th November spoke to his employer. Evans asked for his money making the excuse that he had to post it away. He was told that the money would be paid to his wife as usual on the following day when payment was due. According to Mr. Adler's statement, Evans retorted by saying that if the wages were not paid forthwith, he would refuse to drive for the firm. This threat did not disturb his employer, for during the preceding fortnight Mr. Adler had found Evans neglectful and not as satisfactory in his work as he had been previously. Evans claimed that he had a much better job to go to. This was not true. Mr. Adler paid Evans off and his employment ended. This immediate termination of the employment, although at different times variously described, was a consensual arrangement.

According to Mr. Baker, Evans on his way home called upon a Mr. Macphail who in 1953 remembered that Evans seemed to have something on his mind. He obviously had, for his wife was dead, her death had been concealed and he had just given up his job. He had good cause to be worried about his future. Mrs. Christie in her deposition and in her evidence at Evans' trial said that at about 7 o'clock she overheard Evans, when talking to her husband, say that he had given up his job. Christie in his statement and deposition supported this, but added that the reason given by Evans for leaving his job was that there had been a row at his work because Evans had returned with three orders not delivered. Christie went on to say that Evans announced that he was going to Bristol where he had prospects of a job.

On the 11th November Evans called on Mr. Robert Hookway, a furniture dealer, at his premises at 319 Portobello Road, W.10. It has not been possible to trace

Mr. Hookway, but he gave statements to the police in December 1949. In March 1953 he made another statement. In 1949 Mr. Hookway stated that he was visited by Evans who wanted to sell his furniture which he said had been bought in Cardiff three years earlier. Evans, who knew that he was in arrears with his hire purchase payments for this furniture obtained through a shop in Hammersmith and that his mother was his guarantor, declared that there was no question of the furniture being on hire purchase. When asked by Mr. Hookway for the receipts for the furniture, Evans said that his wife would send them for they were with her in Bristol, where he had to go on Monday 14th November, to a job which awaited him and where accommodation was available through his father-in-law.

The choice of Mr. Hookway as a purchaser is said to be significant and is bound up with the evidence showing when Mr. Hookway first met Christie. At Evans' trial Christie denied advising Evans about a purchaser for his furniture, whereas Evans in evidence said that he had been recommended to Mr. Hookway by Christie. Christie in the witness box said that only three-quarters of an hour earlier that morning Mr. Basil Thorley had admitted to him that he had recommended Mr. Hookway to Evans. No one checked with Mr. Basil Thorley at the Old Bailey in 1950 whether this was right or wrong. In evidence before me, Mr. Basil Thorley said he had neither met nor heard of Mr. Hookway. On 25th March 1953, Mr. Hookway made a statement to the police in which he said that he had known Christie for about three years and that he met Christie at West London Magistrates Court when both gave evidence in the Evans case. Mr. Hookway did not give evidence at the hearing, though he had given statement to the police and may well have been at the Court at the time of the Committal Proceedings

In 1959–1960 Mr. Kennedy saw Mr. Hookway and was told a very different story. At this time Mr. Hookway claimed that he had known Christie for two years before the murder of Beryl Evans, that is to say since 1947, and that Christie had come to the shop before Evans did and said that he was sending a young fellow round who wanted to sell his furniture. Following upon this Evans arrived, and Mr. Hookway remembered that Evans said that he had previously been in Egypt. Mr. Hookway was one of the very small band who seemed to like Christie. Despite the fact that Christie was always short of money, Mr. Hookway spoke appreciatively of Christie's companionship and respectfully of his mind and intelligence. By the time Mr. Kennedy saw Mr. Hookway he was voicing an opinion about Beryl Evans which had not been heard of before by anyone who had interviewed him. Mr. Hookway now described her as a little tarty thing whom he thought was having an affair with Christie with the consent of Evans. If Christie had at any time told this to Mr. Hookway no doubt the latter would have said so to Mr. Kennedy. It stands therefore as no more than an opinion held by Mr. Hookway and of which he had given no inkling in 1949 or 1953. There is no evidence of familiarity between Beryl Evans and Christie.

The only time anything like this was said to have arisen was the tardy revival on 1st December 1965 in Mrs. Evans' recollection of an incident forgotten since it occurred over sixteen years ago. Mrs. Evans recalled in the witness box that Beryl Evans was once very upset because, when she was hanging out washing in the back garden, Christie had put his arms round her.

Mr. Hookway's opinion is not supported by other evidence. Not having seen Mr. Hookway I cannot say affirmatively whether he did or did not know Christie before 1949. I would think that his 1949 statement and his evidence on oath in 1953 are probably to be preferred to a statement made for the first time ten years after when in all probability Mr. Hookway was in an imaginative frame of mind. I do not attach great importance to this matter for Christie could have recommended Mr. Hookway as a purchaser whether Christie had murdered Beryl Evans pretending it was an unsuccessful abortion, or whether Evans had murdered his wife and was leaving London. The recommendation of a purchaser is a neutral act.

According to Joan Vincent, Evans called upon her about this time. She has placed the visit on various dates. On 1st December 1949 she said that it was on Friday 11th November, and thinking that it was because of her that Evans had quarreled with his wife she was somewhat surprised to see him. She said that he told her that his wife and child were with relatives in Bristol and that Beryl Evans would be writing to her. In her evidence Joan Vincent said that she asked Evans whether she was still required to buy a doll which she had previously arranged to obtain for Beryl Evans as a present for Geraldine. Evans said that he wanted the doll and that they would collect it at some future date.

Later Evans met Mr. Basil Thorley in a cafe and said that he was joining his wife and child on the following Monday at Bristol. Mr. Thorley's recollection in 1965 was that Brighton was mentioned at this meeting and Bristol at a later one. According to Mr. Basil Thorley, Evans also called upon Mrs. Barnett in Ladbroke Grove to excuse her granddaughter Beryl Evans' failure to keep an appointment, probably for tea, with her grandmother on the preceding Tuesday. He then told the grandmother that Beryl Evans was in Scotland. Mrs. Barnett's daughter Miss Simmonds sent a statement to the Inquiry saying that her mother had said that her granddaughter had failed to arrive for lunch and Miss Simmonds was present when

Evans said that his wife and child had gone to Scotland.

Mr. Hookway called to examine the furniture and refused to pay the asking price of £65, saying it was only worth £40. But at Evans' request, Mr. Hookway arranged to call upon the following Sunday to see if the two could do business together. Mr. Hookway saw nothing which on later reflection he might have thought was a bundled up body in the Evans' flat.

According to Mrs. Ashby's recollection in 1953 Evans called round at his mother's home on the Friday, looking as she said, like a spiv, and had a meal there.

At about 10.15 a.m. on 12th November, Evans called upon his mother. She, hearing him singing, asked him if he was feeling all right, and he said that he was and that he was going to Brighton the following day to see Beryl and the baby. There is a certain confusion whether Evans saw his mother again on this day, as Mrs. Evans said in 1949, or whether there was but one interview as she now says, and one with his sister Mrs. Westlake. In 1953 at the Scott Henderson Inquiry Mrs. Evans was not very sure of the times of these meetings. In my view, the differences are of no importance. Mrs. Evans now says that later on the same visit her son looked strangely at her and she asked whether he was in trouble. He said that he was not and went on to say that Beryl had written and that the baby was asking for its grandmother. In answer to his mother's question, Evans said that he had sent his wife 30/-, but that he did not know whether he had enough money to go to Brighton the following day. This series of lies completely deceived Mrs. Evans. Evans, undoubtedly anxious to make sure that his plans did not go awry, called upon Mr. Hookway to confirm that he would be making his promised call at 10 Rillington Place on the following day.

Christie meanwhile visited Doctor Odess on this day. The doctor applied strapping to ease the pain which had now developed in Christie's back and was caused by fibrositis.

On Sunday 13th November, Mr. Hookway called at 10 Rillington Place. So did Mr. Mackay an agent for the Provident Club. He told Mr. Baker in 1953 that Christie had opened the door to him and said that Evans was out and that Beryl Evans was in Bristol, but that Evans called from the top window and Mr. Mackay went up. He thought that Evans was in a rather flustered state but attributed it to his drinking on the Saturday night. Evans paid his club contribution and told Mr. Mackay that his wife was in Bristol with the child. Mr. Mackay did not imagine from the appearance of the room that it was shortly to be vacated.

On the Monday morning a rag dealer Albert Rollings, who had met Evans earlier, called at 10 Rillington Place. Mr. Baker saw this man in 1953. He said that he was told that Beryl Evans was on holiday. He was given papers, bottles and clothes in exchange for a drink to be given to Evans later. The dealer picked up a rattle thinking that it might be included in the rubbish, but Evans said that that belonged to the baby and that she would want it.

On Monday 14th November, Mr. Hookway collected the furniture and paid £40 for it. Evans signed a receipt giving his address as 79 Whiteladies Road, Bristol. He showed a roll of notes to Christie but denied saying, as Christie later claimed, that he had said it contained £60. According to Evans he went to the cinema in the afternoon. He had a meal with Mr. Basil Thorley, who was told by Evans that he had received a telegram from his wife saying that Geraldine was ill and that he was joining them at Bristol. Evans had with him a cloakroom ticket from Paddington Station. He left not for Bristol but for Wales arriving at Merthyr Vale early in the morning of Tuesday 15th November.

It is convenient to step back a few days in time to consider a matter which has in the past been thought to be of great importance. It concerns Joan Vincent. In about December 1948 Beryl Evans had renewed a schoolgirl friendship with Joan Vincent. She lived with her husband and baby at 164 Westbourne Park Road. At about the beginning of November 1949, Joan Vincent was told by Beryl Evans of her pregnancy and of her determination to be rid of it because of the living conditions at 10 Rillington Place and her relationship with her husband. This confirms what Mrs. Christie had said of Beryl Evans' feelings at this time. She told her friend of the various things she was taking in an effort to bring about a miscarriage. On the 5th November 1949. Joan Vincent twice visited 10 Rillington Place. Her first visit was to collect some tea which was owed to her. She called again later to collect a shirt which she had arranged to borrow. This was the last time Joan Vincent saw Beryl Evans.

In the statement made by Mrs. Christie to Sergeant Fensome on 1st December 1949 she referred to the frequent quarrels she had heard between Evans and his wife, the last of which being on Sunday 13th November. This date was a mistake for the 6th November. Mrs. Christie described this quarrel which appeared to her to be violent, and she said that it lasted all day on and off. The following day Beryl Evans, who looked "terribly ill", mentioned that a friend of hers called Joan had made trouble between her and her husband: that this friend was coming round that morning but that Beryl Evans did not wish to see her. According to Mrs. Christie, later in the morning of 7th November Joan called, but Beryl Evans locked herself in the kitchen and refused to see her friend. Mrs. Christie did not know Joan's surname but identified her to the police as being married to the son of a nearby shopkeeper. Mrs. Christie, although not wholly accurate, was obviously referring to Joan Vincent. She was not seeking to hide the caller's identity. Mrs. Christie said that she was asked by Beryl Evans during the Monday afternoon to keep an eye on Geraldine and she did so, until Evans returned home at 5.30 p.m.

The police took two statements from Joan Vincent concerning these matters on the 1st and 7th of December. In the second of those statements Joan Vincent mentioned her visit to 10 Rillington Place as described by Mrs. Christie which had been omitted from the first statement. When in her first statement Joan Vincent had described her two visits on the 5th November to 10 Rillington Place, the whereabouts of Beryl Evans and Geraldine were not known. Six days later on the 7th December, it was known that both of them had been strangled. Joan Vincent told the police that she had omitted from her first statement the fact that at 10.30 a.m. on Monday 7th November she had called at 10 Rillington Place to see Beryl Evans. This confirmed Mrs. Christie's account. The front door was open so she went upstairs. The kitchen door of the Evans' flat was shut. Joan Vincent said that she called out "Are you there, Beryl?" and receiving no reply she said "I am sure somebody is there and if you don't want to open the door you needn't." Joan Vincent went downstairs where she met Mrs. Christie in the hall, and according to the statement told Mrs. Christie that she could not get the kitchen door open and had a feeling that somebody was inside. She asked Mrs. Christie if she knew whether Beryl Evans was in, and Mrs. Christie said that she did not know.

On Thursday 10th November, Joan Vincent said that she called again at 10 Rillington Place. Again the front door was open and she went upstairs, but when she reached the second flight of stairs Christie called out from below "Who's there?" and she answered "It's Joan, I want to see Beryl." Thereupon Christie said "She isn't there. She has gone away. I expect she will write to you." Joan Vincent then left.

In 1953 Joan Vincent wrote a letter to the Daily Mirror which she intended for Mr. Baker who had already interviewed her. The letter is dated "7/3/53". Mr. Baker says that that date is wrong but he does not know the date of receipt of that letter. One suggestion was made that the date should read 3/7/53 which would mean that it would have been written two days before Joan Vincent gave evidence at the Scott Henderson Inquiry. In that letter Joan Vincent gave an account of her two visits to 10 Rillington Place, differing from that given to the police over three years earlier. She now wrote that she visited the house on Tuesday 8th November when the kitchen door appeared to be locked. That she heard no sound but had an uncanny feeling that someone was in there. Feeling rather nervous she left the house and called again the following day. On this second visit, the letter continues, she reached the first landing when Christie called out "What do you want?". She replied that she wanted to see Beryl. Christie then told her that Beryl and the baby had gone away to Bristol. She said that she noticed Geraldine's pram and high chair in Christie's sitting room. It will be seen that the dates put in 1949 as 7th and 10th November, had by 1953 become 8th and 9th November. These were the dates which Joan Vincent had given to Mr. Baker in an interview which she had with him in April 1953. In that interview she added that which she looked pointedly at the new pram and high chair which had recently been delivered, Christie said that he was sending them on. Subject to any contrary inference which might be drawn, Evans in his own statement claimed that he was still looking after the baby on 8th and 9th November.

During the day of 1st December, while in Notting Hill the police continued their investigations, in Merthyr Tydfil Constable Evans had been making his own enquiries. He had interviewed Cornelius and Violet Lynch, the uncle and aunt with whom Evans had been staying. Constable Evans learned from them of events which later were to be recorded in their statements and in the evidence given by Mrs. Lynch at the Evans trial. He also learned that on the morning of 30th November Mrs. Lynch had received a letter from Evans' mother in answer to one which Mrs. Lynch had written. Evans had arrived unexpectedly and without luggage at the Lynch home in Merthyr Vale on the 15th November, shortly after 6.30 a.m. For some reason he had left his suitcase in Cardiff, for within a few days of his arrival Mr. Lynch saw a cloakroom ticket belonging to Evans for a suitcase deposited at Cardiff station. His aunt had last seen him three or four years previously. His uncle had not seen him for nine years. Evans said that his employers' car had broken down in Cardiff and he would be in Wales for a few days pending its repair. During breakfast with his aunt he told her that his wife and child were in Brighton until after Christmas. On the 17th November he left for Cardiff to see, he said, if the car was ready. He returned early the same day saying that the repairs were not yet finished. Evans left again on the 21st, returning on 23rd November. On his return Evans brought a suitcase. He said that he had seen his mother in London, and when asked whether he had seen his wife he replied that he had but that when he had entered his flat she had walked out without saying a word, leaving the baby in the cot in the bedroom. When asked what had happened to the baby, Evans said that he had taken her to some people from Newport living in London who were looking after her for him and to whom he had paid £15. He explained that he did not take the baby to his mother as she was working and he did not bring her to his aunt because he did not think of it. During his stay in Wales, Evans was not seen to be upset.

On occasions he visited public houses with his uncle, did his turn at the singsong, and spent many evenings in the company of his cousin and boyhood friend William Costigan and his wife.

On the 18th November, when in a public house in Merthyr Vale, Evans produced a wedding ring and asked his uncle whether he thought that the landlord would advance some cash upon it. He denied that it was his wife's ring and said that he had found it in Gloucester. On another occasion when Mrs. Lynch had seen the wedding ring, he denied to her that it was his wife's and said that he had found it, according to Mrs. Lynch's recollection, either in Gloucester or Cheltenham. Constable Evans learned from the Lynches that the ring had been sold by Evans to a jeweller in Merthyr Vale for 6/-. This was confirmed by a Mr. Scannell who, having refused to buy a wrist watch, bought the ring for 6/- from a man whose description obviously fitted Evans and whose signature appeared on the declaration form which, with the ring, was handed over to Constable Evans at 9.30 a.m. on 2nd December.

Mr. Lynch who was to say in his statement that his nephew was known throughout the family as a liar, told Mrs. Lynch to write to London and find out from his sister what was happening. Mrs. Evans burned the letter which she received but her reply arrived in Merthyr Vale on the 30th November. The letter, which expressed immediate thoughts written in anger reads as follows:

Dear Brother Sister

Just a few lines in answer to your welcome letter which I got safe. Well Vi I don't know what lies Tim have told you down there I know nothing about him as I have not seen him for 3 weeks and I have not seen Beryl or the Baby for a month. Tim came round and told me that Beryl & the Baby had gone to Brighton to her father for a holiday that is all I know about them ask Tim what he have done with the Funichter he took from his flat there is some mirstry about him you can tell him from me he dont want to come to me I never want to see him again as long as I live he have put years on my life since last August he knows what I mean he packed up a good job up here he is like his Father no good to himself or anybody else so if

you are mug enough to keep him for nothing well that
will be your fault I dont intend to keep him any more I
done my best for him & Beryl what thanks did I get his
name stinks up here everywhere I go people asking for
him for money he owes them I am ashamed to say he is
my Son also you can tell him he wont get the loan Club
I am paying his Debts with it the Furniture man have been
here so I payed his loan Club £20 to them so he had it. I
will send him on the bill for it in my next letter so I think
I have told you all the news for now I will close with love
from your
loving sister
Vien (?)

Enclosed in that letter was a note from Evans' sister, Mrs.
Westlake, dealing with private matters but a few lines
reflect her mood:

Mam is going to write to you now Aunty Vi and she will
tell you about Tim. I know if I see him I'll kill him for the
worry he's giving Mam.

Mrs. Lynch read the letter to Evans at the breakfast
table and asked him what he had done with the furniture
from his flat. Evans lied when he answered that it was still
there, and said that his mother was telling lies. He became
agitated and was unable to finish the breakfast that he had
just begun.

At 11 a.m. on 1st December, Constable Evans questioned Evans about the letter. Evans said that he knew that
one had been received and, lying again, said that he did not
know what was in it. Constable Evans then asked when
Evans had last seen his wife's body and whether he had
helped Christie to carry the body down, for Evans had
said that Christie single-handed had moved the body.
Evans now said that when Christie had told him to stop

in the kitchen he heard Christie puffing and blowing and went out and saw him half way down the stairs between the Evans' flat and Mr. Kitchener's flat. His wife's body was then on the stairs, and Evans said to Christie "What's up?" Christie said that he could not move her any more, and asked Evans to give a hand and told him to pick up her legs, which Evans did, and together they carried her body into the kitchen.

Evans was then asked whether he had been back to London since he arrived in Wales, for in his statement he had said that he had been in Merthyr Vale since his first arrival there but the Lynchs had said otherwise. He admitted that he had been back. He went on to say that he had forgotten to mention that on the Wednesday or Thursday of the week after his arrival in Wales he had gone back to see his child and had been told by Christie that he could not see her. Christie had said that it was too early and that the child should be left alone for about three weeks: that Evans should write to Christie who would tell him when he could see her. Constable Evans then questioned Evans about the manner in which he had said that he had torn up his wife's clothes. The officer, hearing the explanation, went on to say, "I do not think you are saying the truth". Evans answered "I may have made a few mistakes but as far as Christie is concerned I have said the truth".

Constable Evans telephoned London, and at about 4 p.m. Evans was interviewed again, this time about the brief case which had been found in his flat. Under caution he made a third statement, in which he said that in August Charles Vincent and his wife Joan had brought a brief case and a small rug, hidden under their baby in the pram, to the Evans' flat. Joan Vincent had asked Evans to look after the two articles. The husband said that they had come from the flat next door. Evans said, as Lucy was to confirm, that the rug was later bought for £3 by her mother to whom he had delivered it. He said that he was told that if he sold the brief case he could keep the proceeds. Joan Vincent and her husband, when questioned at Notting Hill on 1st December, denied all knowledge of the brief case and rug. After making this statement Evans went on to say "It was over Joan the row was on the Sunday with my wife. She was always borrowing off my wife". There had been no mention in his previous statements of a row on the Sunday night and nothing had been said about a row to Constable Evans.

While in Merthyr Vale, Evans spent many evenings with Mr. and Mrs. Costigan, both of whom gave evidence. Although the Evans family and the Lynch family are said to have been in reasonably regular correspondence, William Costigan, who was a nephew of Cornelius Lynch and living only a few doors from him, did not know until Evans' arrival that his cousin was married and the father of a child. Evans gave Mr. and Mrs. Costigan much the same reason for his presence in Wales as he had given to Mr. and Mrs. Lynch. When he told them that his wife was in Brighton they both thought that Evans and his wife had separated, and although Mrs. Costigan says that she thought that this was a permanent separation neither asked Evans the cause of it. Within a very short time of their first meeting Mrs. Costigan asked Evans why he had not brought the baby with him, and he replied that he did not wish to impose upon her. Mrs. Costigan remembers that for about three or four consecutive evenings Evans did not call, and when next seen he announced that he had been to London. No one asked him why and he did not explain. Mr. Costigan recalled that Evans told him that Geraldine was then staying with friends of his at home. He heard no mention of East Acton. Mr. Costigan remem-bered for the first time in 1965 that Evans had suggested that the two of them should go to London and bring back Geraldine to Merthyr Vale. I doubt the accuracy of this recollection. He also says that Evans was suggesting that the Costigan family should eventually move to London and live with Evans and Geraldine at 10 Rillington Place.

On his return from London which would have been on the 23rd or 24th November, Evans made a present of a necklace to Mrs. Costigan, who described it as looking pretty new. It had been an inexpensive gift from Mrs. Evans to Beryl Evans. If the statement made by Mr. Costigan on 3rd December 1949 is correct, Evans had said to Mrs. Costigan after making the gift "Don't ask no questions where it came from because I won't tell you". By the time Mr. Costigan handed the necklace to the police and made his statement he knew that Evans had been arrested, and he thought for murder. Mr. Costigan said that he was sure that Evans did not think that his baby was dead and he also said that he had become aware of Evans' arrest because he had heard at work that there was some mention of Evans in the local newspaper. He therefore decided to go to the police. Before doing so he said that his uncle, Mr. Lynch, asked about the necklace and suggested to him that he should go to the police. Mr. Costigan says that he did. Mrs. Costigan says that she did not tell the police anything as no one came near them. Constable Evans tells a different story. He says that Mr. Costigan was most reluctant to make a statement and that twice at his house and once at the police station he had declined to make one. Eventually Constable Evans refused to accept the necklace which Mr. Costigan offered to hand over and told him to deliver it to the police station. When he did so, Constable Evans obtained a statement from Mr. Costigan. By this time the Evans matter was in the national press. In his statement Mr. Costigan made no mention of Evans telling them about the baby or her whereabouts.

Although Mr. Costigan's mother went to London to be with her sister Mrs. Evans at this difficult time, there is no evidence that any other member of the family heard of Evans' conversations with the Costigans about the child. Why Mr. and Mrs. Costigan were so reluctant to pass on this information I do not know. Mr. Costigan says that he was suffering from nervous trouble and was at the time confused. There is no evidence that Mrs. Costigan was ill. I think that the answer may be that, just as Mr. Lynch said that Evans was generally known throughout the family as a liar, Mr. Costigan may have shared this opinion of his cousin. When Evans was arrested, as Mr. and Mrs. Costigan thought, for the murder of his wife and child, they concluded that Evans had been lying again. They did not know what the truth was and they decided that they could best help him by saying nothing, lest in telling what they knew they did him more harm than good. When information did come through to them I have no doubt that the family thought that Evans was guilty of these offences. In Merthyr Vale, the Lynchs and Costigans must have exchanged amongst themselves their recent experiences with Evans, who was by then in custody in London. Mrs. Lynch was a witness for the prosecution at his trial. I would expect that any information that Mr. and Mrs. Costigan could have given about Evans would have reached the Evans family in London but it is too late now to speculate about what may have been said.

It has been put forward as evidence supporting Evans' ignorance of his child's death that in Wales he spoke and behaved as if she were alive. When Evans was in Merthyr Vale he could not have avoided talking about Geraldine, and on these occasions, whether the child was to his knowledge dead or alive, he would have been bound to have spoken about her as being alive. Standing alone therefore, conversations about Geraldine being alive do not answer the question whether she was in fact alive or dead. These conversations carry as much or as little weight in establishing whether Geraldine was alive or dead as Evans' conversations with Mrs. Lynch about a doll which have in the past been put forward as important. In a pamphlet entitled "The Case of Timothy Evans," by Lord Altrincham and Ian Gilmour, it says on page 20 that while Evans was at Merthyr Vale he bought a teddy bear for his child and this cannot have been a calculated deception on his part because it was not mentioned at his trial. The only evidence that I have heard, which could be said to be related to this is given by Mr. Baker who interviewed Mr. and Mrs. Lynch in 1953. Mrs. Lynch told Mr. Baker that her nephew was always talking about the baby and said, amongst other things, "You wait till you see her, Auntie Vi, she's a smasher". One day according to Mrs. Lynch she went into Woolworths with Evans and he was talking about buying a cuddly doll for Geraldine. Mrs. Lynch said that she would buy one for Geraldine for Christmas, so Evans said that he would buy a teddy bear, and either then or later Evans told his aunt that he would be bringing Geraldine down to Merthyr Vale for Christmas. Mr. Baker cannot remember more of the conversation than that. Had there been anything significant in it to indicate that Mrs. Lynch was saying that Evans had bought a present for Geraldine, I have no doubt that Mr. Baker would have recorded it. It was the sort of evidence he was hoping to find. There was nothing like a teddy bear in Evans' belongings which were handed over in Wales. There is nothing to show that such a present was sent from Wales. I do not think that there is anything significant in this conversation about the doll. As far as the Lynchs knew, the baby was alive and whether according to Evans' knowledge the baby was alive or dead, his comment about buying a teddy bear would have been the same. It is said that the purchase could not have been a calculated deception on Evans' part. No evidence of any purchase has been proved.

The only other evidence relating to this is contained in television interviews transmitted on 20th January 1961. The transcript of the film of the interviews was supplied to the Inquiry by Independent Television for Wales and the West of England. The programme was entitled "In the News" and in part dealt with the publication of Mr. Kennedy's book 10 Rillington Place and included separate interviews with Mr. Lynch, Mrs. Lynch and Lord Altrincham. According to a letter received from the producer of the programme it was with great difficulty that Mr. and Mrs. Lynch were persuaded to take part in it. This was confirmed by Mr. Lynch. His wife died in July 1961, but he gave evidence before me. He was often unreliable in his recollection, I think in the main because he was injured in an accident in the mine two years ago and has forgotten a good deal in consequence. He had been further upset by the effects of a minor traffic accident on the night before he gave evidence. He has unhappy recollections of this interview for television. In the film Mrs. Lynch was asked whether Evans whilst on a walk went looking into the shops for anything for the baby. She said that Evans, when out shopping with her, chose a little cuddly doll that she was to buy Geraldine for Christmas. There was nothing said in the interview to show that Evans ever bought anything for his child. Mr. Lynch told the interviewer that the police did not treat Evans fairly, for the simple reason that he did not know what he was saying because he was frightened. Obviously Mr. Lynch could not know this of his own knowledge. He thinks that he made it clear during the interview that he was only repeating what he had heard, but he did not say so at the time.

Mrs. Lynch said in answer to questions that Evans, when he went to the police station, made two quite different statements because of his fear of Christie. She then went on to say that Christie told Evans that if he said anything about Christie being an ex policeman he would make Evans suffer for it, and Mrs. Lynch said that she thought that Evans was walking in fear of his life. What Mrs. Lynch meant by that and whether it was her own theory or whether it came from someone else or whether Evans told her this, I do not know. She added that after his conviction Evans told her to forget what had happened and that one day his name would be cleared and then his aunt would remember. If Evans did say what is attributed to him by his aunt, it is in some degree in harmony with a recollection of Mrs. Ashby's given to Mr. Kennedy. If not, it is a third explanation given by Evans to members of his family which he did not give to anyone else outside his family.

It will be remembered that on the 1st December, Evans answered Constable Evans' enquiry by saying that he had been back to 10 Rillington Place on a day which was either 23rd or 24th November. In their statements made on 2nd December, Mr. and Mrs. Lynch said that Evans left their home on the 21st November, and was back in Wales in the early morning of 23rd November. That meant that Evans must have been at 10 Rillington Place not later than the 22nd November. Mrs. Lynch gave this evidence at Evans' trial. Christie put the visit on the 23rd November, and in evidence Mrs. Christie, without putting the date on it herself, accepted counsel's date of the 23rd, saying that she did not see Evans on his return but heard his voice. She had given this account and placed it on this date in the first statement which she had made on the 1st December, when Christie had also said that the visit was on the 23rd

November. Where else Evans was in that period of about 48 hours is not known. He lied to his uncle and aunt on his return to Wales, for he told them that he had seen his mother when he had not.

Christie claimed that Evans told him that he had been looking for work and had been visiting various towns without success. Where he went and what he did can only be known by Evans and possibly Christie. At his trial Evans put this visit as being on about the 23rd. Evans said that, after it, Christie went with him part of the way to Paddington Station. Christie said that he went with Evans part of the way on a bus, then left him to visit the doctor.

The doctor's notes show that Christie paid a visit to him on the 22nd November, but not the 23rd. If Mrs. Lynch was right and the visit was on the 22nd, then Christie would be wrong about the date, but right about visiting the doctor on the day Evans called. If Christie is right about the date, then he did not visit the doctor after leaving Evans. The conversation that took place is known only to Evans and Christie, for although Christie had at one time said that his wife was present at it, she did not agree and Evans did not say that he spoke to Mrs. Christie on this visit. Christie recounted how Evans had said that his wife had left him and that he had searched for work. Evans' account was that he went to London to see Geraldine, and Christie had told him that the visit was premature. Since only Evans and Christie know what was said the meeting can prove nothing. On one side, it is said Evans went to see Geraldine. Therefore she was alive as far as he knew. And Christie who knew the child was dead pretended that any visit by Evans would upset the child. On the other, it is asked why did Evans not tell his aunt that the child was in East Acton if this was what he believed? Why say that he had seen his mother when he had not? Only Evans and Christie knew.

＊

On the morning of the 2nd December Chief
Superintendent Barratt and Chief Inspector Jennings visited 10 Rillington Place. They went over the house, they
spoke to Mr. Kitchener, and they looked at the garden. The
wash-house door was firmly closed. In a report made six
years after the event and dated 22nd October 1955, the
Chief Inspector described the wash house in 1949 as a
locked out-building. But in a further report written four
days later, he corrected this when he said that the door was
shut and could not be opened until a piece of metal used
as a spindle was inserted. This, it was explained, would then

withdraw the tongue of the lock. The police ordered the door to be opened. Mrs. Christie, using a piece of metal as a spindle, opened it. A record of what was found was made by the Chief Inspector and appears in his notebook. This book still exists because, being a documentary exhibit in the trial of Evans, it has been preserved. The officer saw the wood stacked around the sink as shown in a photograph taken shortly afterwards. Using a torch he felt behind the wood and touched a large package which was found to contain the body of Beryl Evans, doubled up and wrapped in a blanket enclosed in a tablecloth, all tied with a rope cord. Although Beryl Evans had been dead some twenty four days no smell was detected. Behind the door Geraldine's body was found covered with but not wholly hidden by pieces of timber.

The officers interviewed Christie and Mrs. Christie. The Chief Inspector regarded Christie as a decent type of man. He already knew from the statements taken from Christie that he had been a War Reserve Police Officer, attached to Harrow Road Police Station, and by now Constable Byers would doubtless have made it known that prior to 1943 he had worked with Christie at Harrow Road Police Station, and considered him a capable officer. Sergeant Fensome had perhaps said that he knew Christie as a civilian who made a nuisance of himself bringing trivial complaints to the police. Mrs. Christie was asked about the wash house and her explanations were at first given verbally and later in a statement taken on 5th December 1949. When referring to the wash house she described it as a small out-building which is a disused wash house, situated in the back yard and used for storing wood and other things because the copper was out of order. She said that the building had an outside door which was locked at night. Mrs. Christie has been criticised for this, and it is true that the word "locked" is inaccurate. But many people referring to a door which, when closed, cannot be opened without the insertion of a spindle or piece of metal, might be excused for using the word "locked" in such circumstances. Its meaning at the time when the statement was given would be fully understood by Chief Inspector Jennings who was taking the statement, for he had seen the door closed in this way and was to describe it years later as being locked. Mrs. Christie's account, as recorded in her statement of 5th December, continued by saying that since 8th November 1949 "we have been using this place daily for the purpose of getting water for rinsing the slop pail, when emptying it in the lavatory which is situated next door". The date mentioned would obviously appear in the statement because Chief Inspector Jennings would have asked whether Mrs. Christie had been in the wash house since the 8th November. This was the day when, according to Evans' statements of 2nd December, he had put his wife's body in the wash house. Mrs. Christie has been criticised because in her deposition which is a 16 line precis of some 145 lines of statements, she is recorded as saying the following words: "I didn't use the wash house at the back. The boiler was out of order and hadn't been used for years. The wash house was for the use of all the tenants but only the water tap was used." The criticism was that Mrs. Christie was then saying that she did not use the wash house, that she was lying because she did use it, and that this points to some guilty knowledge in her. I would have thought it obvious that she was saying no more than that she did not use the wash house as a wash house but with the other tenants used it as a water point.

It is further said that Mrs. Christie must have become aware of the presence of the bodies in the wash house during this period if the bodies were there. But the evidence shows that on discovery there was no smell from the bodies. If the bundled body of Beryl Evans had been hidden behind the wood under the sink I see no reason why it should not have gone undetected by Mrs. Christie when she entered the wash house merely to draw water. If Mrs. Christie thought that wood had been stored behind the door, and it turned out that Geraldine's body was beneath the wood, I do not think that it must follow, as is suggested, that Mrs. Christie knew of that.

I do not find on the evidence that Mrs. Christie knew anything about the bodies being there or anywhere else. If, for example, Mrs. Christie had been told that Beryl Evans had died as a result of an abortion, and if Mrs. Christie had been prepared, in order to protect her husband, to keep a corpse in the wash house or in the house, I am unable to accept that she would have been so accommodating if she had known that Geraldine's corpse was also on the premises. For she would known that the child had been murdered. Mrs. Christie does not appear to have created in anyone the impression that she was either intelligent or full of guile; all that the evidence shows about Mrs. Christie is that she was a woman very much dominated by her husband. If she had known that the bodies of either Beryl Evans or Geraldine, or both, were in the wash house, I have little doubt that the many experienced police officers who questioned her when the wash house was opened up, and later, would have detected this. Either by her demeanour or in her answers to questions her knowledge would have been apparent.

The two officers also spoke to Christie who was hobbling about at the time seemingly in pain. As a result of the questioning the Chief Superintendent was satisfied certainly with the answers given by the Christies. It was decided that Evans should be brought back from Wales for questioning without further delay. The bodies were later transferred to the mortuary and Doctor Teare carried out a post-mortem examination on each.

Doctor R. D. Teare, M.D., F.R.C.P., F.C.Path., is now the Reader in the Department of Forensic Medicine at St. George's Hospital Medical School. He saw the bodies at 2 p.m. on 2nd December 1949. Geraldine had died from asphyxia due to strangulation by a tie tied tightly round her neck with a bow knot. At 3 p.m. he began the post-mortem, the first of two to be performed on the body of Beryl Evans. The body was clothed in a dress, blouse and jacket. Doctor Teare's impression was that the clothes were rumpled up round the waist. The breasts, upper abdomen, thighs and private parts were exposed. The body was in a jack-knifed position with the knees up under the chin. Doctor Teare thought that the clothes would have been lifted up for easier bundling, but apart from that was not prepared to make any further assumption. He did not know why the upper clothing should be opened. Doctor Teare although agreeing that it would be more probable for Beryl Evans to have been wearing knickers said that their absence did not greatly startle him. In 1953 Doctor Matheson told the Scott Henderson Inquiry that from his experience in prison many women young and old arrived in prison not wearing knickers.

The ligature which had been used to strangle Beryl Evans was not found upon the body. On the right side of the neck there was an abrasion 3½ inches long, 1¼ inches to 3/8 inch wide tapering to the rear indicating that the strangler had attacked from behind. Doctor Teare thought that the ligature had been a rope of 1/2 inch to 3/4 inch diameter. He could not exclude the possibility that a twisted nylon stocking might have been used in that, being twisted, the grooves in the pressure mark which tend to be seen when looser ligatures are used, would not appear. He thought however, that a twisted stocking would produce narrower marks than the ones found.

A group of old abrasions on the left side of the back of the neck were of no significance but—(*a*) on the left front of the neck just above the collar bone there was an abrasion which Doctor Teare thought could have been made by the hand of an assailant grasping the victim's throat, or by the victim's own finger nails when trying to pull something away from her throat. (*b*) There was a bruise 1½ inches in diameter on the inner aspect of the left thigh 4 inches above the knee and another 2½ inches long by one inch wide on the inner aspect of the left calf immediately below the knee. (*c*) There was considerable swelling of the right eye and upper lip. Doctor Teare thought that the findings in (*a*), (*b*) and (*c*) above were consistent with a struggle having taken place. (*d*) Doctor Teare also found an old scar in the posterior wall of the vagina and beside this a little ante mortem bruising. A sixteen week foetus was found but there was no evidence of interference with the pregnancy. The bruising of the left thigh and calf had not produced the kind of marks that Doctor Teare had seen in cases of forced intercourse. The mark on the thigh was large for a thumb mark although a thumb which dwelt and moved in that area might have caused it. Although Doctor Teare had not seen similar marks produced in such a case, he accepted that these marks were at least consistent with a man trying to force Beryl Evans' left leg with his right hand and right knee.

The considerable swelling of the right eye and upper lip is recorded in Doctor Teare's post-mortem examination report. Evidence of this was not adduced when Doctor Teare's deposition was taken at the Magistrates Court nor was it mentioned at Evans' trial when Doctor Teare was

asked less than thirty questions. The condition of Beryl
Evans' face at the first post-mortem showed blood signs
being the fluid of decomposition lying over and beyond
the area of the mouth. There was no evidence of any fresh
haemorrhage at or immediately before death. If there had
been blood anywhere which had been wiped away it
would have come from the mouth. The upper lip was
markedly swollen and turned upwards virtually touching
the nose. The lip had taken this shape and position in order
best to accommodate the gases and fluids of decomposition. Doctor Teare thought that the facial injuries had been
caused by one blow with the back of a hand or by the less
likely cause of two blows with a fist, and that when
inflicted there would have been little if any blood. He
thought this because in the decomposition he could not
see any gross laceration of the lips. He agreed that to some
extent decomposition might obscure laceration and that
there might have been a small effusion of blood sufficient
to stain the sheets and leave some residual blood at the
bleeding point. Doctor Teare had also said in 1953 that
there might have been blood-stained fluid coming from
the mouth and nose. Doctor Teare was of the opinion that
the swelling caused by the blow or blows would account
for about half that seen after decomposition. Doctor Teare
thought that after receiving the blow Beryl Evans must
have lived for some time for the swelling to develop. He
was not prepared to put a precise time but his estimate was
that the blow or blows probably occurred twenty minutes
before death. As one would imagine a ligature produces
some congestion in the face which would, if anything,
emphasise the marks on the face. On 8th July 1953 at the
Scott Henderson Inquiry, Doctor Teare described the
injuries as being quite evident though probably exaggerated by decomposition and to a certain extent by
strangulation. At that time Doctor Teare said that the

bruising and swelling were virtually typical of blows from the fist of which he thought there had been two. At the same time with reference to all the bruises Doctor Teare said that it was stretching his memory too much to try and remember then whether it was a matter of minutes or hours before death that the bruises had been caused. In his evidence Doctor Teare said that the body after strangulation would be seen to be deep blue by reason of the post-mortem staining. No doubt to a person unfamiliar with the normal appearance of a dead body who did not see those parts of it which most clearly show the post-mortem staining such as the back, the signs might be missed; equally they might be if the bruised face was turned away from the onlooker and if the neck weal in its most obvious areas was somehow not easily visible. But if all was as Doctor Teare suggests, then a person seeing the body some hours after death must have been very unobservant to have associated its appearance with abortion and not with violence.

At the first post-mortem Doctor Teare, alive to the question of abortion, examined the vagina visually using a magnifying glass. In 1949 the prevailing medical opinion was that vaginal semen would not survive for a period such as the three weeks between the death of Beryl Evans and the first post-mortem. (I use the word semen throughout where on occasions spermatozoa would be more accurate because the experts have used the words synonymously.) In 1949 it was not generally realised that in a cold body in a reasonable state of preservation semen could be recovered after a relatively long period. In the light of further knowledge Doctor Teare considers that his visual examination in 1949 would have disclosed the presence of semen if sexual intercourse with Beryl Evans had taken place at about the time of death. Professor Camps gave confirmatory evidence on this matter. He said that when Doctor Teare was looking for the visual signs of abortion fluid his mind and eye would be directed to the surface of the vagina, and if on that surface there had been a recent deposit of semen of any quantity, Doctor Teare would have spotted it immediately. Professor Camps pointed out that because the possibility of abortion had to be investigated the vagina had been opened up, thereby permitting the bruise to be seen. If there had been semen present and visual examination had not detected it, a swab might well have done so. It cannot be stated affirmatively that, because semen was not seen, therefore none was present, but Professor Camps' firmly held opinion was that it would have been seen.

In accordance with Chief Superintendent Barratt's order, Inspector Jennings telephoned to Merthyr Tydfil. He says that he spoke to Inspector Black who agrees with this, remembering that he broke off an interview with Evans to take the call. Chief Inspector Jennings, not wishing to discuss details on the telephone, told Inspector Black that the bodies had been found, that he was to stop questioning Evans, bring him to London, and to keep all newspapers from him and not to discuss the case at all with him. A matter which is material only on the recollection of the witnesses is that Sergeant Fensome claims that he made this telephone call and passed the message to Sergeant Corfield, who however denies receiving it, but agrees that Inspector Black took the message and passed on the orders received from London. I am quite sure that the Chief Inspector would not have permitted anyone else to pass a message of this nature to Wales. Inspector Black says that the call came during his first interview with Evans. This sufficiently coincides with the Inspector's recollection in 1953 that the message came about dinner time, for the interview is shown in the Occurrence Book as taking place from 11.45 a.m. to 12.20 p.m. The Chief Inspector thinks that the call was made later than this but I think that Inspector Black is right. There can be no certainty about it and the timing is not important. The interview which was so suddenly ended had not in Inspector Black's view been productive. He described Evans as being unco-operative and evasive and thought that both by his attitude and his expression he was sullen. The Inspector agreed that it could also have been the attitude of one who did not wish to be interviewed or was tired of being interviewed. Inspector Black considered that he had got nowhere with Evans when the interview ended.

There is a later entry made by the station officer in the Occurrence Book at Merthyr Tydfil which shows Sergeant Corfield as visiting Evans in the cells from 2.55 p.m. to 3.35 p.m. No one can now remember this visit or its purpose. It is possible that a delay in returning a key by Sergeant Corfield or a failure by the Station officer to note that a key had been returned earlier might have affected the time when the interview was booked as ending, but it is now impossible to discover the reason for this visit and nothing seems to turn on it. Evans had meals at 9.30 a.m. and 1.45 p.m. on this day, and a third meal at 4.10 p.m. prior to being handed over to the officers from London at 4.30 p.m. At some time Evans would have been told that he was being taken to London in connection with enquiries about the brief case. At the hand-over Sergeant Corfield and Evans signed a form headed Personal Property Found on Prisoner. Its contents accord with the entry in the Occurrence Book made when the articles were taken off Evans on his arrest at 6.0 p.m. on 30th November. The documents show that Evans had no money on his arrival at the police station. Seven articles which he would have had in his pockets when arrested, and his belts, collar, tie and scarf were signed for. There was no mention of a wrist watch. Constable Evans said that a wrist watch should have been taken off Evans and placed in the bag with the other articles. If so it would have been recorded and signed for but the Constable also said that it is possible that if someone had brought it in and left it at the Enquiry Office, the watch might have been handed to Evans and not to the police officer. It is Inspector Black's experience that a wrist watch would not be taken off the prisoner in such a case. The Inspector cannot now say that he saw Evans wearing one, for he has no more than a vague recollection of seeing one.

The party went by car to Cardiff Station. On the train the three men occupied a reserved first class compartment. Evans was handcuffed to Sergeant Corfield who thinks that during the journey the Inspector again asked Evans about his wife's whereabouts. The Inspector says that he did not. Inspector Black described Evans' demeanour during the journey as sullen and very depressed, and once or twice he noticed that Evans had tears in his eyes. The Inspector said that he tried to bring him out of himself, and eventually from being dejected and worried Evans brightened up at the mention of Queens Park Rangers Football Club, in which he was interested. Whether or not the Inspector's use of the word sullen is appropriate to describe Evans' demeanour, it is not a description of Evans under questioning, for I am satisfied that Evans was not asked any questions about his wife or child during the journey. I feel that Inspector Black would have hesitated to disobey a direct order from the Chief Inspector. The Inspector also kept all newspapers away from Evans and said nothing to him of the finding of the bodies. Of all the events concerning Evans and the police which have been the subject of criticism or inquiry, one matter that is clear beyond doubt is that Evans liked Inspector Black. There is no evidence that Evans ever changed his mind about this officer. Mrs. Evans said that her son described Inspector Black as a gentleman and I think that the Inspector is right when he says that, after Mrs. Evans had visited her son in the condemned cell for the last time, she passed to the Inspector Evans' kind regards. This is no small compliment to one who saw so much of Evans and probably spoke more to him than any other police officer.

The train arrived at Paddington Station at about 9.30 p.m. where photographers were awaiting it. Whether the news was leaked to the press in London, or whether it had been passed to London from Merthyr Vale or Merthyr Tydfil where some would by then have known that Evans had been taken to London, cannot now be known. The party stepped from the train in the order: Inspector Black, Evans and Sergeant Corfield. At this time a photograph was taken which has been referred to as Photograph A. It was supplied to the Inquiry by Photo Services Associated Newspapers Limited and has been given national publicity. It has also been reproduced in several books including "The Man on your Conscience" by Michael Eddowes, and a memorandum by the same author which was submitted to me. It appears in "10 Rillington Place" by Ludovic Kennedy and was submitted with a memorandum by Mr. H. M. Wolfe who, challenging Chief

Inspector Jennings' statement that Evans did not appear to be frightened or nervous when he arrived at Notting Hill Police Station, says that this photograph disproves it and that Evans was obviously frightened and nervous. Mr. Kennedy wrote of it "The photograph too is revealing: the haggard, hag-ridden expression like that of a hunted animal gives some idea of the strain and anxiety he was suffering." Another photograph taken at Paddington Station that night was supplied to the Inquiry by Camera Press Ltd., and was referred to as Photograph B. It matters not which of the two photographs was taken first, for it is clear from the position of the three men that the two photographs were taken within seconds of each other. I think that they make it apparent that Photograph A registers Evans' facial reaction of surprise to a flashbulb being used to take another photograph. In photograph B Evans' expression appears natural and bears no indication of strain or anxiety. Doctor Hobson, who as a witness could not more strongly support the case that Evans did not kill either his wife or child, said of these photographs when seeing them both that he did not think one can place a lot of reliance on the expression. I do not think that any reliance should be placed upon it.

Chief Inspector Jennings says that he met the train. Inspector Black agrees with this and so did Evans at his trial. The matter was questioned because Sergeant Fensome's recollection, in part supported by the vague recollection of Sergeant Corfield, is that he drove the car to the station and that the Chief Inspector was not there. Sergeant Corfield, in a statement made in 1953, said that the Chief Inspector was at Paddington, but when giving evidence before me he thought otherwise. I am in no doubt that Chief Inspector Jennings was at Paddington. He was in command. He had decided what was to be done and what was to be said, and more important to him, what was not to be said. It would be contrary to his nature not to be present to supervise a situation which he intended to control, for according to his plan there was to be what has been called in criticism a "confrontation". He also said that as the officer in charge and available to go it was his duty to be there.

The journey to Notting Hill police station would take about ten minutes or so. The station record shows that Evans was brought to the station at 9.45 p.m. On arrival the party went into a room called the D.I's office. With the passing of time some of the witnesses had forgotten the internal layout of the station, thinking that entry to this room was made through the C.I.D. Office. A plan of the station showed that both the D.I's office and the C.I.D. office had a separate door off the passage. On arrival Inspector Black asked for tea to be brought. In the D.I's office the handcuffs were released by Inspector Black, and Sergeant Corfield, without having to be told, left the room. Another officer whose identity is neither agreed upon nor important, took from a cupboard in the room the clothing, rope and wrappings which had been around the body of Beryl Evans and the clothing and tie which had been taken from the body of Geraldine. The two piles of clothing were placed side by side, their separate identities maintained. Nothing was said to Inspector Black about events which had happened in his absence or of those to follow. The Inspector, no doubt by experience sensing that something was afoot, having removed his máckintosh produced his notebook. At this time Evans would not know the identity of the silent Chief Inspector. According to both officers whilst all three present were standing up, the senior officer then spoke saying. "I am Chief Inspector Jennings in charge of this case. At 11.50 a.m. today I found the dead body of your wife Beryl Evans

concealed in a wash house at 10 Rillington Place, Notting
Hill, also the body of your baby daughter Geraldine in the
same outbuilding and this clothing was found on them.
Later today I was present at Kensington Mortuary when it
was established that the cause of death was strangulation in
both cases. I have reason to believe that you were responsible for their deaths." Evans answered "Yes".

As the Chief Inspector was speaking Inspector Black
said that he wrote down what was said in his notebook.
He wrote quickly, abbreviating words where necessary, so
that nothing would be missed. The Chief Inspector then
cautioned Evans and Evans made a verbal statement which
each officer said that he recorded in his own notebook.
This statement reads: "She was incurring one debt after
another and I could not stand it any longer so I strangled
her with a piece of rope and took her down to the flat
below the same night whilst the old man was in hospital.
I waited till the Christies downstairs had gone to bed, then
took her to the wash house after midnight. This was on the
Tuesday 8th November. On Thursday evening after I came
home from work I strangled my baby in our bedroom
with my tie and later that night I took her down into the
wash house after Christies had gone to bed." Chief
Inspector Jennings' notebook shows his entries. On page 3
there is written '9.45 p.m. on 2.12.49 at F.H. Stn. saw
Evans', followed in the Chief Inspector's handwriting by
the statement made by Evans. At the end is Evans' signature, with the time and date '9.55 p.m. 2/12/49' both
written by Evans in the notebook. Chief Inspector
Jennings said that he wanted the time of signature
recorded and that Evans looked at his wrist watch to
check the time. Inspector Black could say no more than
that he had a vague recollection that Evans had a rather
large new-looking wrist watch. To decide whether the
time was taken from a wrist watch or not is, I think,

impossible on the evidence at this length of time. Then follows 'He signed this statement, then added "It is a great relief to get if off my chest. I feel better already. I can tell you the cause that led up to it." 'After this follows an entry relating to the making of a second statement. Having therefore recorded the events from the time Evans first spoke, there follows the entry by the Chief Inspector of his own words spoken earlier, but not recorded by him at the time, before Evans made the first statement. The whole sequence of events is then written out again in the notebook.

Inspector Black's notebook, not having been made an exhibit at the Evans trial, is no longer in existence. It did exist on 9th July 1953 when it was produced at the Scott Henderson Inquiry where the officer's evidence was confirmed in that, according to the transcript of that Inquiry, he had written part of his note in pencil and later repeated the same entry complete and in ink. According to the transcript of that Inquiry the pencil note started: '9.45 p.m. 2/12/49 F.H. followed by Chief Inspector Jennings' words, followed by Evans' reply, the first statement and ending '9.55 p.m. 2/12/49.', all in Inspector Black's own handwriting. Whereas the transcript of the Scott Henderson Inquiry explains the form in which the note was taken, there is also a written statement still in existence, dated 3rd December 1949 and made by Inspector Black, containing the information already referred to and which the Inspector said was made from his notebook. Inspector Black when asked in evidence why Chief Inspector Jennings did not write down his own introductory remarks, said that the Chief Inspector would know what he was going to say before he spoke and would have memorised his words beforehand.

The officers say that Evans was upset in that he cried a little after making his first statement, and that when all three were standing up, the Chief Inspector thinks that Inspector Black put an arm round Evans' shoulder. He said that Inspector Black was that type of man. It was at this time that Constable McCann took in the tea. His recollection in evidence was that the Chief Inspector had an arm on Evans' shoulder and that both of them were sitting at the desk with Inspector Black standing or sitting on the other side of it. I do not think that Chief Inspector Jennings would have had his arm around Evans' shoulder. He said that it was Inspector Black who told Evans not to upset himself. In a statement made shortly before he gave evidence, Constable McCann could not recall what Inspector Black was doing when he entered the room. Constable McCann did not notice the clothes which were on the floor but remembered that he handed the tea to Inspector Black. Although the officer puts the time of his entry at 10.30 p.m., he also said that it was shortly after Evans' arrival at the station. This quick entry and exit sixteen years ago by Constable McCann on such an everyday errand as bringing in the tea, cannot be expected to have left more than a most general picture on his mind. Since the time of arrival at Notting Hill Police Station is fixed with reasonable accuracy, his timing of 10.30 p.m. is wrong.

After this Chief Inspector Jennings says that he again cautioned Evans asking him if he wished to have his explanation taken down in writing. Evans assented and the second statement was taken down by Inspector Black. Its contents are set out later in this Report. Inspector Black confirms this evidence. The officers both say that the statement ended at 11.15 p.m., having taken from 10.0 p.m. or from just after 9.55 p.m. to write and read back. They both say that they were surprised that Evans confessed so readily. Inspector Black says that he had to write fast and at times was unable to keep up, for Evans was very voluble and Chief Inspector Jennings had to hold up the dictation. Inspector Black made a note of the time of 11.15 p.m. in his notebook. The time when the statement started and finished is not recorded at the end of the statement and this was not necessary in the endorsement. In 1949 however, there was a current Home Office recommendation directing that the times be recorded in the notebook of the officer concerned. Inspector Black said that after the statement was read over he made his entry in his notebook 11.15 2nd December. In 1953 at the Scott Henderson Inquiry an answer given by the Inspector appeared contradictory to it but it was made clear that he was saying that the writing of the statement took until about 11 p.m. Both officers give similar evidence about this, and say that no questions were put to Evans, and that the statement was made as it was dictated. Inspector Black says that from the time he left London until he heard the statement he knew nothing about events save that the bodies had been found and that he was learning of them as the statement unfolded, just as he had first learned that Beryl Evans and the child had been strangled when Chief Inspector Jennings made his short speech to Evans.

In order to check on the time when the second statement was finished, various officers were asked at the Inquiry to try and remember their own times of departure that night, for all records and diaries have long ago been destroyed. In the case of all or most of them this would have been the first time since 1949 that they have been asked to do this. Sergeant Corfield had a recollection that he left the police station at 3 or 4 a.m. when Inspector Black told him to get home and be back in the morning. He said that it would be reasonable to suppose that Evans had confessed by then. Sergeant Fensome could not say when he left the station: he thought probably later than midnight; 2 a.m. at the earliest: possibly as late as 6 a.m. As far as Sergeant Corfield is concerned this would have been his third successive night spent wholly or partly out of his bed. The recollection of both these officers has failed them about the earlier events of the day, of the evening, and I think of the night also.

Constable Hammond was present when Evans was brought into the police station. He said that he was told to wait until the Chief Inspector gave him permission to go. Constable Hammond pointed out that he had nothing to do at the time and that he had been on duty since 9 a.m. He feels, for his recollection cannot help him positively, that if he had been sent home late for no good reason he would have resented it after being kept idly waiting. He said he remembered that the Chief Inspector came in to the C.I.D. office and said that Evans had made a statement admitting that he had killed his wife. The Constable said that about half an hour later he was told that he could go and that he was to be back at 7 or 8 o'clock in the morning. He puts his time of departure at between midnight and 1 a.m. He also had a vague recollection of seeing Sergeant Corfield come out of the Detective Inspector's office and of hearing from him about the instructions received in Wales. He also remembers the C.I.D. room without Sergeant Corfield being in it, but no more. Inspector Black says that he left the station nearer to midnight than 2 a.m. and that Evans had gone to the cells at 11.30 p.m. at the latest. Chief Inspector Jennings thinks that he probably got home between midnight and 1 a.m. and he does not agree that such was inconsistent with a reference in his statement for the Inquiry that it was well after midnight when he went home.

Criticism of the evidence that Evans was returned to the cells before midnight is made by Mr. Kennedy in his open letter to the Home Secretary. He there calls attention to a newspaper article in the News Chronicle of 3rd December 1949, which he claimed was a piece of evidence which had hitherto escaped notice. It is a short article of nine sentences, the last of which reads 'Early today a man was being interviewed by Notting Hill police'. In 1959–1960 Mr. Kennedy interviewed the Chief Sub-Editor of the News Chronicle whose name he does not now remember. He told Mr. Kennedy that the article was in the edition which went to press at 3 a.m. and that the phrase 'Early today' would not have been used unless a telephone message had been received by the newspaper after midnight that a man was still being questioned. Therefore, it is said, Evans must still have been under questioning after midnight. Inspector Black explained that if a journalist telephoned the press bureau at Scotland Yard a telephone call would have been put through to Notting Hill Police Station. If the man had not been charged the message given out would be the familiar one 'a man is assisting the police with their enquiries'. Evans was not charged until 10.50 a.m. on the 3rd December. Chief Inspector Jennings said that a newspaper would not be told what actually was being done but merely that enquiries were still proceeding. The newspaper article is inaccurate in several respects. It stated that the post mortem examination was 'made last night'. It was carried out in the afternoon. Both bodies, it is said, had been found under the sink. Only one was found there. It said that they had been dead for about fifteen days when in fact they had been dead for over three weeks. It was also stated that Beryl Evans had lived in the flat since her marriage two years ago. Beryl Evans and her husband had not lived there since their marriage, nor had they lived in the flat for two years. I would not place reliance on this article if it purports to show accurate timings of events inside a police station of which the reporter could have no direct knowledge.

When a person is held pending a charge of murder he is kept under supervision at all times. It was necessary for various officers to take their turn at this duty. One such officer who retired form the police force in October 1964 was Inspector Trevallian who in 1949 was a Sergeant in the uniformed branch. He gave evidence because having repeated once again, as he had done many times before, an account of his short association with Evans, he was told that it was his duty to give evidence. Sergeant Trevallian says that he sat at the entrance to Evans' cell keeping observation and talking to Evans. He does not know at what time of day he was on duty and he does not know who relieved him. The circumstances that brought him there and the general background of events are now very vague. The details have gone from his mind. To him they are unimportant; it is his own experience which has stayed with him. He thinks the incident occurred after 6 a.m. He remembered clearly that Evans was sitting down and was quite relaxed and that he had said to Evans words to the effect that he could possibly understand the murder of a wife but not the murder of a baby. Evans replied that it was the constant crying of the baby that got on his nerves and he just had to strangle it as he could not put up with the crying. At this time Sergeant Trevallian did not know whether Evans had made a formal statement, but he knew about Evans being brought in and that from the station gossip the case was, as he said settled. When the opportunity presented itself, Sergeant Trevallian spoke to a senior officer, he thinks that it may have been Inspector Black, and he repeated what Evans had told him. This officer said that they knew all about it as Evans had made a statement. The witness said that at the time he thought that Evans was speaking the truth, nor does he now doubt it. The strength of this witness's evidence is that the nature of the conversation has remained firmly in his mind although over the years the surrounding and related details, which are unimportant to him, have been forgotten. He told me that when he heard of this Inquiry he was so confident of his experience that he thought that any Inquiry was a waste of time and it was when he was giving his reasons for this opinion that his listener told him that it was his duty to give evidence.

Another officer at Notting Hill at this time was Constable Strait. He too kept observation over Evans. He talked to Evans on general matters only. It was during the night, but he is not sure of his watch. He does not know whether he was on duty before or after Sergeant Trevallian. He thinks that he did duty for about an hour. He remembered that on the following day, Sergeant Trevallian asked him whether Evans had said anything about the murder. When Constable Strait said that he had not, Sergeant Trevallian then told of his experience and of Evans' admission of guilt.

On the following morning at about 9.30 a.m. Mrs. Evans went to the police station to see her son. On the previous day, having read in a newspaper that bodies had been found at 10 Rillington Place, Mrs. Evans had gone there to find out what she could, but the policeman on duty would not permit her to enter. At the police station she was told, and Mrs. Evans thinks that it was by Chief Inspector Jennings, that Evans was about to be taken to Court, and that she could see him there or at Brixton prison on Sunday, the 4th December. The officer told Mrs. Evans that her son would be granted legal aid and made

the suggestion that she should see him on the Sunday. This
Mrs. Evans did.

On the 3rd December at 9.40 a.m. Evans was told that
he was going to be charged with the murder of his wife
by strangulation on the 8th November. He answered "Yes,
that's right". Just before leaving the police station for the
Court, he was formally charged with that offence, and
made answer "I have nothing to say". Evans was not at this
time charged with the murder of Geraldine. He was driven to the Magistrates Court in company with Inspector
Black and Sergeant Corfield. The evidence heard on the
3rd December was formal, and Evans was remanded until
15th December 1949. He was given a legal aid certificate
and taken to Brixton prison. There are two incidents
which took place at about this time, one on the way to
court and one after Evans had been remanded, about
which much has been written and alleged. The first is a
conversation that took place in the car carrying Evans
from the police station to court; the second concerns a
conversation between the police and Mrs. Ashby about the
tie which had been found round Geraldine's neck.

On the journey to court Evans said to the Inspector,
"There is something I meant to tell you, Mr. Black",
whereupon the Inspector interrupted and reminded Evans
that he had been cautioned and he need not say anything.
But Evans continued . . . "Yes, I know but I meant to tell
you this. After I killed my wife I took her wedding ring
from her finger and sold it to Samuels at Merthyr for 6/."
Evans was unaware that the police knew about the wedding ring and had it in their possession, for when
Constable Evans recovered it from Mr. Scannell in Wales
he did not question Evans about it. On arrival at the
Court the Inspector reported this conversation to Chief
Inspector Jennings. It is the latter's recollection that at the
time he happened to be speaking to Mr. Freeborough who

was in court on other business but was later to become Evans' solicitor. Inspector Black took the ring to Evans who on being further cautioned said, "That's the one I sold and told you about". An account of this conversation was included in a statement which Inspector Black made on the same day. On 22nd December, at the committal proceedings the Inspector gave his evidence on oath. It was confined to this incident alone. Sergeant Corfield, whose unaided recollection of earlier events has often faded, remembers making an entry of this conversation in his note book when he arrived at Court. He also made a statement about it. The original of that statement and the notebook no longer exist, but a copy of the statement does.

This evidence, which on the face of it is an unequiv-ocal admission of guilt in respect of the death of Beryl Evans was not given in evidence at Evans' trial. The reason for its omission is, I think, clear. Evans was tried on the indictment alleging that he had murdered Geraldine. The defence objected to the admission of evidence in respect of the murder of Beryl Evans which the prosecution sought to adduce in proof of Evans' guilt of the murder of his child. During the legal argument on the admissibility of the evidence in respect of Beryl Evans' murder, counsel for the defence, in addition to taking the general point on admissibility, urged that the evidence with regard to the selling of the ring, relating as it did to the death of the wife only, was such that its prejudicial effect outweighed any probative value that it might have. It will be realised that the sale of the ring might be given an importance which it did not warrant. Selling a ring does not itself go to the issue whether Evans killed his wife, still less his child. Mr. Justice Lewis ruled that in law the evidence in respect of the killing of Beryl Evans was admissible on the count before the jury. The prosecution however, although calling other evidence in respect of the death of Beryl Evans did not lead any of the evidence relating to the wedding ring which was to be found in the depositions of Mrs. Lynch, Constable Evans and Inspector Black. In the brief delivered to Junior Counsel for the Prosecution it can be seen where he has crossed this evidence out of his copy deposition. The result was that this particular statement by Evans was not considered by the jury and Evans was not called upon to explain the making of it or its meaning, or when he obtained the ring. It was suggested at the Inquiry that the two police officers may not have recorded Evans' exact words and that he might have used some other phrase such as 'after my wife died', which has been wrongly and inadvertently recorded as 'after I killed my wife'. The conversion of a phrase referring to the death merely as a point of time and made by a person charged with murder into a plain admission of guilt could not, in my view, occur by mistake save in exceptional circumstances. Either Evans said this or the police officers deliberately attributed to him an admission of guilt which he had not made. I have no doubt that the police officers in evidence were telling the truth to me as they did in 1949, when the one gave this evidence on oath and both made statements about it.

Mrs. Ashby remembers that on this day—the 3rd December—Chief Inspector Jennings and Inspector Black called at 11 St. Marks Road to tell Mrs. Evans what had happened in Court. Mrs. Ashby said that she told the officers that she could not believe that her brother had murdered his child as he loved her too much. She says Chief Inspector Jennings answered by saying that there was no doubt about it, that the baby was strangled with a tie, and that the poor little mite's head was nearly off. Mrs. Ashby said that she asked if she could see the tie and the

Chief Inspector said that he did not have the tie with him but that he would show her a photograph. This offer, she said, caused Inspector Black to say "For God's sake man, don't show the girl that," for the photograph showed the tie around the baby's neck. Mrs. Ashby said that she was interested in the tie because she usually bought the few which her brother owned and that he had three coloured ones at this time. Inspector Black does not recall this conversation at all and says that in any event, the words are not his for he would not have used the phrase "For God's sake" which is attributed to him. In 1953 at the Scott Henderson Inquiry Mrs. Ashby had said that Inspector Black's comment was "I do not think I should show her that". Mr. Baker's notes made in 1953 under the name of Mrs. Ashby, read as follows:- "Jennings offered to show Eileen (Mrs. Ashby) the photos. Said 'Baby's head nearly cut off by tie'. Tuesday Old Bailey Jennings said he would show mum photos. Black said 'no'."

It seems a little unusual that during the trial at the Old Bailey a police officer engaged in the case would be offering to show a photograph to Mrs. Evans. It is also surprising that the same sort of offer should be made by that officer in the presence of the same Inspector some weeks later. It exemplifies, I think, how one incident may with time be multiplied. This demonstrates the other possibility which must be considered when accounts of events are recorded as given by Mrs. Ashby and Mrs. Evans, for in recounting them they tend to refer to the experience of another member of the family as the experience of the speaker. When the note taker does not accurately distinguish the source of his information confusion arises. Chief Inspector Jennings could not be blamed for not having in his own possession an exhibit such as a piece of clothing when calling at the Evans' home after the first formal remand. It may be said that offering to show a photograph of a tie around the baby's throat showed a lack of sensitivity; on the other hand, there was no attempt to prevent Mrs. Ashby from seeing the photograph of the tie if she could face up to it. Mrs. Ashby admits that it was more than likely that when giving her account of this incident to Mr. Kennedy on 24th May 1960 she had told him that the Chief Inspector would not listen to her. This Mrs. Ashby said in evidence, but it amounted to no more than that she was saying that it was beyond her belief that her brother could have murdered Geraldine and the police officer was saying that he was sure that Evans had. This incident is taken to its most exaggerated conclusion by Mr. H.M. Wolfe who in his memorandum says that if a police officer was prepared to produce a photograph in these circumstances, conclusions could be drawn concerning methods when dealing with a man whom he believes to have murdered his wife and child.

During the period December 1949 to January 1950 Mrs. Evans and her daughters must have been suffering great distress. For a decent family to find one of its members charged with a capital offence must have meant a continuous and dreadful ordeal for all, the more distressing in this case as the victims were a daughter-in-law and an only grandchild. With that knowledge the actions of the Evans family must always be judged with understanding and sympathy and as taking place within the confines of this tragedy.

Mrs. Ashby says that Chief Inspector Jennings told her that the tie was a dirty one, and she said that she described to him the colour of her brother's ties. Mrs. Ashby did not at any time after 3rd December attend at the police station to look at the tie. She did not attend the trial, giving as the reason for her non-attendance the fact that she was working. I did not believe that answer when Mrs. Ashby gave it. The real reason for her non-attendance was that Mrs.

Ashby thought that her brother was guilty. It was not until her last visit to Pentonville Prison that she thought otherwise. For Mrs. Ashby said that she was the last to take leave of her brother and she asked him "Please tell me before we go, did you or did you not touch that baby?" In answer, said Mrs. Ashby, her brother looked her straight in the eye and said "I did not touch her, Eileen", and she believed him. No question was asked about Beryl Evans. At this time Mrs. Ashby was about 27 years of age. I make every allowance for the general circumstances in which the Evans family found itself and bear in mind the strangeness that they must have felt particularly in those days, in meeting lawyers, to them strangers, for the first time. I realise that they probably felt diffident and lacking self confidence in knowing how to go about making enquiries of others or presenting their views to the lawyers who might seem somewhat remote from their ordinary lives. None-the-less I do not think that Mrs. Ashby would have failed to examine the tie if she had thought it worth while to do so. Thinking as she did during the preparation for, and the period of the trial, the tie was of no importance in Mrs. Ashby's mind. She cannot have spoken about it much at home for her sister Mrs. Westlake does not remember the tie being discussed. When Mrs. Ashby visited Evans' solicitor's office about another matter she did not mention the tie.

In 1953 the tie seemed for the first time to be important. It was then, when others had urged their opinions upon her, that Mrs. Ashby gave details of the colour of her brother's ties to the Scott Henderson Inquiry. In July 1953 Mrs. Ashby herself wrote a petition to the Queen complaining, amongst other things, that at the Scott Henderson Inquiry she asked if she might see the tie, but was told that by then it had been destroyed. Mrs. Ashby's complaint was that the destruction of it was most convenient for the law and that the tie was one of the most vital parts of the case. But under the regular police procedure an exhibit such as a tie would have been destroyed long before 1953. The information on this is that in March 1950 Chief Inspector Jennings was given authority to destroy the tie and also certain other clothing. This authority would in the normal way be entered in the Prisoners Property Office Authority Book. This book was, in accordance with established practice, destroyed in 1961. The complaint then was the failure to preserve the tie until 1953, not the failure of the police to show it in 1949.

But criticism of the police officer in respect of the tie did not end in 1953, for in that year the Evans family was being advised by a firm of solicitors who still act for them, and the partner who handled their affairs was Mr. Morley Lawson. Unknown to him and within a very short time of the Scott Henderson Inquiry, at least one other non-lawyer was giving advice and preparing documents about the Evans matter for the Evans family. On 11th August 1953, a typewritten letter bearing the letter heading, 11 St. Marks Road, was posted in North Kensington to Chief Inspector Jennings. The letter made requests for exhibits, statements and the like to be sent. The letter was signed by Mrs. Ashby. Mrs. Ashby cannot type but she must have known who prepared the letter for her signature, and after some hesitation due to reluctance rather than lack of recollection she gave the name of the person whom she thought was the author of the contents of the letter. He is a person who seems to be well known as one nursing his own private discontents.

Over two years later, in January 1956, a lengthy petition, also typewritten, was sent to the Queen through the Home Secretary. This was signed by Mrs. Evans who at the Inquiry acknowledged her signature but denied knowing anything about the document. It appears to be related to the letter of the 11th August 1953, in that it makes reference to the failure of Scotland Yard to supply certain documents and in both letter and petition the word wash house is spelt with one h, and the word miscarriage is hyphenated. Mrs. Evans said that she had signed her name so often for people writing books and papers that she does not know what she has signed. She maintains that all correspondence was done with and through Mrs. Ashby, and that without Mrs. Ashby's consent she would not sign any paper. Mrs. Ashby said that she knows nothing about the petition, yet one of the complaints in it was the Chief Inspector Jennings refused to show the tie to Mrs. Ashby, as it had become an exhibit, although the same tie had been shown to Christie and Mrs. Christie. I can well understand that Mrs. Evans did not read every one of the many documents placed before her for signature and may have no recollection of the contents of this lengthy document. I find it difficult to believe that Mrs. Ashby knows nothing about it.

There is no evidence of any refusal to show the tie to Mrs. Ashby. This is a wrong emphasis given to an interview when the police officer, not having the tie in his possession, offered to show a photograph of it to Mrs. Ashby. I think that this is one of several incidents which with the change of opinion that some people have had about Evans' guilt, has been turned over, discussed and exaggerated in an effort to put blame where none should lie.

When Evans was taken to Brixton Prison he was seen on arrival at 1 p.m. by Doctor J.C.M. Matheson, then the Principal Medical Officer at the prison who has now retired. Evans was admitted to the hospital ward. At the time of this first interview Doctor Matheson had no information about how Evans was alleged to have killed his victims, other than that which he might have read in the newspapers. Doctor Matheson would be the first to interview Evans in the ward as it was not the custom for a subordinate to hold a preliminary interview or supply any information to the Doctor. The meeting with Evans took the usual form. It was private. Doctor Matheson and Evans were seated on different sides of the desk. Doctor Matheson thought and still thinks that he established the doctor patient relationship which he sought to achieve. His main purpose in interviewing Evans at this time and in this way was to form an opinion whether or not Evans was fit to plead to the indictment and to stand his trial. The doctor said that he gave Evans a warning that he need not say anything but that if he did, the doctor would have to report it if need be when Evans came to trial. The account of this interview is recorded in Doctor Matheson's own handwriting in the Hospital Case Paper relating to Evans. It starts with details of a physical examination. The report continues under headings of Family History, Personal History, School, Spare time and Sex. Doctor Matheson said that save for prompting where necessary with a phrase such as "What next?" he allowed Evans to tell his own story at his own speed. The notes made by the Doctor are not a verbatim record of Evans' or the Doctor's exact words. They are in places a paraphrase of what was said but as an accurate reproduction of the interview the notes speak for themselves.

"Married 1947. Knew her 9 months before marriage. She was 18 yrs. He was 23 yrs. No premarital sexual intercourse. Marriage happy at first. Wife then started incur debt, rent and furniture. Living in own flat. She did not drink. Baby, female 1948 (October 14th). Wife then got jealous of baby—rows—at first he ignored her but she kept it up and he got fed up with it. She kept at it until Tuesday 8.11.49 and he killed her. It all happened in a fit of temper. He came home from work a row started on debt, he lost his temper and strangled her. Put body in wash house. Stops at this and says 'Do I have to go through all this? I have told it all to the police'. He says it distresses

him to think of it but there are not many signs of great distress. Baby disposed of on Thursday 20.11.49. Went to
Wales on following Sunday. He looked after baby himself
from the Tuesday to the Thursday. On Sunday went to relatives in Wales. Gave himself up in Wales before the bodies
were discovered. Gave himself up last Wednesday 30.11.49.
Didn't tell anyone about it until he gave himself up . . ."

The date written as Thursday 20.11.49 should have read
10.11.49. Doctor Matheson said that this was his mistake
in quickly and wrongly guessing at a date when only the
day of the week had been mentioned by Evans. Doctor
Matheson said that when Evans started talking about the
crime with which he was charged he then got tired and
resistant to any further questions or interventions. It was
the conduct, said the Doctor, more or less of a normal man
who appreciated what was happening at the interview and
the position he was in. When saying that there were not
many signs of great distress the Doctor accepted that it was
not a happy situation, awaiting prosecution for murder.
Evans had shown signs of quite deep emotion at the mention of the baby and appeared to love the baby very much.
He had the appearance of being mentally and physically
tired and worn out, and the Doctor thought that there was
a good deal of mental dulling due to shock. Doctor
Matheson said that save for trying to find out whether
Evans was suffering from any insane delusion or impulses
there was no cross examination of him and the nearest that
could be said to be cross examination would be when the
Doctor asked how the baby's presence went unnoticed by
others, when the baby was left unattended all day. This particular questioning would, I think, have occurred at a later
interview when, as the notes show, this matter was discussed. When the account reached the stage of going to
Wales, Doctor Matheson said that Evans seemed to

brighten up. Doctor Matheson thought that Evans was telling him the truth. In coming to this conclusion he was making what he called an ordinary human appreciation of Evans. The Doctor agreed that he had made mistakes in judging whether a person was speaking the truth or not. At the end of this interview Doctor Matheson recorded under the heading First Impression—"Some emotional dulling. Not intelligent. ?M.D. high grade." M.D. here means Mental Defective.

Evans was received into the ward at 1.30 p.m. In the Hospital Ward a book called the Hospital Occurrence Book is kept. The first entry relating to Evans was made on this day and reads: "... Appears cheerful and converses with others. Watches games." Doctor Matheson said that he would see Evans in the ward and ask him how he was, and he said that whenever he saw Evans and had an interview with him he would record it in the Hospital Case Paper. On 28th December 1949, Doctor Matheson wrote a report on Evans. It would in the main be based on the notes which had been made on 3rd December, and anything else reported in the meantime. Doctor Matheson recorded that he had not seen the depositions to check Evans' story. In this report he gave his first impression of Evans as an inadequate psychopath with schizoid traits. Doctor Matheson described a psychopath as one who tends always to want to get his own way and who will act without any foresight, regardless of possible consequences to himself. He stressed this lack of foresight and lack of reasoning power. A person so described might make a statement to his own detriment just as a perfectly normal person who had committed a serious crime might do. The Doctor said that such inadequate people do not worry at the right time or over the right things. They might take trivial matters too seriously and serious matters too lightly.

∘∘⊰⊱∘∘

During the morning of the following day, Sunday the 4th December, Mrs. Evans, accompanied by her husband, went to Brixton prison to see her son. They were the first members of the family to see him. A 1953 record of this visit appears in Mr. Baker's notes, where Mrs. Evans is reporting that she asked her son what had happened and he replied:

"I did not touch her, Mum, Christie did it. I didn't even know the baby was dead until the police brought me to Notting Hill. Christie told me the baby was at East Acton.

Don't trust Jennings, Mum, he's a swine. Black's a gentle-man."

Mr. Baker's other note is:

"Tim said in Court Cops kept him up all night trying to get him to confess to baby murder. Finally Jennings threw baby's dress in his face. I signed it because I didn't care if I lived or died when I knew my baby was dead."

Nothing of this was said in Court at Evans' trial in January 1950 as the transcript of the evidence shows. Mr. Baker says that the words "in Court" were not in his original notes but appeared in his typescript of them, which is an expansion of the original note, putting it into story form. But Mr. Baker understood that the inclusion was what Mrs. Evans had told him. At one time in her evidence Mrs. Evans said that she did tell Mr. Baker that Evans had said in Court that the cops had kept him up all night trying to get him to confess. Similarly, the words "trying to get him to confess to baby murder" are not found in Mr. Baker's original notes. Mr. Baker cannot be criticised for expand-ing or adding to his notes as he wishes, but the fact that he has done so must be borne in mind when these notes are considered for the purpose of record, for in some ways they appear misleading.

In her proof of evidence prepared by her solicitors for the Scott Henderson Inquiry in 1953, this interview of 4th December was dealt with in some detail by Mrs. Evans. After hearing how he had blamed Christie, Mrs. Evans asked her son why he had made the statements which she knew he had made to the police and Evans replied "I know I made all them statements, Mum, but only one of them is true. The one in which I said that Christie had done it". Mrs. Evans then remarked: "You have made so many statements that when you tell the truth they won't believe you". Thereupon Evans answered "See Christie". Mrs. Evans told the Inquiry that this was one of several visits on which her son had said that Christie had done it. Mrs. Evans' proof continues with her saying that her son told her that at Notting Hill the police had "kept him at it" until about 5 o'clock in the morning: that he did not know that his baby was dead until he got to Notting Hill Police Station and that at one stage when he was being cross examined, Chief Inspector Jennings threw the baby's clothes in his face and said "Your baby is also dead". Evans told his mother that he had signed the statement containing the confession because he had nothing left to live for now that Beryl and the baby were dead. The procedure which Mr. Scott Henderson followed resulted in Counsel for Mrs. Evans putting leading questions to her. These, as one might expect, were in the main answered by the word "Yes". In this way Mrs. Evans explained that Evans had said that he did not know of his child's death until his arrival at Notting Hill and that he had been at the Station until about 5 o'clock in the morning, and that whilst he was being questioned the baby's clothes were produced to him by Chief Inspector Jennings, and that the officer had then said, "Your baby is also dead". The suggestion that the clothes were thrown in Evans' face was omitted from Counsel's questions.

When Mrs. Evans gave evidence before me she said that to her Evans denied killing his wife or child saying that he did not touch them, that he did not do it, and that until he got back to London he did not know that his baby was also dead. She repeated that on 4th December 1949 Evans had complained of being kept up until 5 o'clock, and that the police, meaning thereby Chief Inspector Jennings, kept telling him to confess, and threw the clothes at him saying "Confess, you bloody liar, you baby is dead as well". Mrs. Evans said that on this day her son did not look fully sane. Although these accounts vary in detail, the general picture is of a protracted cross-examination during which the baby's clothes were produced and thrown at Evans at the moment chosen to tell him of the death of his child and to demand a confession from him. When Evans gave evidence at his trial he made it plain that he was told about the death of the wife and the baby as soon as he arrived at Notting Hill Police Station.

After the first visit to Brixton Prison made by Mrs. Evans and her husband other members of the family visited Evans. On either the 5th or 6th December, his two sisters visited him. Mrs. Westlake, who was then only 20, was distressed and crying, and Evans seeing this, asked his elder sister the reason for her tears. Mrs. Ashby said, "Well what do you think she is crying for. It's because of what you've done" and Evans replied, "I haven't done anything. Christie done it". Mrs. Ashby says that either on this visit or at a later one Evans said that he was not responsible, and he went on to say that Christie knew all about it and had medical books described as black ones with a white cross on the front. These were undoubtedly Christie's handbooks from the St. Johns Ambulance Brigade which to Evans, unable to read or understand, would be as convincing a proof of learning as any medical text book.

At some time which cannot be accurately fixed, either at Brixton or Pentonville prison, Mrs. Ashby must have asked her brother why he had admitted the murders if he had not committed them. I would have thought that this was more probably said at Brixton than at Pentonville because by the time Evans was at Pentonville he had given his reasons during the trial. In any event, in view of the many visits made by the family to Evans it seems to me that from the start this must have been the burning question that they would be asking him and each other, since the family knew from the police in the early stages that Evans had made several statements.

When Mrs. Ashby was seen by Mr. Kennedy in 1959/1960 he may well have asked her a similar question, for Mrs. Ashby told him that they had asked Evans if he had done it, to which he replied that Christie had done it. When Evans was then asked why he had said that he had done it, he gave the answer that Christie had said that if Evans confessed, everything would be all right. I find it difficult to believe that Mrs. Ashby would be making up that answer for she must have asked some such question. If this was in fact said by Evans, he was offering a reason for the making of his confession of guilt which was different from the reason that he gave to his mother on the 4th December, and was again different from any of the three which he gave at his trial. Making all allowances for the fact that Evans was a liar who no doubt said things which came most readily to his tongue, it is somewhat strange that at whatever stage in these events this conversation took place Evans to his own family should be incapable of telling a consistent story to explain his conduct. The meaning of that remark by Evans must be that at some time in London Christie had told him that this was what he was to say if questioned about the death or deaths.

One of the matters that I find strange in the interviews which took place between Evans and his family was his way of making cryptic remarks in explanation of his conduct. On the 15th December for example, his mother said that he made the remark "Have you seen Christie, he is the only one who can help me". In addition to saying "Christie done it" he was heard to say "Get Christie". When it is remembered that Evans was a fluent talker these answers seem to show an economy of language and thought which I would not have expected in a person such as he, in view of his predicament. I would have expected him to have poured out his heart and his anger and not to have confined himself to these somewhat strange remarks. To none of the family did he repeat what happened. No member of his family has said that he mentioned an abortion or told his family anything about Beryl Evans' death save that in Mr. Baker's notes there is an entry that Evans is reported as having said that when he came home on 8th November he found Beryl Evans with blood all over her.

Evans' explanations to his family about the events which had brought him to Brixton Prison should be considered in the light of other explanations which he was giving during this period. It was Inspector Black's duty to take Evans to Court and to return him to Brixton prison. The Inspector says that Evans was always very friendly towards him and told him that he was the only person he could trust and that he would never lie to him. On one occasion he remembers that Evans had asked whether it was right for the prison doctor and officials to have questioned him. Inspector Black said that he told Evans that it was right and that he should tell them the truth and that he should also tell the truth to his legal advisers and his family. Evans, according to the Inspector, went on to tell him that he did intend to tell his mother and sisters the truth, but at the last minute he could not bring himself to do so as he felt so awful about it. And he told the Inspector that his trouble was that he had never had any money, that he had married too young, and that marriage had kept him poor. Inspector Black considered that he got to know Evans well and won his confidence, and the Inspector always thought that Evans treated him as a friend. He disagrees with the suggestion that Evans was a timid little man, and says that as he knew him he was reserved until you got to know him but then he would talk freely. One of his main subjects of conversation was football, and in particular the club he supported, and he would talk of the things that he had done when he had some money to spend, and how he managed when he was hard up. Inspector Black gave his opinion of Evans as a person able to hold his own in any company having, as the Inspector described it, average intelligence for his class and district. I understood the Inspector to mean any company which Evans was likely to keep. Inspector Black said that Evans, when speaking of the committal proceedings, had said that everyone had been very fair and that everything that had been said was the truth. This, I think, would only have been said once and whatever the language used it is probable that it would have been said, if at all, of the evidence called on the day when the words were spoken. This is born out by the fact that when appearing before the Scott Henderson Inquiry in 1953, Inspector Black's evidence fixed this conversation as being on 22nd December 1949, for he then said that Evans had spoken in this way after he had been committed for trial. This was also the day upon which Inspector Black had himself given evidence. Inspector Black says that he would have told Chief Inspector Jennings the substance of the various conversations that were passing between himself and Evans on these journeys. No report of the conversations was made by Chief Inspector Jennings to his superior officer and the suggestion is made that since the conversations were not reported in writing in this way they did not take place. Inspector Black said that he would not expect this type of conversation to be the subject of any report particularly when the hearing had begun. I would have thought that it would have been unlikely that these conversations would have been recorded in view of the confessions which had been made and the conversation in court between Chief Inspector Jennings, Mr. Crump and Mr. Freeborough which is dealt with later.

The Inspector also described how he parted from Evans at Brixton Prison on 22nd December after Evans had been committed for trial. He said that they shook hands and Evans wanted to know when they would next meet and the Inspector told him that this would be in Court at Evans' trial, but that then they would be on opposite sides of the Court and they would not be able to talk to each other. According to the Inspector, Evans using both hands, gripped the Inspector's hand and said "I'm sorry", meaning that he regretted that they would not be talking together again.

It is suggested that these conversations were either invented or imagined by Inspector Black in 1953 in that being so certain in his own mind that he had at all times behaved properly, he decided to add this evidence which could not be challenged and was to him no more than an underlining of what he knew to be right. In this way those who enquired might be silenced or presumably would know that another evidential barrier had to be removed. If that be right, it means that, having imagined or lied about these matters in 1953, Inspector Black is therefore committed for ever to this story and is persisting to the end in its truth, or alternatively that with time he has come to believe it to be true. I have to decide whether or not I believe Inspector Black: whether these matters about which he speaks were or were not said, for there is no direct evidence to support or challenge these conversations. There is corroboration of the nature of the relationship existing between the Inspector and Evans in that at some time or other, both Mrs. Evans and Mrs. Ashby repeated that Inspector Black was a gentleman in the eyes of Evans and it was after these incidents that Evans was to speak of Inspector Black with warmth to Counsel. This tends to support Inspector Black's evidence that he won Evans' confidence. It does not support that he heard

what he claims to have heard from Evans. At the Scott
Henderson Inquiry, Inspector Black gave evidence of all
these conversations in the motor car; he also said that he
had no idea that Evans was retracting or intended to
retract the statements which he made at Notting Hill
Police Station. If, as I think is the fact, Evans sent a farewell
message to Inspector Black from the condemned cell
which was carried to him by Mrs. Evans after her last visit
to her son, it would not be unlikely that Evans would take
his farewell of the Inspector in the manner which has been
described. When Evans shook hands with Inspector Black,
he had on that day heard the Inspector give evidence of
the admission made on 3rd December, "After I killed my
wife . . .", in respect of the wedding ring. I believed
Inspector Black. I do not think that he invented the substance of these conversations in 1953 and is persisting in
lies. Nor do I think that he has imagined these conversations and retained them in his memory as a shield against
those who have challenged his conduct or recollection.

On the 4th January 1950 Doctor Matheson had a second interview with Evans, and by this date the Doctor was in possession of the depositions and the police reports. At this interview Evans told the Doctor that his wife did not to Evans' knowledge try to abort herself but that she asked him to get an abortion carried out upon her. The Doctor not unnaturally asked Evans why he had told different stories to the police. Evans did not explain but answered "I do not know". Later on in the report appears the entry "... After wife was dead he used to feed the baby in the morning before he went to work, tuck her up in the cot and leave her in the room alone. Did not feed her again until he got back from work in the evening about 6.30 p.m." The words "after wife was dead" were an abbreviation of Doctor Matheson's phrase "After your wife was dead". Doctor Matheson said that he deliberately referred to the death of Beryl Evans in this way because he did not wish to appear accusatory. He did not take any initiative in inviting further information from Evans as to the manner in which the child was killed because he did not think it right, in his position, to keep bothering Evans after he had told the Doctor everything that was necessary for the Doctor's purposes in determining Evans' mental state. Evans who on 3rd December had already told the Doctor about killing Beryl Evans said nothing to correct this admission at this second interview.

During his first interview with Evans, Doctor Matheson tested Evans' mentality and fixed his intelligence quotient at 65, which he said was rather low, and put Evans' mental age at about 11 years. Doctor Matheson's opinion was that the defect in Evans was an educational one and not an innate defect. He was a dullard, due largely to his educational defects and to that period of time towards the latter end of his married life which had been unhappy. The Doctor found that Evans was not unintelligent in answering questions. Tests carried out by a Doctor Read record that he had assessed Evans' mental age as 14 years, according to his estimated total vocabulary of 9,000 words. His report was included in the Hospital Case Book, where he went on to say "The Healy Form Board he did very well and accurately. Memory and attention good. Weak in simple arithmetical problems. Reasoning was poor".

On 22nd September 1955 Doctor Matheson wrote to Sir Frank Newsam, the Permanent Under Secretary of State at the Home Office, summarising his interviews with

Evans. In that letter the Doctor ends by saying "At all my interviews I always got the impression that Evans, in talking of the crime, was telling me the truth". Doctor Matheson agreed that the word "all" refers to the two interviews of 3rd December 1949 and 4th January 1950. In his report to the Director of Public Prosecutions dated 9th January 1950, Doctor Matheson wrote that he had had further interviews with Evans. Today there are only written records of one further interview, namely that of 4th January. It may well be in fact, that Doctor Matheson had more interviews with Evans than he now remembers but that he did not make any written entry about them. Doctor Matheson ended his letter by saying "But he said 'She would never stop once she started a row'. In conclusion, I feel, if I may use popular language, in my "heart of hearts" Evans did murder his wife and child".

At some date after 3rd December 1949, the defence of Evans was undertaken by a firm of Solicitors, Freeborough, Slack & Co. In the main the matter was handled by Mr. Saunders, the Managing Clerk. He was then over 80 years of age. He had spent his lifetime in the law. Mr. Freeborough, the senior partner, spoke highly of Mr. Saunders, describing him as a first rate man who had joined this firm in 1937 and had been largely responsible for holding the practice together during the war when Mr. Freeborough was away. Mr. Freeborough said that he had never found Mr. Saunders wanting in any way. Mr.

Saunders interviewed Evans at Brixton Prison. This is apparent from the Brief which he drew for his principal who was to conduct the case during the committal proceedings on 15th December 1949. The Brief is still in existence, the only alterations to it being those made so that it might in part become the basis of the Brief which was to be delivered to Counsel for the trial. The Brief sets out the history of the marriage and a short account of Beryl Evans' death as set out in Evans' statement in Merthyr Tydfil, and it also says that the police have interviewed Christie who denies the whole story connecting him with the death, that the police accept his denial and that they will no doubt produce him as a witness in the Police Court. At this time, according to the Brief, Evans was saying that he had first made a statement admitting the strangulation and then on the 2nd December he had made a statement in accordance with his instructions. In other words he was saying wrongly that his statement in Notting Hill Gate was made before his statement in Merthyr Tydfil. The Brief ended with the statement that cross examination and defence must be reserved. There had no doubt been some conversation between the Solicitors and someone on behalf of the Prosecution because, although the Brief refers to Evans being charged with both murders, he was not formally charged with the murder of Geraldine until 15th December 1949, which was the date of hearing for which the Brief had been prepared.

At some time, probably immediately after accepting the Defence, Mr. Freeborough said that he saw Chief Inspector Jennings whom he was meeting for the first time. Mr. Freeborough thought that the meeting was in the Warrant Office. The Chief Inspector confirmed to Mr. Freeborough that Christie had been a war reserve policeman and, according to Mr. Freeborough, described Christie's evidence as being either "as good as gold" or "as pure as snow", meaning thereby that Christie would be a very good witness. Chief Inspector Jennings denies that he ever used these phrases to Mr. Freeborough. Mr. Freeborough thought that this interview took place at a time when the Chief Inspector had not yet checked Christie's record. The Chief Inspector indicated, so Mr. Freeborough told me, that the case was "buttoned up", and Mr. Freeborough was therefore led to believe that Christie was a man of good character. Mr. Freeborough thought that before the hearing at the West London Magistrates' Court on 15th December he would have been supplied with the contents of Evans' various statements. There is some confirmation of this in a minute to Mr. Crump who was to conduct the prosecution on behalf of the Director of Public Prosecutions, which would seem to have been written between the 8th and 15th December. It says of Mr. Freeborough, "He has asked for copies of the prisoner's statements and I see no objection." Mr. Freeborough gave an account of these events when on 9th July 1953 he told the Scott Henderson Inquiry that the police were very helpful to him and that he could remember quite clearly that they showed him all their statements unofficially before the hearing to assist him. They were, he said, most helpful too, in that they told him the things that they knew. In evidence before me, Mr. Freeborough thought that he had been given a preview of the statements of some or all of the witnesses who were to be called in the case. Mr. Freeborough says that he saw Evans at the West London Magistrates Court before the Court sat on the 15th December and went through the matters raised in the Brief with Evans, who was quite adamant that he had nothing to do with the killings.

At this interview Mr. Freeborough said that Evans made no complaint to him about the police or their methods. He admitted to Mr. Freeborough that he had made the various statements and there was no suggestion that they were obtained by force, or fear, or fraud. Mr. Freeborough did not ask Evans to explain the contradictions in those statements, or to explain why he had admitted the killings. The reason for this reluctance was that Mr. Freeborough found the matter a little frightening. He said that he did not want to receive a bad answer to his questions, so he decided to leave what he considered to be a very difficult matter to Counsel to deal with in conference with the accused. Mr. Freeborough said that the matter was made more difficult because Mrs. Evans was not able to assist for she had given a statement that was itself unhelpful, and he says that he had no knowledge of the visits of Mrs. Ashby or of Mrs. Westlake to 10 Rillington Place, nor did he know that workmen were on the premises. In the circumstances Mr. Freeborough did not intend to limit Counsel's conduct of the defence by asking questions at the Committal Court. I imagine too that Mr. Freeborough realised that on the evidence Evans was bound to be sent for trial and Mr. Freeborough did not therefore ask any question in cross examination.

Mr. Crump, now the Assistant and Deputy Director of Public Prosecutions, knew Mr. Freeborough quite well professionally. Mr. Crump said that the case as it then stood was one in which there were certain inconsistencies in the evidence, though these were not of a crucial nature and were of the kind which not infrequently arise because witnesses are confused over dates. Mr. Crump said that Evans' case also had its inconsistencies in the statements about the disposal of the body, but apart from these matters, from the Crown side the case seemed cut and dried. Despite reservations which naturally exist when looking back sixteen years, Mr. Crump has the firm recollection that he was invited by Mr. Freeborough to lead the witnesses for the Prosecution, namely to ask them leading questions. Mr. Crump said that he was absolutely sure of this and that he would not have led the witnesses without this consent. He recalled only one other case in which the penalty was death when this had happened to him in his 30 years experience; that was at a committal in Leeds prior to 1939. He said that the reason for this was that he had mentioned to Mr. Freeborough that there were some inconsistencies in the evidence, but Mr. Freeborough told him there was no dispute about the killings, as the sole issue in the case would be insanity. Mr. Crump thought that this was said to him at the end of the first remand. He did not thereby mean the 3rd December for he not unnaturally thought that there must have been another remand before the evidence was taken on 15th December, since usually the intervals between remands would not be for as long as twelve days. Enquiries at the Court failed to show any intermediate remand and the Hospital Occurrence Book has no record of Evans leaving the Ward to go to Court until 15th December.

As a result of Mr. Freeborough's invitation Mr. Crump said that he led the witnesses more than he otherwise would have done. When Mr. Freeborough was questioned about Mr. Crump's evidence he first said that he could not remember but he had no reason to doubt Mr. Crump's word, as he did not think Mr. Crump would say this if it did not happen. Later Mr. Freeborough did doubt it, stating that he probably told Mr. Crump that he was not intending to ask questions saying "I am not cross examining in this Court." It would seem however that this information had been passed to the office of the Director of Public Prosecutions before the 15th December for in the minute to Mr. Crump to which I have referred, the first sentence states, using abbreviations, that Mr. Freeborough is defending and is not going to cross examine at the Police Court. This information in this minute may well have started a conversation about the case between Mr. Crump and Mr. Freeborough. Mr. Freeborough said that he might also have told Mr. Crump that the defence had a formidable case to meet. Mr. Crump however goes further still for he says that Mr. Freeborough asked him if the prosecution could give any help on the question of insanity, whereupon Chief Inspector Jennings was called over and Mr. Crump put the question to him. The Chief Inspector said that he had not found anything yet and either that he had to see the mother again or the mother could not help, but said that he would do his best. Chief Inspector Jennings remembered being called over by Mr. Crump. His recollection is that one or the other, he thinks Mr. Freeborough, said that the facts on the killings were not being disputed, and asked whether there was any evidence of insanity in the family. The Chief Inspector says that he said that there was none, but in fact by then Mrs. Evans had given her recollection of her parents' account of the death of her paternal grandfather in an asylum in Ireland. Mr. Freeborough does not dispute with any certainty that the Chief Inspector was called over but says it is possible that it happened but he cannot remember it. Neither Mr. Crump nor Chief Inspector Jennings would have known that so much of the brief to be delivered later to counsel would deal with insanity.

If Mr. Crump or the police misled Mr. Freeborough, I find it difficult to understand why Mr. Freeborough did not at least complain about this. Mr. Freeborough says that he has never known the prosecution not to tell the defence of the criminal record of a prosecution witness and he did not ask about Christie's record as he assumed it was a good one. He said that he was perfectly sure that Mr. Crump would have given him any information that he could. There is no doubt that at this time Mr. Crump had details of Christie's criminal record and the records of all others whose names figured in the case, for they had been supplied by Chief Inspector Jennings to the Director of Public Prosecutions with his report dated 8th December 1949. This would probably have reached the Director of Public Prosecutions' Office by the 12th December, after being seen by the Chief Superintendent and the Assistant Commissioner of Crime. Probably Chief Inspector Jennings would take the papers from Scotland Yard to the Director of Public Prosecutions' Office to discuss the case.

I find it difficult to understand how Mr. Freeborough could speak as he does about Mr. Crump if he, contrary to his practice, had withheld information from Mr. Freeborough. If either Mr. Crump or the police had mis-led Mr. Freeborough by wrongly withholding Christie's criminal record, I would have expected that to have ran-kled with Mr. Freeborough for ever and I do not see how he could then have brought himself to tell Mr. Scott Henderson, as he did in 1953, that the police had given him so much assistance. I think that the true position is that when on some date shortly after 3rd December Mr. Freeborough accepted the defence of Evans, he may have asked the police what the case was about. Inspector Jennings, in those early days, if asked would tell Mr. Freeborough what the police knew including no doubt the fact that there were conflicting statements that Evans had made. At a later date Mr. Freeborough telephoned Mr. Crump leaving a message asking for copies of Evans' statements. At this time as Evans had made his written confessions the Chief Inspector might well, if asked, have said that as far as he knew Christie was likely to be a good witness, for at this time the police would not be thinking of any conflict in the evidence in the light of the admissions that Evans had made, and until his record was known that would be the general opinion of Christie. If anything had been said after the police had the particulars of Christie's record, Chief Inspector Jennings would not have pretended that he was either a man of good character or a potentially good witness. I do not believe that the Chief Inspector used any of the phrases which Mr. Freeborough now says were used.

At the trial Christie's record was given to the defence. When Mr. Freeborough later heard of this he would have known, if his evidence is correct, that Chief Inspector Jennings had misled him. The reasons given by Mr. Freeborough for not complaining to Chief Inspector Jennings about this were first, that the case would be out of his hands when next they met, and secondly that the omission was not serious as the defence had the record at the time of the trial. I do not think that either of those reasons would have restrained Mr. Freeborough from challenging the police officer. Mr. Freeborough did not take up this matter with Mr. Crump who had failed to disclose what he knew about Christie. On the contrary, Mr. Crump says that he had handed over the case to someone else and was not present at the trial. When he heard of the defence that had been raised he chided Mr. Freeborough good-humouredly when next they met about the unexpected change in tactics, and he says that Mr. Freeborough was apologetic. He is not suggesting that Mr. Freeborough did anything that he was not entitled to do, but was explaining why there had been this change of defence.

I think that Mr. Crump's recollection is reliable and that he was told that the defence would be one of insanity and that he was asked if the prosecution could give any help on this issue. This is borne out by the Brief which was later delivered to Counsel. As Mr. Saunders was handling the case he may well have told Mr. Freeborough that the only defence could be insanity. In 1953 he was still saying that Evans was guilty. What is not clear, and I do not think matters, is at what precise stage in the proceedings this was said. It is because of what was said that Mr. Crump did not give Mr. Freeborough the information about Christie's character which he had; it would not occur to him in the circumstances that the matter was material, for all that was to be in issue was the state of Evans' mind. I consider that all the evidence points to the accuracy of Mr. Crump's recollection. I do not believe that Chief Inspector Jennings said anything that Mr. Freeborough would have criticised. In 1953 Mr. Freeborough spoke appreciatively of the help the police had given in 1949.

This matter is bound up with the further allegation which was first made by Mr. Geoffrey Bing, Q.C. in the House of Commons on 29th July 1953, when he said that statements were suppressed in 1949. Mr. Baker said that Mr. Bing's view was that some of the police were inaccurate or lying, and others have made allegations about the suppression of statements by the police. When the police make a report and hand over the papers to the Director of Public Prosecutions all decisions thereafter are made by the Director of Public Prosecutions, or later, when Counsel is instructed, by him. The duty of the police is to arrange for the attendance of such witnesses as those in charge of the case direct, to see that the exhibits are available and otherwise carry out the orders given to them. The decision about the calling of witnesses has nothing to do with the police. There is no evidence that the police or anyone else suppressed any documents. The Director of Public Prosecutions was in possession of all relevant documents.

On 4th January 1950, the Brief for the defence was delivered to Counsel. It covers six and a half pages of Brief paper. Four pages contain information obtained from Mrs.

Evans. The instructions draw attention to Evans' doubtful mentality and the fact that there had been two cases of insanity in Mrs. Evans' family, namely her paternal grandfather and an uncle, both of whom were said to have died in asylums. Mention is made of the epileptic attacks suffered by one of Mrs. Evans' brothers and of her father's acts of criminal violence towards his wife. Mrs. Evans denied in evidence that her paternal grandfather had died in an asylum and she says that she knew nothing of the circumstances of her uncle's death. It seems unlikely that Mr. Saunders would have imagined, still less invented this, particularly as in her second statement to the police made on 6th December 1949, Mrs. Evans said . . . "but my father's father, Timothy Lynch, died in an asylum somewhere in Ireland many years ago, according to what my Mum and Dad used to tell me. . . . So far as I know there is no mental history on my mother's side." Whether the statement that her grandfather had died in an asylum is true or not I cannot say, but I have no doubt that Mrs. Evans must have twice given that account of the medical history of the deceased members of her family. The information was given to different people on separate occasions. The reason why those things were said is that, although Mrs. Evans will not admit it now, even to herself, she then thought, as the members of her family thought, that Evans had killed his wife and child. Mrs. Evans also thought that, because he loved the child so much, to have killed her her son could not have been sane.

After explaining about Evans' upbringing and marriage, the Brief then refers to Joan Vincent and to Evans' dislike of her and how he had ordered her from the house. It is also stated that Joan Vincent had been interviewed by the police. There then follows an account of the trouble over Lucy. Beryl Evans' short-comings as a housewife are next set out. She was dirty in her habits and she failed to feed her husband properly or generally look after him or the home. A reference is made to the violence used by Beryl Evans in the quarrels between her and her husband, although Mrs. Evans said that that was a mistake by Mr. Saunders as only once to her knowledge was violence used—when Evans came to 11 St. Marks Road with a bruised or cut head caused by Beryl Evans throwing a jar of cosmetics at her husband. Beryl Evans' behaviour with the painter is referred to and the fact that there were debts for rent and furniture. Mention is made of a visit to 10 Rillington Place which probably refers to that of Mrs. Westlake on the 29th November, and finally it is stated that Mrs. Evans believed that if her son killed the baby he must have been mad.

There is no mention in the Brief of what Evans is alleged to have said on 4th December, with reference to the questioning until 5 a.m., the throwing of the clothes, or the call for a confession. Mrs. Evans said that she told Mr. Saunders about this on her second visit to see him. This would probably have been on the 15th December. The remainder of the Brief is repetition of the contents prepared for Mr. Freeborough, stating Evans' case in conformity with his statement in Merthyr Tydfil. The instructions continued with the comment—"In the facts stated so far, it will be a matter for serious consideration whether it will be possible to set up a defence of insanity, or to let the prisoner pursue his somewhat wild story of abortion, or endeavour to put to the jury the possibility of an alternative verdict of manslaughter. The later could clearly only be an alternative as regards the wife. The destruction of the poor little girl baby can only be accounted for—if in fact the prisoner strangled her—by insane impulse, possibly induced by fear of discovery of the murder of the wife. Counsel's advice on this head is desired."The Brief ends with the criticism of Doctor Tear's evidence at the Magistrates Court. There is no explanation in the Brief of Evans' several admissions of guilt in his statements made in Notting Hill Gate or of the evidence contained in the depositions, including the admission made to Inspector Black. All this, as Mr. Freeborough said, was deliberately left for Counsel to deal with in conference.

After delivery of Briefs to Counsel on 4th January 1950, Mr. Malcolm Morris, Q.C., then a member of the Junior Bar who was to lead for the defence, saw Evans in Brixton prison. Mr. Malcolm Morris cannot now say whether he saw Evans once or more than once. Evans' defence to his Counsel was that he did not commit the murders and that Christie did. There was no medical evidence on the question of insanity, and Mr. Malcolm Morris thinks that he must have discussed the matter of insanity with his instructing solicitors but it came to nothing, no medical reports having been obtained. This is not surprising for there is no evidence of insanity other than that attributed to the recollection of Mrs. Evans. There is certainly nothing to show that this defence could have been established.

Mr. Malcolm Morris thinks that the details of the defence were obtained by him direct from Evans. This must be right, for otherwise Counsel could not have obtained Evans' explanation of his statements. Evans explained his admissions, particularly those made in Notting Hill Gate, by saying that he had made them because when he heard that his daughter Geraldine was dead he had nothing left to live for, and secondly, that he thought that the police had decided to beat him up if he did not confess his guilt. This was a case in which the admissions appearing on the depositions in one form or another were so complete, repetitive and damaging for the defence that anyone conducting it must have been alert to the hope, if not the possibility, of challenging the voluntariness of the statements. For if the prosecution could not prove, as it must, that a confession was voluntary, that confession would be excluded. Even if the chances of successfully challenging the confessions seemed remote, this matter must have been in the forefront of Counsel's mind. No doubt with an accused who is known to be a liar, Counsel would have been careful when questioning Evans, lest the form of his question suggested an answer which Evans, with his propensity for lying, might have thought would help him in his defence. Mr. Malcolm Morris said that he would have asked Evans fairly formally about any threats that might have been used, but that there was no doubt in his mind that Evans would have been asked about them. Mr. Malcolm Morris was equally certain that Evans made no such suggestion, for had he done so, Mr. Malcolm Morris said that he would have used that evidence to challenge the statement. Mr. Malcolm Morris cannot actually remember asking the question about this but he is satisfied that he would have done so. So am I.

When Evans alleged that he feared that the police would beat him up if he did not admit his guilt he did not mention any particular police officer, but as he spoke of Inspector Black with affection, Mr. Malcolm Morris deduced that Evans feared Chief Inspector Jennings. Although Evans was asked about the conduct of the police he did not tell his Counsel anything about Chief Inspector Jennings throwing the clothes at him or saying "Confess, you liar." Nor did he say that he was kept up until 5 a.m. This is confirmed in that Mr. Malcolm Morris did not challenge the statements in Notting Hill Gate, nor did Evans during his trial when stating his reasons for making these statements ever say that which he had said to his mother and not to his legal advisers.

Two visits made in 1949 to 10 Rillington Place, the first by Mrs. Ashby and the second by Mrs. Westlake, have over the years been said to be visits of considerable importance. One was in part dealt with at Evans' trial, the other was not. The first was on 27th November. Sunday 20th November was Evans' birthday. It had been his habit to call at his mother's home on his birthday to collect his presents. Mrs. Ashby had customarily visited 10 Rillington Place on Sunday mornings. Evans did not call on his birthday and Mrs. Evans, no doubt annoyed because she had not seen her son for some time and had heard nothing from her daughter-in-law, would not permit Mrs. Ashby to take the birthday presents to 10 Rillington Place. Mrs. Evans was unaware that her son was in Wales. On 27th November the newsagent complained that Evans had not collected his newspapers, so Mrs. Ashby took them for him and called at 10 Rillington Place. This visit is said to be important for two reasons. First in that it shows that Mrs. Christie was deliberately misleading Mrs. Ashby in giving an account of Beryl Evans' alleged departure which differed from that given by Mrs. Christie to Mrs. Westlake two days later, and secondly because the solicitors acting for Evans in his defence, and the police, failed to act upon the information supplied to them by Mrs. Ashby and Mrs. Westlake.

The accounts of this visit given by Mrs. Ashby have varied. The earliest accounts are the ones given to Mr. Baker in 1953. Despite apparent contradictions between the first and second accounts, Mrs. Ashby was saying that Christie had said that Evans was in Bristol and Beryl Evans in Brighton, and that Mrs. Christie had said "I know she's gone because I helped her downstairs with the case." Christie had also said he thought they had had a row. The next account appears in a proof of evidence prepared for Counsel at the Scott Henderson Inquiry, where, according to Mrs. Ashby, Mrs. Christie said that she helped Beryl with the case down the road to the station. At that Inquiry the station was not mentioned but Mrs. Ashby said that prior to this visit a letter had arrived from Mrs. Lynch in Wales. This, as Mrs. Ashby now admits, was wrong, for if she had known that Evans was in Wales there would have been no point in her taking the newspapers round to his home. At that Inquiry Mrs. Ashby said that when told that Beryl Evans was in Brighton she remarked that it was mean of her not to have brought the baby round to her grandmother before going away. In evidence before me, Mrs. Ashby said that there was no reply to her three knocks, which was the signal to the top flat, and that Mrs. Christie then answered a single knock for her flat. Mrs. Ashby asked Mrs. Christie where Beryl was and was told that she had gone to Brighton to visit her father. Thereupon Mrs. Ashby expressed surprise and asked when she had gone, saying "she never came and told us." Mrs. Ashby said that she was surprised to hear this about Beryl. This evidence could hardly be right because it was on the 9th November that Mrs. Evans had been told about this by her son, and the Evans family must have known from that date that Beryl Evans was supposed to be in Brighton with her father. When asked to explain her surprise, Mrs. Ashby unconvincingly suggested that Beryl Evans might have come back and then gone away. That might be more probable if she had been told that Beryl Evans had gone to Bristol and not to Brighton and Mrs. Ashby had confused the two towns.

This becomes more confused by the information recorded by Mr. Baker in 1953 which must be wrong, that on a Saturday it was learned that Beryl Evans had not been to her father's at Brighton. The latest possible Saturday for receipt of this news must have been 26th November. Therefore, when visiting 10 Rillington Place on 27th

November, and receiving the reply from Mrs. Christie that Beryl Evans was in Brighton Mrs. Ashby would know that the information was wrong. The information was not received until after the 27th. Later Mrs. Ashby could not explain why she should have been surprised at hearing of Beryl Evans' departure. Mrs. Ashby had said that when she arrived home and told her mother that Beryl Evans was in Brighton with her father, Mrs. Evans had replied "He's got bloody generous all of a sudden." This is a strange comment for Mrs. Evans to make at that time, for she had been told some weeks before about Beryl Evans' departure. These were the words which, according to Mr. Baker's notes, were used by Mrs. Evans to her son when on 9th November he first told his mother that his wife had gone to Brighton to stay with her father. It is not possible to tell whether these inaccuracies emanate from Mrs. Christie or Mrs. Ashby or from Mr. Baker's notes. It is however, common to all Mrs. Ashby's accounts that Mrs. Christie was saying that she gave some assistance to Beryl Evans with her luggage. This could not be true, and to the police and in evidence Mrs. Christie did not say this but in fact said the contrary, when she claimed that it was from Evans that she learned that Beryl Evans had gone away without telling her. There is no evidence that this matter was brought to the notice of the police. Mrs. Ashby referred to a discussion which she had had with Chief Inspector Jennings upon another matter, as being the only time she had held a conversation with that officer.

Mrs. Ashby said that, obeying her mother's instructions, she called upon Mr. Saunders at his office and told him of her experience on the 27th November. Mrs. Ashby called during her lunch break without an appointment, and waited until about 2.45 p.m. when she saw Mr. Saunders. The interview lasted about three quarters of an hour. Mrs. Ashby is not sure of the date of this call but thinks that it was during Evans' trial, but before his conviction. Mrs. Ashby said that during the interview Mr. Saunders did not write down anything. When it was over he made a remark which she thought ridiculous, for it was something to the effect that she was not to worry too much about her brother as he would most probably be sent to Australia. Mrs. Ashby said that Mr. Saunders was drunk or had had enough to drink. She took this a stage further when, in 1959–1960, she saw Mr. Kennedy. She then described Mr. Saunders as being drunk most of the time. When asked in evidence to explain what she meant by that remark, having seen Mr. Saunders on one occasion only, Mrs. Ashby said that she must have been referring also to the occasions when her mother, and perhaps her sister, had told her this. Mrs. Ashby says that they did. Neither Mrs. Evans nor Mrs. Westlake had said this in evidence, nor is there any record that it has ever been said by either of them at any time. In 1953 at the Scott Henderson Inquiry Mrs. Evans was complaining that her son's case had not been properly gone into. When referring to the evidence which she said had not been but ought to have been collected, she mentioned the evidence of Joan Vincent and Mrs. Westlake in this context. No mention was made about Mr. Saunders being drunk. If it were true it could not have been forgotten. At that time he was alive. If there had been any basis for this suggestion I am sure that Mrs. Evans would not have failed to comment on it between 1949 and 1965. I think it is an exaggeration by Mrs. Ashby, made at a time when encouraged by what she had heard and read, all who touched the Evans case were being blamed. Mr. Freeborough denied this suggestion, saying on the contrary that Mr. Saunders was an industrious man who would often be working in the office until 8 p.m. If Mrs. Ashby is capable of such an exaggeration her evidence about the remark of Evans being sent to Australia may be suspect. It obviously was not intended to be taken literally. I think that something of the sort probably was said, but I think that it must have been a well meant but, to the hearer, ill chosen method of saying in a light-hearted way that Evans would not in the end be hanged. It is clear that Mrs. Ashby would have seen Mr. Saunders at a time when, according to her, she thought that her brother was guilty. When asked in evidence how important did it seem to her at the time that Mrs. Christie had said that she had helped Beryl Evans to the station with the case, Mrs. Ashby said she did not think that she even thought about it. It gives some idea how three years later a conversation is given an importance which it did not possess when spoken.

In the petition dated January 1956, to which reference was made previously, a complaint is made that Mrs. Ashby made a statement of her conversation with Mrs. Christie to both Chief Inspector Jennings and Inspector Black which they ignored. There is no evidence that Mrs. Ashby ever mentioned this interview to those officers. Someone must have fed the information to the person who composed, typed and sent the petition. I think that the reason why in later years the Evans family blame the police for this is shown in the statement made to Mr. Kennedy that they all hated Chief Inspector Jennings, although when giving evidence, Mrs. Evans said that she had nothing to say against the police in their conduct towards her.

During the afternoon of Tuesday 29th November, Mrs. Westlake called at 10 Rillington Place. By this time the letter from Mrs. Lynch had been received and answered. The furniture salesman, wanting his money had called at her mother's home, for Mrs. Evans, unbeknown to her husband, had guaranteed Evans' hire purchase agreement. It was from her husband that Mrs. Evans learned that

Evans' furniture had gone. Mrs. Westlake knew this when she made her call, and that her brother was in South Wales, and she also knew as a result of enquiries that had been made by this time, that Beryl Evans was not at Brighton with her father. The purpose of this visit must have been to discover what she could of the whereabouts of Beryl Evans and Geraldine. Mrs. Westlake relies for her recollection of this visit in the main upon a statement which she made to Inspector Kelly on 20th June 1953. In that statement Mrs. Westlake said that she was told by Mrs. Christie that Beryl Evans had put the baby in the pram on Tuesday, saying that she was going away and that she would write to Mrs. Christie, but that nothing had been heard from her. Mrs. Christie then criticised Beryl Evans' conduct in leaving the child unattended and returning home smelling of gin. Mrs. Westlake challenged this and defended her sister-in-law, but Mrs. Christie insisted that Beryl Evans did go out leaving the baby alone. Christie then arrived. He said that Beryl Evans had gone away without saying good-bye. This contradiction about the departure caused Mrs. Westlake to say to the Christies that one of them must be lying. Mrs. Christie was about to say something about Beryl Evans when she was rudely silenced by Christie. According to one exaggerated account of this given by either Mrs. Westlake or Mrs. Evans to Mr. Baker in 1953, Christie went to hit his wife. Mrs. Westlake said that Evans was in Wales and that Beryl Evans was not in Brighton as Christie had mentioned. He then went on to say that the departure had been planned: that Evans owed a lot of money, and that the two of them had probably gone to different places intending to join up later. Tempers were no doubt rising. Mrs. Westlake understandably but illogically rebuked Christie for permitting the furniture dealer to enter the house. Christie made Mrs. Westlake more angry by saying that her mother had interfered in the marriage

and he further went on to say that when he was in the
police force he knew about Evans. Mrs. Westlake, knowing
that this could not be true, called Christie a bloody liar
and left him, saying that if nothing was heard by the following Friday the police would be told. Christie, then
being angry too, said that Evans would not thank his sister
for that and that he, Christie, knew more about it than
Mrs. Westlake thought he did. Christie did not explain
what he meant nor did Mrs. Westlake enquire, for she told
Christie that she was not worried about him or Evans but
was concerned about Beryl and the baby. Thereafter
Christie would not permit Mrs. Westlake to go upstairs
and collect the bills which he said were there.

Mrs. Westlake said that in 1953 she told the police that
she probably got the conversation with Mrs. Christie
mixed up and may have forgotten one or two things.
When giving evidence at the Scott Henderson Inquiry,
Mrs. Westlake said that she reported this conversation to
Sergeant Corfield when he came to her mother's house on
the night of the 30th November/ 1st December, and at
some unspecified date she told Inspector Jennings about it
but that he said it was irrelevant. In evidence Mrs. Westlake
could not remember saying anything to the police when
they called in the early hours of the 1st December. She
said that she only remained in the room for a little while.
Mrs. Westlake had substantially repeated the details of this
incident in a letter which she wrote to Mr. Kennedy in
February 1960. This matter was raised at Evans' trial with
Christie, who when giving his explanation about his
arrival when Mrs. Westlake was talking to Mrs. Christie
and about what Christie claimed was said, was cut short as
Counsel cross-examining him said that he did not want to
hear all the details. Counsel put to Christie that he had
refused to permit Mrs. Westlake to visit the empty flat. This
Christie denied. Inspector Kelly who retired from the

police ten years ago thinks, but cannot put it any higher, that when he took Mrs. Westlake's statement he was the first one to have been told about it. He cannot remember one way or the other whether he asked a question about this but he said that the type of question he would have put would have been one to enquire whether Mrs. Westlake had told anyone about this matter at the time. Since he was recording events of three and a half years before, he said that had Mrs. Westlake made any reference to telling someone else about this he would have incorporated it in the statement.

Mrs. Westlake remembered visiting Mr. Saunders with her mother and telling him of the events of the 29th November. He did not, she said, make a note of what she told him, saying that what she said was irrelevant. Evans said at his trial that he lied when he told Mrs. Christie that his wife had gone to Brighton and would write. In whatever manner Beryl Evans had died, Mrs. Christie must have been wrong when she said to Mrs. Westlake that Beryl Evans had said goodbye before leaving. Since Mrs. Christie was prevented by her husband from saying anything further in answer to Mrs. Westlake's accusation that either she or Christie must be lying, it is not surprising that Mr. Saunders thought that the evidence was not likely to be helpful on this point. It was dealt with by Counsel on the point of Christie's refusal to permit Mrs. Westlake into the house. Mrs. Christie, if asked, had only to say that Evans had brought his wife's message of goodbye for the matter to be explained. No one has shown with any conviction what would have happened if Mrs. Christie had been seen about Beryl Evans' departure. She would I suppose have given the account which she gave in evidence. I can find nothing in the evidence before me to show that Mrs. Christie knew anything about the death of Beryl Evans or Geraldine, prior to the discovery of the bodies.

Evidence that Mrs. Christie was involved in an abortion comes at its highest from a witness, Mrs. Hide, whose evidence by now is understandably a little confused for she is 85 years of age. She said that she recalled being told by Mrs. Christie that either Evans or Beryl Evans had asked Christie or Mrs. Christie if they could help her bring about an abortion, and Mrs. Christie's comment to Mrs. Hide had been "Fancy asking my Reg such a thing." Mrs. Hide thought that she remembered telling Mr. Baker in 1953 that it had been Mrs. Christie who had said that Beryl Evans had asked Christie to carry out an abortion on her.

A considerable amount of evidence was adduced in respect of the activities of workmen employed at 10 Rillington Place at the time of the deaths of Beryl and Geraldine Evans. This evidence was at one time considered to be one of the most important features of the Inquiry. By the time it had all been heard almost all the issues arising from it had shrunk to minimal proportions. When the bodies were found the wash house was tidily arranged. The door opened inwards swinging to the left. Facing it, in the left corner there was a misused copper; in the right corner there was a shallow sink with a single tap fixed on the wall above. Resting against the sink were some pieces of wood, each of a different length and most of different widths. They formed an apron of wood around the sink and created a hiding place beneath it. In front of the wood were some old paint tins and brushes. On top of the copper there were bottles, tins and rubbish. Behind the door and against the copper was another length of wood. It was under the sink hidden by the wood that Beryl Evans' body was found. Geraldine was found behind the door under pieces of wood, mostly small. The Kensington Borough Council had served a written intimation notice requiring the landlord to carry out certain works at 10 Rillington Place, including work on the wash house. The work was done by Larter and Sons (referred to as Larters) of Holland Park Avenue, W.11, at a fixed contract price of £57, such work being called a contract job. The workmen employed were Mr. Willis the plasterer and his labourer Mr. Jones, Mr. Anderson the carpenter, Mr. Smith the plumber, all under the supervision of Mr. Phillips the Manager.

The work started on the 31st October and finished on 14th November 1949. Evans in his statements had said that the body of Beryl Evans was put into the wash house during the night of Tuesday 8th November and that of the child on the night of Thursday 10th November. On 29th July 1953 in the House of Commons Mr. Geoffrey Bing, Q.C., who had been assisted in his enquiries by Mr. Baker, covered most of the points relating to this matter. He stated (*a*) that it was quite clear that the timber behind which the bodies were found was the old timber taken by the carpenter from the floor of Christie's flat and the floor of the hall; (*b*) that the carpenter's time sheet gave in detail the times at which he took up the timber and that his recollection was perfectly clear; (*c*) that the timber which was given to Christie could not have been given to him before Monday 14th November, the day upon which Evans left

London. Mr. Bing also stated: (*d*) that the time sheets were given to the Police and that (*e*) they were returned after the Evans trial, but that one, and unfortunately that of the plasterer, was missing from the pile when it came back from the police; and that the plasterer's time sheet was considered by those interested in the defence of Evans to be the most material of all the documents.

Mr. Jones, the labourer, is dead. His time sheets almost invariably read "taking materials to job, waiting on plasterer, bringing back rubbish". Occasionally only two of these entries appear. On Friday 4th November Mr. Anderson, the carpenter, spent 8 hours fixing the external shuttering for the new roof of the outhouse. Mr. Willis, the plasterer, now thinks that the internal shoring which he would erect would have been positioned at the same time and completed on the morning of Saturday 5th November. Larters' materials book shows that the shingle for the concrete was issued on 4th November and two cwts. of cement on the 5th. Therefore, according to the documents, by Saturday 5th November all the material for the roof was at the site, but according to Mr. Phillips a date in the materials book may not necessarily be the actual date of issue. On Monday 7th November Mr. Jones' time sheet shows that he was working elsewhere and Mr. Willis says that he would have been working with his labourer. It is Mr. Willis who claimed that his own time sheets, which are missing, would have shown in detail what was done and when. Mr. Phillips disagreed. He said that he had worked with Mr. Willis before either man went to Larters, and that Mr. Willis never did supply the kind of time sheets he now claims to have completed. Mr. Phillips was disarmingly frank about time sheets, for which he has scant respect and which he considered immaterial on a contract job. It would not matter to him what was on the time sheet for he is interested in seeing that the work is done in the time allotted by the contractors for its completion. He does not think that time sheets provide a good timetable in any building firm.

Mr. Phillips explained that, save when he may specifically ask a man to keep an accurate time sheet, the only occasions when he would speak to a workman about errors in them would be if the man put himself down as working at the wrong site or doing a job outside the contract. Mr. Phillips' own time sheets on occasions did not accurately record his movements. He may be recorded as visiting a site which he has not visited. Mr. Willis gave some evidence tending to support what Mr. Phillips said, for he stated that if, for example, on the Saturday morning it had not been convenient to start the next stage of the work the men might work out their time sitting in a cafe but recording on the time sheet "clearing up site". At the Inquiry attempts were made to determine when the concrete roof was poured and the date when the work on the wash house roof would have finished. It is not necessary to decide this for the important question is when did the workmen cease to use the wash house.

On 6th December Mr. Phillips made a statement to the police. Despite his doubts I think that it was at Larter's premises that it was taken by Sergeant Fensome and written by Sergeant Corfield. At that time as his statement records Mr. Phillips handed to the officers a copy of the specification of the work. It would appear that Mr. Phillips, in order to help his recollection and before making the statement, probably obtained information either from a book which he kept himself or the time sheets in the office. After describing the work done earlier, Mr. Phillips said that the wooden shores were finally removed during the morning of the 8th November and until then no one could enter the wash house; that thereafter Mr. Willis completed the ceiling on 9th November, working there until about 11 a.m., and that from then until 11th November the men worked on the ground floor front room. Mr. Phillips said that on 12th November the carpenter spent four hours repairing the timber in the hall and that on 14th November the carpenter completed his work and the job by 10 a.m. Mr. Phillips is more likely to be right than the others, as he did obtain such information which he thought that he required before being interviewed.

On 7th December statements were taken by Sergeant Fensome and Sergeant Corfield from Mr. Jones and Mr. Willis respectively. Both agreed that they finished working in the wash house during the morning of 9th November. Mr. Jones said that until then it would have been impossible for anyone to have put anything in the wash house, and that until the afternoon of Friday 11th November, nothing but their materials and tools were in there. He said that before leaving he cleaned out the copper and the wash house. Mr. Jones went on to say that at about 10 a.m. on Wednesday 9th November he saw a woman, young, small and thin, come downstairs with a baby and accompanied by another young woman. The baby was put in the pram. Mr. Jones warned the woman against tripping over a ladder when she returned. By the description this was Beryl Evans and as she was supposed to have died on the 8th November it is not surprising that Sergeant Fensome should question the date given by Mr. Jones. He repeated that he was positive about the date and he gave as a reason that on the following morning, just before lunch, he saw a man, obviously by description Evans, who stood for ten minutes in the street after coming downstairs. On this day, 10th November, Evans was in fact driving in the Brighton area. Mr. Jones said that he did not speak to Evans but that on the following afternoon at 2.30 p.m. this man came downstairs again. They did not speak. No doubt in answer to a further question from Sergeant Fensome, Mr. Jones said that he was positive that he saw and spoke to the woman on Wednesday 9th November. Mr. Willis said that his tools were in the wash house until the morning of the 11th, when it was cleaned and left completely bare. Christie in his statement dated 8th December said that he heard the shoring being knocked down on 8th November, on which day the builders' tools and materials were moved into the front room. If the evidence given by the two workmen is right, then the body of Beryl Evans could not have gone into the wash house on the 8th/9th November, nor could the unwrapped body of the child have been put there on 10th November.

On reading the statements from the workmen Chief Inspector Jennings noticed that there were discrepancies between them and the other evidence available, in particular Evans' own admissions and the statements by the Christies of sounds heard in the night of 8th/9th November. Chief Inspector Jennings told Sergeants Fensome and Corfield to arrange for the three men to be brought to Kensington Police Station, where they were seen by the Chief Inspector and Inspector Black on the afternoon of the 8th December. All three resented this inconvenience, none more than Mr. Phillips, for he had to pay Larters' men later in the afternoon and did not want to be delayed. Not unnaturally all three wished to know why further interviews were necessary. Both the detectives seem to think that they said little if anything in answer to this question, as Chief Inspector Jennings had not given them the reasons. I accept that they were given an order without any information, but as detectives they must have realised that there were discrepancies somewhere, particularly as Sergeant Fensome knew that in the statement which he had taken on the previous day Mr. Jones had insisted three times that he had seen Beryl Evans alive on the day following the probable date of her death. Although I do not think that either Mr. Phillips or Mr. Willis remember the words of the answers given to their complaining questions, I have no doubt that the gist of them was that the Chief Inspector was not satisfied with some parts of their written statements and wanted to interview all three of them himself to sort out the matter. Mr. Phillips and Mr. Willis each claims to have been the third of the trio to be interviewed, Mr. Willis saying that Mr. Phillips was first.

It was not until more than three years after these events that Mr. Willis' time sheets were found to be missing. Their history was investigated at the Scott Henderson Inquiry, where on 10th July 1953 Mr. Willis was questioned generally about this interview of 8th December 1949 and with particular reference to his own time sheets. Mr. Willis then said that when Mr. Phillips went for the first interview he took time sheets in with him, and that when the police interviewed Mr. Willis they had his time sheets and that although he did not see the time sheets when he was being questioned by the police Mr. Phillips was reading them out. Mr. Willis said that he did not read them himself, but Mr. Phillips was there with them and they were referred to. In evidence Mr. Willis had a different recollection. He said that as he never saw his time sheets he did not know whether the police had them. He did not know whether his time sheets had been taken to the police station that day, but that as the police had some time sheets he assumed that his own had been taken in by Mr. Phillips. His explanation of the statement that his time sheets were referred to was not that they were examined but that their existence was mentioned.

At this interview on 8th December 1949 both Mr. Willis and Mr. Jones made statements varying those they had made the previous day. The statements were taken by Chief Inspector Jennings and written by Inspector Black who cannot remember whether he was in the room for the whole of the interview. Mr. Willis in his second statement said that it would have been possible for anything to have been under the sink with the timber in front, as wood flooring had been left behind for tenants to use as firewood. He had not previously brought this fact into his recollection as he gave only a cursory look round. This explanation is difficult to reconcile with his earlier statement saying that the wash house was completely bare when cleared during the morning of 11th November. Mr. Willis was asked about this statement at the Scott Henderson Inquiry. He explained that he was shown a photograph of the wash house and that he told Chief Inspector Jennings that it did not represent the state of the wash house as seen by him. He also said that the timber there shown had not come from the floor but that the Chief Inspector had said that the timber could have been put there later. Mr. Willis gave much the same evidence before me, saying that after Chief Inspector Jennings had asserted that the bodies were in the wash house whilst Mr. Willis was there, he first denied it but eventually he made his second statement. Mr. Willis said that he thinks that this statement merely meant that as he personally did not enter the wash house on the Friday he could not have known whether there was anything under the sink. I do not believe that Mr. Willis was seeking to convey this meaning when he made his second statement. Chief Inspector Jennings genuinely thought that what Evans said was true, he challenged Mr. Willis' recollection, and Mr. Willis considered that any protracted argument over such a detail was of little moment and said what he thought would meet the situation.

Mr. Jones was unwilling to alter his statement. He was described as a conscientious workman and, being sixty-seven years of age, was much older than his workmates. His deafness did not make questioning easier, and his first statement contained several obvious errors. In so far as Mr. Phillips remembers, he was called in and told by the Chief Inspector that the statements made by Mr. Willis and Mr. Jones contained mistakes, and that Mr. Willis had acknowledged that he could have made a mistake. Mr. Phillips was asked to have a word with Mr. Jones, for as he was deaf it was difficult to make him understand; he was told that Mr. Jones was disinclined to change his statement, and would Mr. Phillips try and convince Mr. Jones that he could have made a mistake. Mr. Phillips says that the police officer told him that at least twenty or more witnesses could prove that there must have been something under the sink when Mr. Jones left the wash house. Mr. Phillips said that he tried to persuade Mr. Jones to change his statement. Mr. Phillips agrees that he stated that the police must be right, but he denies that he ever told Mr. Eddowes that Mr. Jones was shaking all over at this time. Mr. Jones eventually said that he might have made a mistake, and made another statement. By this statement Mr. Jones altered the date when he saw Beryl Evans from the 9th to the 8th November. He altered the date when he saw Evans from the 10th to the 9th. He put the time of seeing Evans at about 10 a.m., where earlier he had said "just before lunch" which meant just before noon. He added that it was on 8th November when he cleaned out the wash house, and that he took no particular notice of it when he collected his tools on 11th November. In his first statement Mr. Jones had said that he did not speak to Evans. He did not alter this in his second statement, yet at the Scott Henderson Inquiry in 1953 he recounted a conversation in which Evans had offered him a cigarette and asked when the job would finish and was told by Mr. Jones that they would be out by Friday.

Mr. Jones had told Mr. Baker that Evans in the presence of Christie asked this question. Chief Inspector Jennings' recollection is that he was mainly interested to fix the dates of death of the victims, which he thought was the 8th November in respect of Beryl Evans but which Mr. Jones by his insistence was putting not before the 9th November. Chief Inspector Jennings said that if the workmen were right in what they had said about their use of the wash house, the body could have been placed there as late as the 14th. He agrees that he may well have said that something could have been under the sink, but he denies that he said that there were 20 or more witnesses to prove it. Both the police officers say that these statements were obtained as a result of questions and answers and that the form of the statement would reflect the language used by the police officer when questioning the maker of it. This is not unusual in a witness statement. After returning from the police station Mr. Larter says that Mr. Jones was very disturbed at being kept there for such a long time and was not very happy about the alterations he had made to his statement, while Mr. Willis was said to be taciturn and uncommunicative. In 1964 Mr. Eddowes recorded that Mr. Larter remembered that both Mr. Willis and Mr. Jones felt that pressure had been put on them by the police to change their statements, and that the police had claimed to have fifty other ways of proving the matter, and that they felt that they had been unjustly treated by the police because what they had said originally was true.

It should be remembered that by now much publicity had been-given to these events, and exaggeration occurs easily when events of little importance at the time are later presented as being of great importance, and when the information is second hand. Although Mr. Larter says that

Mr. Eddowes' notes substantially express the conversation which they had together, he points out that he was being questioned years later about events which at the time were not so important. Mr. Smith the plumber remembers that, about a month after the event Mr. Jones said that the wash house had been cleared when he left the house.

I am in no doubt that Chief Inspector Jennings did make it clear that he thought that both Mr. Willis and Mr. Jones had made mistakes in their statements made on 7th December 1949 and that Mr. Willis after little argument was prepared to alter his statement. Chief Inspector Jennings was right in thinking that Mr. Jones' statement contained several obvious mistakes. The Chief Inspector also thought that Mr. Jones was wrong about the state of the wash house prior to his departure. The Chief Inspector made the mistake of thinking that Evans had told him the truth when he said that the bodies went into the wash house on 8th and 10th November respectively. I also think that the Chief Inspector did say that there was other evidence to prove the point that he was making. It was because of the strength, as he saw it, of that evidence that he was making the point with the workmen. If the number of witnesses was stated as twenty, thirty, forty or fifty—the number has been raised with the years—Chief Inspector Jennings would have been using an obvious exaggeration to make his point. I think that Chief Inspector Jennings was too determinedly impressing his views upon Mr. Willis and Mr. Jones and that they came into line with his suggestion, the one easily, the other on the advice of his Manager.

At various times until the plastering was completed, Mr. Jones would have to go to the wash house for water to make the mix outside the front room window. It would have been about midday or shortly afterwards on the 11th

November when the wash house was last visited by Mr. Jones, and I do not think there were any bodies in it at that time. I think that most of the wood was placed around the basin on or after the 11th November, after the departure of these two men and when the contents of the wash house which had been temporarily stored in the yard were replaced. After his first visit to 10 Rillington Place on the 4th November, Mr. Anderson the carpenter did not return until the 11th. His time sheet for this day shows that his day was evenly divided between 105 Holland Road and 10 Rillington Place. Mr. Anderson's recollection is that he worked first at 10 Rillington Place, although a statement which he made on 13th July 1953 to the Solicitors acting for Mrs. Evans said otherwise. He spent four hours pulling up rotten joists and flooring on the ground floor. He estimates that he pulled up about twelve to fourteen lengths and offered about nine or ten short pieces of old floor boards, called scrag ends, to Christie who took them for firewood. The larger boards which were going back to Larters were put outside the house. Those given to Christie were placed, according to Mr. Anderson, by him in Christie's front room. Mr. Anderson says that he required the narrow hall passage to be cleared so that he could work without being impeded. Having seen that narrow passage I can well imagine why Mr. Anderson would want it to be clear of wood. The relaying of the new floor was completed on the morning of the 12th and on Monday 14th Mr. Anderson says that he returned for 2 hours to fit some skirting boards and, according to his time sheet, some beading also, but Mr. Anderson cannot remember the last item. I do not think that there is any inconsistency in Mr. Anderson's evidence that he gave this wood to Christie who took it from the front room out to the back of the house, and a sentence in Mr. Anderson's statement already referred to "my normal procedure always would be to pull up the rotten boards, put in the new ones and then deal with the debris after I had finished the job". This, it is said, means that if Mr. Anderson had been minded to give Christie some wood he would not give it away until the particular job was completed. In this statement, Mr. Anderson is referring to his practice when returning debris to his employer's yard. It does not exclude the giving of scrag ends for firewood to a householder whilst the work is in progress. The sentence in the statement is an answer to a general question on the removal of debris from the site.

I find that the wood from the flooring was given to Christie on the 11th November and the suggestion that it could not have come into his hands until 14th November is wrong. It seems to have been assumed that the different lengths of wood placed around the sink were pieces of the old floor boards. Mr. Anderson, who now can only give his opinion upon the wood as seen in the photographs, said that he thought that two of the pieces of wood could have been flooring. On the evidence most of the timber which hid Beryl Evans' bundled-up body did not consist of old floor boards. No one else can say that the other pieces were old floor boards. It is more likely that they were pieces of wood already in the possession of Christie and stored in the yard pending their return to the wash house. Mr. Anderson has no recollection of being interviewed by the police. The police evidence is that he was. On 10th July 1953 Sergeant Corfield's notebook was in evidence with the name of Mr. Anderson the carpenter and Mr. Smith the plumber recorded in it. The reason why statements were not obtained from them presumably was that neither at the time had anything helpful to say. Mr. Anderson would have known nothing about the inside of the wash house, for he was never in it and doubtless said so. Mr. Smith was only at 10 Rillington Place from 8.30

a.m. to 9 a.m. on 12th November when he worked on the main stopcock, then laid bare by the removal of the floor boards on the previous day. The work was done before Mr. Anderson put in new boards on the same morning.

In 1949 the time sheets had not assumed the importance with which some have now sought to endow them. At Larters the time sheets were filed by the week in the order corresponding to the list of workmen in the Wages Book. This was not in alphabetical order but by wage scales in descending order so that, for example, the time sheet for Mr. Willis the skilled man would be filed before Mr. Jones his labourer. The time sheets for the current quarter were kept in a cupboard in the office. At the end of the quarter they would be collected into a separate bundle, and at the end of the year the four quarterly bundles would be parcelled together and stored away. Mr. Larter took an interest in the filing of these time sheets. He thinks that when they came back from the police station that he would probably have replaced them, but he has no recollection of so doing. If he did, it is surprising that he did not notice that Willis' time sheets were missing when the others were returned. The time sheets were stored in their parcels for about six years. It was in 1953 for the first time that Larters' time sheets attracted attention when various people wanted to see them. Mr. Larter thought that he had first produced them for Mr. Furneaux and Mr. Eddowes. He had forgotten that some months earlier those that had been found had been taken to and brought back from the Scott Henderson Inquiry. He had also forgotten that even earlier he had opened up the parcel for Mr. Baker and found that the time sheets were then collected together and marked "Re Rillington Murder". If in 1949 those time sheets had been put away and tied together, they had not been filed in accordance with the firm's practice which is itself some indication that Mr.

Larter himself did not receive them back or file them in 1949.

When Inspector Black wrote the statements made on 8th December taken by Chief Inspector Jennings, he did not see any time sheets. He maintains that if time sheets had been produced and taken into the possession of the police, they would have been referred to in the statement. This had been done earlier, when, in Mr. Phillips' statement, the specification was recorded as so produced. If taken into possession in this way the time sheets would be sent to the Director of Public Prosecutions. But the production of a time sheet by the maker of a statement does not mean that the time sheet would necessarily be taken into possession by the police. This is shown by the fact that the relevant time sheets which are in existence were returned to Larters. Both Chief Inspector Jennings and Inspector Black said in their evidence that time sheets are unreliable documents and had been proved wrong time and time again. On 21st August 1953 Chief Inspector Jennings made a report to Chief Superintendent Barratt. In that report he said that on the 8th December he saw some rough pencilled notes and checked them with the statements. Since then he had seen his official diary which showed a visit by the three men on 8th December, followed by one on 9th December. He thought at the time that the three men had been brought back on the 9th for their original documents to be checked. The diary has been destroyed like so many other records and no one else now remembers the visit on 9th December.

The evidence does not show who collected Mr. Willis' time sheets, who handed them over, who returned those that were returned, whether they were all returned, who received them back, or who filed them. The only relevance of the time sheets is that in 1953 word was spread around that Mr. Willis' time sheets were the ones which so

accurately particularised the work at 10 Rillington Place
that from them its progress and state could have been readily determined. I do not believe it. Mr. Willis has a failing
recollection in certain matters and has too often said that
which he thinks the questioner wishes to hear. Mr.
Kennedy says that in 1959–1960 Mr. Willis said that he
was browned off at being detained at the police station for
four hours. Mr. Willis says that he may have said that he
was browned off, but not for a delay of that length, since
they were at the police station for two and a half hours.
Other matters have been alleged which are without foundation, namely that the police promised to provide
transport only when statements had been made. Mr.
Kennedy was told by Mr. Willis that he was shown by
Chief Inspector Jennings a photograph of a child that had
died of starvation. Mr. Kennedy made a note that this was
presumably done to put pressure on Mr. Willis. Mr. Willis
had not suggested this. This presumption was developed by
the author in his book. The officer's name was not given
but it was said that the obvious inference was that the
police were trying to trade on Willis' sympathies and so fill
him with horror and disgust at the murder of Geraldine
that he would do all he could to help them secure a conviction.

In evidence Mr. Willis recalled being shown the photograph, but said that this was after he had made his second
statement. Mr. Willis also agrees that he offered Christie
some short ends of timber but said that Christie refused
them as he was suffering with arthritis or something like
that and could not use a chopper. Mr. Willis relates the
offer to the time when the shores were being erected. At
that early stage in the work Christie was not suffering
from fibrositis. I think that at that time Christie would
have said that his complaint was enteritis, but hearing later
of arthritis from some other source Mr. Willis has confused

one complaint with the other. Alternatively Mr. Willis made the offer towards the end and not the start of his time spent at 10 Rillington Place.

Evans' trial started at the Old Bailey on 11th January 1950. The case for the Crown was conducted by Mr. Christmas Humphreys Q.C., then Senior Counsel to the Crown at the Central Criminal Court, and Mr. Henry Elam. Before the trial started Mr. Humphreys told Mr. Malcolm Morris, who was leading Mr. Evelyn Russell, that it was intended to proceed first on the indictment charging Evans with the murder of Geraldine. The reason for this was that in respect of that death the defence of provocation could not be raised. There appears to have been no other discussion between Counsel about the case before it started, and Mr.

Humphreys said that he did not know what the defence was going to be, the prosecution case being in the main based upon Evans' own statements.

In accordance with the practice then followed there were two indictments, each containing one count of murder. Evans would have been tried separately on each indictment. Today, Evans could have been tried on two counts of murder in the same indictment. As has already been mentioned, Mr. Justice Lewis ruled after legal argument, that in law the evidence in respect of the death of Beryl Evans was admissible on the count charging Evans with the murder of Geraldine. The Brief for the Prosecution contained a short note to Counsel. This referred to a similarity, as far as the bundling of the body was concerned, to the Setty case in which the wrapped up and mutilated body of a murder victim had been dropped from an aeroplane. At the time when Beryl Evans' body was discovered, the police thought that its disposition had been planned on the lines of the Setty murder. It was thought that Evans intended to carry away the bundle on his van and get rid of it somewhere, but that when his employment terminated on the evening of the 10th November, he could not dispose of it in that way. The note to Counsel pointed out that this was conjecture and therefore no evidence had been called in respect of it.

Apart from this note to Counsel there were no other instructions with the Brief. It contained the enclosures usually found in a Brief delivered by the Director of Public Prosecutions, including the depositions, the statements made by the persons called at the Magistrates Court, and the statements of 23 persons who had not been called, including those of Mr. Phillips, Mr. Jones and Mr. Willis. It also included a copy of the Police Report compiled by Chief Inspector Jennings on the 8th December, in which it was pointed out that Christie had a criminal record and short details of it were given.

Mr. Humphreys' recollection of the Evans case is hazy. This is understandable. He said that at this time he was much engaged in the Hume case which was then pending and in which he had been briefed at short notice. Mr. Humphreys said that he may not have read the police report for as a general rule he did not do so, as such reports at times contained a great deal of matter which had not been and would not be put in evidence, and therefore their contents, if read, tended to confuse the mind during the conduct of the case. He further said that it was his usual practice to read all the statements including those of the witnesses not called at the Magistrates Court, and to give to the defence the contents of any statement which helped the defence. This was more than he need have done, but it was his practice to hand over the statements. Mr. Humphreys had no recollection of the workmen's statements until told about them before he gave evidence at the Inquiry. He said that if he did not show them to the defence either he did not realise how they were relevant to the defence, or he may not have read them with particular care. He said that looking through them again he does not see how they would be relevant to any defence that he could have envisaged, for the Prosecution had no idea that it was going to be said that Christie was the murderer. Mr. Humphreys said that had he seen any relevance in those documents or had his attention been brought to some inconsistency in respect of them, then he would have shown them to the defence. In the event Christie's record was given to the defence in the early stages of the trial and Christie was cross-examined about it. In 1953 Mr. Malcolm Morris and Chief Inspector Jennings both thought that it was the police officer who handed the copy of the record to Counsel in the Court.

The evidence against Evans was of two kinds. There was the positive evidence of his confessions, his departure from London and his arrival in Wales. This evidence did not include other confessions which had been made by Evans. Matters so excluded were his remarks to Sergeant Trevallian, his reference to killing his wife made to Inspector Black, and his admission of guilt as to the killing of his wife and the disposal of Geraldine which he had made to Doctor Matheson. Nor did the Jury hear of Evans' inability or refusal to explain to Doctor Matheson on the 4th January why he had told different stories to the police. Certain of this evidence was inadmissible then but is relevant now.

Christie had a criminal record. In 1921 he was sentenced to three concurrent terms of three months imprisonment for stealing postal orders. He was bound over in 1923 for false pretences. In 1924 he was sentenced to nine months hard labour for stealing money and goods. In 1929 he was sentenced to six months hard labour for malicious wounding. In 1933 he was sentenced to three months hard labour for stealing a motor car and fined for other offences committed in connection with the use of the vehicle. At the outbreak of war Christie joined the War Reserve Police. No doubt at that time the checking of records was either ignored or faulty and Christie slipped through and served in the force until December 1943. In 1950 he presented all the outwards signs of being a man who, having committed crime, had rehabilitated himself. He appeared to have had almost seventeen years of unimpeachable behaviour behind him. Not only had he succeeded in becoming a War Reserve policeman but he had earned two commendations. The jury at the trial were invited to remember his Great War service, his wounds, his rehabilitation and most of all the fact that he was by reason of his back injury physically disabled at the time and that this disability made it impossible for him to do that which it was alleged he had done.

Christie's doctor at this time was Doctor Odess. He held a morning surgery from 10 a.m. until noon and an evening surgery from 6 to 7.30 p.m. A record of Christie's visits to Doctor Odess is in existence. They make it clear that Christie was a frequent visitor to the surgery. The records show that on 1st November 1949, Christie was given a certificate to enable him to remain off work. He had been treated for diarrhoea on 29th October. If Christie had wanted to remain off work still longer it would have been necessary for him to obtain another certificate on the 8th November. It is not known from the records whether he attended the morning or evening surgery to obtain this but Christie himself on occasions spoke of his evening visits to the doctor and of a visit on this day. When Christie gave evidence for the prosecution at Evans' trial, he maintained that on Tuesday 8th November he was feeling "pretty bad": that he went to bed and was taking milk food. He said that he was resting as much as possible on this day because of enteritis and fibrositis in the back. He described himself as being on a starvation diet and said that he could scarcely bend and that to pick anything off the floor it was necessary for him to get down on his hands and knees. He claimed that for these reasons it would have been impossible for him, even assisted by Evans, to have carried Beryl Evans' body from the top flat to the flat below. This matter was relied upon by the prosecution to show that Christie could not on the 8th November have done what Evans alleged.

In his second statement in Merthyr Tydfil Evans had said that about a week before his wife died he had been told by Christie that he was training to be a doctor before the war. When he gave evidence Christie denied that he had said this or that he had stopped his training because of an accident or that he had had an accident sometime just before or at the beginning of the war.

When Mrs. Christie gave evidence at Evans' trial she was cross examined about an accident which Christie had sustained. She was asked whether Christie had had an accident just before or at the beginning of the war. Counsel was in a difficulty because he had no more detailed information about the accident than Christie had given to Evans. To a general question whether she could recollect any accident happening to her husband Mrs. Christie said she could not recollect anything at all. The other questions were in respect of an accident round about 1939. Mrs. Christie said she did not know of one.

Evans' position at his trial with regard to Christie was an impossible one. He was alleging that, unknown to him, Christie was a strangler who had arranged to abort Beryl Evans. But there was no sign of abortion. Why, it was asked, should this man Christie carry out an abortion and even if he were an abortionist, why should he strangle Beryl Evans? Why should he strangle a child? In addition therefore to the positive case against Evans there was the apparent absurdity of the allegation made against Christie

At his trial Evans was the only witness for the defence. He denied that he strangled his daughter or his wife. He said that he first knew from Chief Inspector Jennings of the death of his daughter when he arrived at Notting Hill police station. He agreed with the evidence of events in Merthyr Tydfil. Evans said that he did not put his wife's body down a manhole, but had said that he did because Christie had told him that that was what he was going to do with the body. He then gave evidence in accordance with his second statement at Merthyr and elaborated a little upon it. He said that Christie had told him that he had been obliged to give up his medical training because of an accident just before the war. He said that Christie would not say how he would bring about the abortion, but said that only a doctor and himself would know how to do that sort of thing. He further explained what he saw when he arrived home on the Tuesday saying that his wife's body was lying on her right side. Evans also added that he saw blood on the pillow slip, which appeared to come from his wife's mouth and nose. He does not seem to have asked or been told why his wife, who had had an abortion, should be injured in the face. He said that at the bottom of the eiderdown and the top of his wife's legs there was some staining, and that he noticed blood there. He agreed, as he had told Constable Evans in Wales, that it was about seven o'clock when, hearing Christie puffing and blowing, he went and helped to carry his wife's body to the kitchen of the flat below. At Merthyr Evans said that he was told that the body would be disposed of down the drain and later, in answer to his enquiry, he was told that Christie had so disposed of it. In evidence he said that he did not ask about the body after helping to carry it, and Christie did not speak about it again. Evans also said in evidence that he did not see his wife's body again. The question of the removal of the wedding ring from her finger was not raised and has never been explained. In accordance with the same statement Evans also dealt with the arrangement about Geraldine, the furniture, the rag dealer, and that it was Christie who told him that if anyone asked him any questions about his wife and daughter he was to say that they had gone on holiday. He spoke of his return on about 23rd November, when he saw only Christie, and then of being brought back to London by the police, and the events in the police station.

The most cogent evidence against Evans at his trial was that of his own admissions in the two statements he made in Notting Hill police station, for they were at that time the basis of the case against him. They should be examined in turn.

In considering the first statement three matters arise:—(1) When was the statement made? (2) What was said by Chief Inspector Jennings? (3) What, if anything, was said by Evans? It will be remembered that the car bringing Evans from Paddington arrived at Notting Hill Police Station just before 9.45 p.m. In evidence at Evans' trial, Inspector Black said that they arrived at Paddington about 9.30 p.m. and at the Police Station about ten minutes or so after. In Chief Inspector Jennings' notebook Evans' signature at the end of the statement attributed to him is timed in Evans' writing 9.55 p.m. According to the transcript of the Scott Henderson Inquiry when Inspector Black's notebook was produced and examined it had written in it '9.45 p.m. 2/12/49 F.H.' and at the end of Evans' statement as recorded was the time 9.55 p.m. All the above was written in Inspector Black's handwriting. One way of checking the time when the first statement (Exhibit 8) finished is to fix, if possible, when the second (Exhibit 9) began. This can be found in the transcript of Evans' trial. During the cross-examination of Chief Inspector Jennings, after he had said that Exhibit 8 had finished at five minutes to ten, the following questions appear:—

Q. When did Exhibit 9 start?

A. Within two or three minutes afterwards.

Later:

Q. And Exhibit 9 must have started after 10 o'clock.

A. Somewhere around about 10, yes.

Q. And what was the time when it finished?

A. I should say about 11 o'clock.

When Inspector Black gave evidence, he was not questioned about the time when this statement was taken, for Chief Inspector Jennings' evidence had not been challenged. When Evans gave evidence he was asked in examination in chief:

Q. Did you then some time after 10 o'clock make this statement which is Exhibit 9 ?

A. Yes, sir.

It may be said that some time after 10 o'clock means any time after 10 o'clock. I think that the questions and answers are obviously related to the earlier ones and that Evans was saying that the second statement started shortly after 10 o'clock. Evans' evidence, therefore, agrees with that of the police officer that by 10 o'clock the first statement was finished. It confirms the more accurate timings recorded in both notebooks, one written by Inspector Black, the other by Evans himself, that the first statement finished at 9.55 p.m.

What Chief Inspector Jennings said to Evans is disputed. Inspector Black said that he took down the words uttered by the Chief Inspector as they were spoken. The notebook containing this entry was produced and examined before the Scott Henderson Inquiry, as can be seen from the transcript. The statement which Inspector Black made on the 3rd December and which he said was copied from his notebook still exists. Chief Inspector Jennings' entry of his own words was not made as he spoke them but later.

According to these records Chief Inspector Jennings did not tell Evans that either body was concealed behind pieces of timber. The word 'timber' does not appear. Nor, according to those records, did he mention the tie. Chief Inspector Jennings also asserted these facts in evidence at Evans' trial. Inspector Black was called to give evidence in that trial. He was not examined in chief but was presented

for cross-examination only. According to his deposition
Inspector Black's evidence was confined to the admissions
made to him by Evans on the 3rd December in relation to
the wedding ring. When crossexamined, after agreeing that
the journey to the station took ten minutes or so he was
asked:

Q. And there did Mr. Jennings tell him (Evans) that he,
   Mr. Jennings, had first found the body of his wife
   concealed underneath the washbasin or the sink in
   this outhouse?
A. Yes, sir.
Q. Did he also tell him that he found the body of his
   baby concealed behind some timber in the outhouse?
A. Yes, sir.

The Inspector is there agreeing with the suggestion that
Evans was told that the baby's body was concealed behind
some timber. When Evans gave evidence, he was asked:—

Q . . . did he tell you when he said the bodies had been
   found in the wash house whether they had been
   concealed or not?
A. Yes, sir; he told me they had been concealed by timber.

Inspector Black therefore agreed in part with what Evans
was saying, and in the answers of both the word timber is
mentioned. On the face of it therefore, it can be said that
no adverse inference should be drawn against Evans for
saying, as he did in his second statement, "I then blocked
the front of the sink up with pieces of wood so that the
body would not be seen". On the other hand, if Evans had
not been told that his wife's body was hidden by pieces of
wood, his statement that it was would indicate that he
knew what had in fact happened to the body of his wife.

There is great force in the argument that as Inspector Black said what he did, the word 'timber' must have been mentioned, otherwise why the mistake? Inspector Black said that after giving evidence at Evans' trial and when told of what he had said he checked his notebook, which he had not been using in the witness box, to refresh his memory. He says that when he checked his notebook he realised that he had made a mistake, and he said that he had accepted too readily the words of Counsel. If it was a mistake, it was one that favoured Evans before the jury. I think it is right that the Inspector did not know what he was going to be asked about when he was presented for crossexamination, but he must take the blame if he has been guilty of inaccuracy. Contrary to what the Inspector had said in his evidence, the word 'timber' did not appear in his own contemporaneous note seen in 1953 and as corroborated by his statement of the 3rd December 1949. The word 'timber' did not appear in Chief Inspector Jennings' notes which was not contemporaneous but made not long after the words had been spoken.

I have already stated that I consider Inspector Black to be an honest and in the main a reliable witness. His evidence was unreliable in the same way as would be the evidence of any person trying to remember details of events over so long a period. I also formed a favourable opinion of Chief Inspector Jennings as a witness. These two officers were in the witness box for many hours. They were cross-examined vigorously, at length and with variations of technique. No other witnesses were so tested. I had the opportunity therefore of watching them for a long time. I bear it in mind that both officers before their retirement had great experience in giving evidence and it can happen that such experience may disguise the weaknesses of testimony and give to it an appearance of reliability out of proportion to its worth. I thought that both officers were good witnesses. They made mistakes, in particular Inspector Black when he sought to marry certain events to others in the past outside the scope of the Inquiry. If the evidence of these officers had been free of such mistakes and if, after all these years, nothing had been forgotten or had required correction, I would have found their evidence suspect. In forming this view I have also borne in mind that I have not heard Evans and can only see his answers from the transcript of his trial and through the recollections of others. I think that it is more probable that the word 'timber' was not mentioned by Chief Inspector Jennings, despite the fact that in evidence Inspector Black said that it was.

I do not attach great importance to the question whether or not Chief Inspector Jennings told Evans that Geraldine was strangled with a tie. It was his evidence that he did not, and despite certain comments on an answer by Inspector Black, I read his evidence as saying that the tie was not mentioned. Nor is it mentioned in his contemporaneous record. When Evans gave evidence, not only did he say that the tie was mentioned, but that the rope also had been mentioned. For after saying that he was told that both deaths had been caused by strangulation he was asked:

Q. Did he say with what?
A. Well, a rope, sir, my wife, and my daughter had been strangled with a neck-tie.

I think that the reliable documentary evidence points also to the fact that the tie was not mentioned. When, however, Chief Inspector Jennings told Evans that the cause of death was strangulation in both cases, the child's clothing was in a separate bundle, with a tie on top of it. The tie had been cut by Doctor Teare leaving the knot visible and its purpose obvious. Evans would not have failed to realise that a tie had been used to strangle the child, even though nothing had been said about it.

The third question is what was said by Evans in his first statement at Notting Hill.. It was suggested to Chief Inspector Jennings in evidence that he used the words attributed to Evans and later, as now, said that they were Evans' words. This is also the view expressed by Mr. Kennedy when he says in his book:

"Yet we are solemnly asked to believe that Evans made this statement 'voluntarily, spontaneously and without any preliminary questioning' (to quote the words of the late Home Secretary Sir David Maxwell Fyfe) and within a few minutes of arriving at Notting Hill Station."

I have already explained why I think that on the evidence it was virtually agreed and is certainly established that the first statement, whatever it was, was made within a few minutes of arrival at the police station. At his trial Evans, when answering his Counsel, said that he answered "Yes, Sir" when told that the officer believed that Evans was responsible for causing the deaths of his wife and child. The following questions and answers then appear:—

Q. Did you then make the statement which the Chief Inspector took down in his notebook?
A. Yes, sir.
Q. Before we go to that, was there any other reason why you said "yes" as well as the fact that you gave up everything when you heard that your daughter was dead?
A. Well, sir, I was frightened at the time.
Q. Why were you frightened or what were you frightened of?
A. Well, I thought if I did not make a statement the

police would take me downstairs and start knocking me about.

Later:

Q. Did you then make this statement saying that your wife was incurring one debt after another, "I could not stand it any longer so I strangled her with a piece of rope"?

A. Yes, sir.

Q. And later that you had strangled your baby on the Thursday evening with your tie?

A. Yes, sir.

Later in cross-examination:

Q. You were then saying that you were responsible for causing their deaths?

A. I did say it, yes.

Mr. Justice Lewis:

Q. What did you mean by that? What did you think the police officer meant by saying he thought you were responsible for causing their deaths?

A. In other words, in my opinion good enough to say as I had done it, sir.

Mr. Humphreys:

Q. Yes, you were saying you had done it were you not?

A. I did say I had done it, yes.

Q. Later you signed a written statement in some greater detail, did not you, Exhibit 8 saying of your wife she was incurring one debt after another, "I could not stand it any longer so I strangled her with a piece of rope and took her down to the flat below the same night whilst the old man was in hospital, waited till the Christies downstairs had gone to bed, and then I took her to the wash house after midnight. This was on Tuesday, 8th November." Did you say that?

A.   I did say that.

Q.   Then you go on to say "On Thursday evening after I came home from work I strangled my baby in our bedroom with my tie and later that night I took her down into the wash house after Christies had gone to bed." Did you say that?

A.   Yes sir.

Q.   Why?

A.   Well, as I said before sir, I was upset and I did not know what I was saying.

Evans' own evidence therefore is in agreement with that of the police officers that he said that which he is recorded as having said and which he signed at the time. The disputes concerning the evidence of Evans and the Police Officers were not about what Evans said but about what the Chief Inspector had said to Evans about timber and the tie. Evans' own evidence, given on 12th January, to which I have referred was that he did make that statement and said the words himself. He did not suggest then that the statement was made in a way which would indicate that it was not a voluntary one, made spontaneously. Nor did he suggest that there was any preliminary questioning other than that to which I have referred. Nor did he say that he did not himself use the words spoken. He said that he did. Making every allowance for Evans' illiteracy and his need to rely upon his memory only, if evidence means anything it is all one way—that Evans admitted saying what he is alleged to have said at the time when he is alleged to have said it.

The second statement is a lengthy document. It runs to about 1,940 words. For convenience I have divided it into five paragraphs. It reads as follows:—

I have been cautioned by Chief Inspector Jennings and told that I am not obliged to say anything unless I wish to do so and that anything I say will be taken down in writing and may be given in evidence.

(Signed) T. J. EVANS.

(i) I was working for the Lancaster Food Products of Lancaster Road, W.11. My wife was always moaning about me working long hours so I left there and went to work for the Continental Wine Stores of Edgware Road. I started at 8 a.m. and finished at 2 p.m. and the job was very nice there. In the meanwhile my wife got herself into £20 debt so I borrowed £20 off the Guvnor under false pretences, so he give me the £20 which I took home and gave it to my wife. I asked her who she owed the money to but she would not tell me, so a week later I got sacked. I was out of work then for two or three weeks. In the meanwhile I had been driving for two or three days a week. I was earning 25/- to 30/- a day. This was for the Lancaster Food Products I used to give her this money and she was moaning she wasn't getting enough wages, so one of the regular drivers at the Lancaster Food Products left so the Guvnor asked me if I would like my regular job back at a wage of £5 15s. 0d. a week. I was doing quite a lot of overtime for the firm working late, which I used to earn altogether £6 to £7 a week. Out of that my wife used to go to the firm on a Friday and my Guvnor used to pay her £5 what she used to sign for. Perhaps through the week I would have to give her more money off different people from which I used to borrow it. I used to pay them back on a Friday out of my own pocket. I had to rely on my overtime to pay my debts and then I had a letter from J. Brodericks telling me I was behind in my payments for my furniture on the hire purchase. I asked her if she had been paying for the furniture and she said she had, then I showed her the letter I had received from Brodericks then she admitted she hadn't been paying it. I went down to see Brodericks myself to pay them my £1 a week and ten shillings off the arrears so then I left the furniture business to my wife.

I then found she was in debt with the rent. I accused her of squandering the money so that started a terrific argument in my house. I told her if she didn't pull herself together I would leave her, so she said "You can leave any time you like," so I told her she would be surprised one day if I walked out on her. One Sunday, early in November, I had a terrific row with her at home so I washed and changed and went to the pub dinner time. I stopped there till two o'clock. I came home, had my lunch, left again to go out, leaving my wife and baby at home, because I didn't want any more arguments. I went to the pictures—A.B.C. Lancaster Road, known as Royalty, at 4.30 p.m. I came out when the film was finished, I think about 7.15 p.m. I went home sat down and switched the wireless on. I made a cup of tea. My wife was nagging till I went to bed at 10 p.m. I got up at 6 a.m. next day, made a cup of tea. My wife got up to make a feed for the baby at 6.15 a.m. She gets up and starts an argument straight away. I took no notice of her and went into the bedroom to see my baby before going to work. My wife told me she was going to pack up and go down to her father in Brighton. I asked her what she was going to do with the baby, so she said she was going to take the baby down to Brighton with her so I said it would be a good job and a load of worry off my mind, so I went to work as usual so when I came home at night I just put the kettle on, I sat down, my wife walked in so I said, "I thought you was going to Brighton?" She said, "What for you to have a good time?" I took no notice of her. I went downstairs and fetched the pushchair up. I come upstairs she started an argument again. I told her if she didn't pack it up I'd slap her face. With that she picked up a milk bottle to throw at me. I grabbed the bottle out of her hand, I pushed her, she fell in a chair in the kitchen, so I washed and changed and went out. I went to the pub and had a few drinks. I got home about 10.30 p.m. I walked in she started to row again so I went straight to bed. I got up Tuesday morning and went straight to work.

(ii) I come home at night about 6.30 p.m. my wife started to argue again, so I hit her across the face with my flat hand. She then hit me back with her hand. In a fit of temper I grabbed a piece of rope from a chair which I had brought home off my van and strangled her with it. I then took her into the bedroom and laid her on the bed with the rope still tied round her neck. Before 10 p.m. that night I carried my wife's body downstairs to the kitchen of Mr. Kitchener's flat as I knew he was away in hospital. I then came back upstairs. I then made my baby some food and fed it, then I sat with the baby by the fire for a while in the kitchen. I put the baby to bed later on. I then went back to the kitchen and smoked a cigarette. I then went downstairs when I knew everything was quiet, to Mr. Kitchener's kitchen. I wrapped my wife's body up in a blanket and a green table cloth from off my kitchen table. I then tied it up with a piece of cord from out of my kitchen cupboard. I then slipped downstairs and opened the back door, then went up and carried my wife's body down to the wash house and placed it under the sink. I then blocked the front of the sink up with pieces of wood so that the body wouldn't be seen. I locked the wash house door, I come in and shut the back door behind me. I then slipped back upstairs. The Christies who live on the ground floor were in bed.

(iii) I went into the bedroom to see if my daughter was asleep. When I looked in the cot she was fast asleep so I then shut the bedroom door and laid on the bed all night fully dressed until it was time to get up and go to work. I then got up, lit the gas and put the kettle on. I made my baby a feed and fed it. I then changed her and put her back into the cot wrapping her up well so that she would not get cold, then went to the kitchen and poured myself out a cup of tea. I then finished my tea and slipped back into the bedroom to see if the baby had dropped off to sleep. It was asleep so I went off to work. I done my days work and got home about 5.30 p.m. that Wednesday evening. I come in, lit the gas, put the kettle on and lit the fire. I fed the baby, had a cup of tea myself, sat in front of the fire with my baby. I made the baby a feed about 9.30 p.m. I fed her then I changed her, then I put her to bed. I come back into the kitchen sat by the fire until about twelve o'clock, then went to bed. I got up at 6 a.m. next day lit the gas put the kettle on, made the baby a feed and fed it. I then changed her and dressed her. I then poured myself out a cup of tea I had already made. I drank half and the baby drank the other half. I then put the baby back into the cot, wrapped her up well and went to work. I done my day's work and then had an argument with the Guvnor then I left the job. He give me my wages before I went home. He asked me what I wanted my wages for. I told him I wanted to post some money off to my wife first thing in the morning. He asked where my wife was and I told him she had gone to Bristol on a holiday. He said "How do you intend to send the money to her" and I said, "In a registered envelope." He paid me the money so he said "You can call over tomorrow morning for your cards."

(iv) I then went home picked up my baby from her cot in the bedroom, picked up my tie and strangled her with it. I then put the baby back in the cot and sat down in the kitchen and waited for Christies downstairs to go to bed. At about twelve o'clock that night I took the baby downstairs to the wash house and hid her body behind some wood. I then locked the wash house door behind me and came in closing the back door behind me. I then slipped back upstairs and laid on the bed all night, fully clothed.

(v) I got up the following morning, washed, shaved and changed, and went up to see a man in Portobello Road about selling my furniture. I don't know his name. During the same afternoon he came to my flat, looked at it and offered me forty quid for it. I told him I would take £40 for it and then he asked me why I wanted to sell it. I told him I was going to Bristol to live as I had a job there waiting for me. He asked me why I wasn't taking the furniture with me. I told him my wife had already gone there and had a flat with furniture in it. He then asked me if it was paid for. I said it was. He said he would call Sunday afternoon to let me know what time the driver would call on Monday for it. I said I would wait in for him. Between 3 and 4 p.m. on Monday this man took all the furniture all the lino, and he paid me £40 which I signed for in a receipt book. He handed me the money which I counted in his presence. I waited till he went then picked up my suitcase which I took to Paddington. The same night I caught the 12.55 a.m. train from Paddington to Cardiff and made my way to 93 Mount Pleasant, Merthyr Vale, where I stayed with my Uncle, Mr. Lynch. The rest I think you know. I have been asked to read this statement myself, but I cannot read. It has been read over to me and it is all the truth.

(Signed) T. J. EVANS.

Statement taken by Chief Inspector Jennings, C.I.D. "F"
Division, written down, read over and signature witnessed
by James N. Black, Detective Inspector "F" Division.

Chief Inspector Jennings and Inspector Black say that
it took an hour and a quarter to an hour and twenty minutes to take and read back to Evans. In his notebook,
Inspector Black had recorded the statement as finishing at
11.15 p.m., it having started, he says, just before 10
o'clock. It is said that such a statement could not have
been recorded in so short a time. Further it is claimed that
when the police officers say that it was obtained without
questioning by them, they are attributing to Evans a lucid-
ity of expression, an ability to marshal facts and to
expound them in chronological order when he possessed
neither the intelligence nor the capacity to do so. On the
question of timing, Mr. Kennedy and Mr. Eddowes carried
out an experiment on 5th November 1965, when under
fast dictation it took them an hour to write the statement
and 11½ minutes for it to be read back. When Evans gave
evidence, he said that Inspector Black took down the
statement and that the 840 words in paragraph (i) were
true and that he had said what was in it. A good deal of
the information in this part of the statement was already
known to the police when Evans was interviewed, but, in
so far as I can judge from the statements then in existence,
a considerable amount of the matters set out in paragraph
(i) was not known to the police at that time, for the statements containing the information had not then been
obtained. It is suggested that possibly, as may well happen,
the police had learned of these matters but had not taken
written statements in respect of them, and that later when
Evans was questioned about the matter and his statement
had been obtained, the police took written statements
from witnesses to confirm the knowledge they already
had. In one part of paragraph (i) Evans explained, for

example, how he had borrowed £20 off his previous employer under false pretences. The person referred to was Mr. Esposito who during his employment of Evans was told by him that he had to travel to Ramsgate to bring back his child suffering from measles. Mr. Esposito advanced £10 and later a further £7 to pay doctor's bills. Afterwards he learned from Beryl Evans that she had not been to Ramsgate, that the child had not been ill, and that her husband was a liar, and, she claimed, that he had not given her any money for a fortnight. Mr. Esposito discharged Evans who gave an I.O.U. for his total indebtedness of £20. Beryl Evans asked Mr. Esposito not to be too hard on her husband, and although Evans obtained another job and promised to repay the loan at £1 a week, he did not pay anything and Mr. Esposito wrote it off as a bad debt. There is no indication that the police had information of this before the 8th December. There are several such explanations of matters contained in paragraph (i) of the statement, showing that the police probably did not previously know about all the matters contained in it. What is said is that they did not need to know very much, for clever questioning would produce all the information, whether it was known beforehand or not. Certainly Inspector Black could not have known a good deal of what was in this part of the statement, for he had been in Wales and rightly stated that he was learning about events as they were described.

Evans said that everything in paragraph (i) was true and that he had said it. When he came to deal with paragraph (ii) Evans gave reasons for having said that which he claimed was untrue. They were that he was upset, having previously thought that his daughter was still alive, and that he did not think that he knew what he was saying: that he made it up and that he was afraid that the police would take him downstairs and beat him up. This paragraph, with paragraph (iv), is an enlargement of the essential parts of his previous statement. To explain the making of that statement, made within a few minutes of arrival at the police station, Evans gave similar reasons, namely, that he was upset and did not care what happened and that he was frightened that he was going to be beaten up. It means on his evidence that, for the reasons which he gave, Evans made the first statement which was untrue, then paragraph (i) of the second which was true, then paragraph (ii) which was untrue and made for the same reasons which had affected his mind earlier but had not affected it during the making of paragraph (i). Similarly paragraph (iv) is untrue between paragraphs (iii) and (v) which are true. Evans admitted at his trial that he did say everything contained in both statements for the reasons which I have mentioned. He did not include as a reason that the police kept questioning him, or that they put words into his mouth or treated him badly. The police officers say that Evans spoke very quickly and at times had to be restrained to permit Inspector Black to take down the words. Both officers say that there was no questioning save to remove any ambiguities.

On the 9th September 1953, the two police officers attended the Home Office. In the presence of the Home Secretary and Sir Frank Newsam and Mr. Fitzgerald, Inspector Black took down the statement dictated by Chief Inspector Jennings. It took an hour to write and ten minutes to read back. Therefore the writing and reading back were completed within the time which was stated in 1949. When on the 30th August 1953 someone had dictated the statement to Chief Inspector Jennings, the times for his writing and reading back were the same. In one sense it does not matter how long it took to take the statement, for Evans said that he uttered every word in it and he did not attribute any impropriety to the officers in the

taking of it. There could therefore have been no objection
if the officers had said that the statement had taken an
hour longer to write than it did. If, prior to the statement
being taken, Evans had been subjected to the long interrogation which Inspector Jennings expected would be
necessary, there could have been no objection. What is said
is that the police, having taken longer than the time stated
because of the delay in getting the story from Evans,
decided on the times given so that it might be put abroad
as a quickly taken statement. In their determination to
underline the point, they made a mistake, obvious now but
not realised when it was made, that they had cut the time
too much. In other words, they had overdone it.

If a statement taken in 1949 is not challenged until
1953, any minor departures from regularity that there
might have been would probably by then have been forgotten. It is quite possible that the wish to remove an
ambiguity might be given a wide interpretation by some
and a police officer might have included some phrase such
as "What did you do next?" "Where did you go from
there?" I would not be surprised when a quickly spoken
account is being recorded if the writer instinctively put 8
p.m. when 8 o'clock was spoken, and the abbreviation
being accepted as right by the person making the statement at the time would for ever be accepted by both as
being an accurate record of what was said. It might well
have happened that in the pauses necessary for Inspector
Black to keep up with Evans' words, Chief Inspector
Jennings would have contained the chronology without
influencing the contents of the statement. Three and a half
years later, the statement not having been challenged, a
person would not remember whether there had been
these minor efforts to achieve orderliness. At this stage of
time I do not see what difference a strict test of voluntariness, according to the Judges' Rules, would make, save on

credibility, since Evans admits that he said everything that
he is alleged to have said. According to his mother, if Evans
was lying he was very hesitant but if he was speaking the
truth he would go straight on. This is confirmed in that
when he lied he was very slow and hesitant as Constable
Evans found earlier when taking the first statement in
Merthyr. He was not quick in dictating the second.

Since Evans admitted that he said everything recorded
in the second statement at Notting Hill, I am not prepared
to find merely on the question of time and the formation
of some of his sentences that the statement was not a voluntary one when Evans made no criticism of the manner
of its taking, a matter which must have been in the forefront of the mind of his Counsel when he saw Evans in
conference before his trial. Although the Brief did not
seek to give an explanation of the conflicting statements,
it did say that the statement of the 2nd December was a
full confession of murder. This matter must have been fully
discussed with Counsel. It is clear that there was nothing
which could be called an interrogation, for had there been
there would certainly have been included in the statement
an explanation why Christie had been protected in the
first statement at Merthyr, blamed in the second, and
exculpated in the second statement at Notting Hill police
station. It would have been in respect of paragraphs (ii) and
(iv) that interrogation would have taken place, not in
respect of paragraph (i). The fact that Evans told his
mother of the treatment which he said that he had
received at the hands of Chief Inspector Jennings and
failed to mention it to his legal advisers, and that he also
made the finer point, not that the police did anything to
him but that he feared that they would, shows that the
question of police behaviour was considered by Evans.

For some reason he decided not to tell his legal advisers that which he had told his mother, and not to mention

at his trial the reason which he gave to his mother, and the different one which he gave to his sister, to account for what he had said when statements at Notting Hill were made. I accept what Evans and the police officers said in 1949, namely that Evans did say all that is contained in those statements. It is necessary, however, to decide what weight there is in the reasons which he gave for saying that which was false, thereby incriminating himself, and not pointing the finger at Christie who Evans, if innocent, must have known was the only person who could have been responsible for what had happened to his wife and child. I consider that in the reasons given by Evans for saying that which was false there is a contradiction. It is not easy to reconcile the one explanation that he did not know what he was saying because he was upset with the other that he said what he did because he feared that the police would beat him up.

The statement that he was afraid of the police and therefore made statements false in part is capable of being tested on the evidence showing Evans' experience of the police. Before Evans made the first statement at Notting Hill he had been with the police for about 55 hours; for some 52 of them he was detained under arrest. Over 49 of those hours had been spent in Merthyr Tydfil, the remainder on the journey to London and to Notting Hill police station. At Merthyr Tydfil, although Evans was seen by several officers, he was in the main seeing and talking to Constable Evans. When I was questioning this witness about the conditions existing and the treatment meted out to Evans at Merthyr Tydfil, Counsel for the Evans family made it clear that no criticism was made about the police in Merthyr Tydfil and said that Constable Evans' conduct was impeccable. It is none the less important to bear in mind what was happening to Evans in that police station, for prior to reaching Notting Hill all his imprisonment in a cell took place there and his experience of the police was gained there.

The records kept at Merthyr Tydfil and the evidence of the officers show that Evans was fed regularly and that the prescribed visits were paid to him. His food was cooked at a nearby Inn and brought to the station. The times of his meals appear in the Occurrence Book. He was allowed to wash frequently. Constable Evans said that he on occasions would go to the cell and tell Evans that he wanted to have a talk with him, and he thought that Evans rather welcomed the trip upstairs as a change from his cell. There would be little for Evans to do in a cell, being unable to read. Constable Evans described his association with Evans at this time in the words "I lived with him". He said that he had never before or since spent so much time with a person in custody, and that when Evans left, the officer felt sure that they were sick of the sight of each other. There was nothing solitary about the confinement. Constable Evans did not think that Evans was at any time in fear of the police at Merthyr Tydfil. During the time that he was held at Merthyr Tydfil Evans had made three written statements in the space of two days. There is nothing to suggest that anything in the taking of those statements could or did frighten Evans. There was no compulsion, Evans saying only what he wanted to say and only being urged on when the pauses were long. He made those three statements without anyone threatening him, and in the making of them he had acquired some experience of giving statements to the police.

Evans was handcuffed on the journey to London. It is no doubt both an annoyance and an embarrassment to be kept handcuffed to a police officer during a journey, but it is a necessary and well known procedure and as such would have caused no surprise to Evans. Evans first met

Inspector Black at 11.45 a.m. on 2nd December, during an interview which ended when the telephone call came from London. Inspector Black travelled with Evans to London. They travelled in a reserved first class compartment. The evidence demonstrated that Inspector Black cannot have said or done anything to hurt or frighten Evans, for Evans was to speak warmly of the Inspector thereafter. From the time of departure from Wales to the moment when Evans was taken to his cell after making his statements, Evans was in the company of Inspector Black. There is no suggestion that Sergeant Corfield did or said anything which would frighten Evans. In his six car journeys with Evans between the 3rd and 22nd December, Evans gave no indication to Inspector Black that he had been afraid at any time when in his company.

The other person introduced into these events was Chief Inspector Jennings. In the car from Paddington to the police station his silence meant silence for all. I have found it proved that Evans made the first statement within minutes of his arrival at the police station. That statement, though short, deals with the strangling of his wife, her removal to the flat below, thence to the wash house and the strangling of the baby and her removal to the wash house. Chief Inspector Jennings was strongly criticised when giving evidence for staging what was called a brutal confrontation. The criticism was that, on the assumption that Evans was innocent of the murder of his baby, short of putting the corpse on the floor the officer could not have thought of any more cruel way of telling Evans that his child was dead. It was later said that it was not suggested that the method was conceived in or motivated by brutality but that it was so brutal to Evans that it must have had a shattering effect upon him. Chief Inspector Jennings did not think so. He said he had reason to believe that Evans might have caused the deaths. Obviously if he had not thought so, he would not have accused him. He would not have been making any assumption of Evans' innocence. From the various things that had been said he had reason to believe that Evans must have known something about the death of his child. He said that Evans had told two different stories in Wales and he wanted the truth and that was what he was after. Chief Inspector Jennings agreed that Evans may have been shaken by what happened but said that he did not thereby have "to tell stories" about it. Inspector Black, who was in no way responsible for this procedure adopted at the police station, did not consider it brutal, saying that some might have done it that way, others might not.

One of the two principal criticisms is directed to the showing of the tie which had strangled the child. Having listened to and read some of the criticisms which have been made directly and indirectly against the police in the conduct of the Evans case, I suspect that if the tie had not been shown to Evans the criticism would now be made that at the outset he was prevented from denying ownership or knowledge of the tie which was used as a ligature on the baby. It should not be forgotten that Chief Inspector Jennings knew that a baby and her mother had been strangled and that the husband and father described by his family as a liar had already given the police two conflicting statements about the death of his wife. The Chief Inspector wanted the truth and decided that, if he showed Evans the evidence which the police had, he was most likely to be given a truthful answer. Evans did not say that the police either threatened to or did beat him up. He went no further than to say that he thought that they were going to. I can find nothing in the evidence to indicate why he should have thought that or that anything was done that would lead him to think it. In view of his immediately recent experience at Merthyr Tydfil with Constable

Evans and of the journey with Inspector Black, I do not see any grounds to support Evans' contention that he was frightened by or of the police.

Some cross-examination of Inspector Black was directed to the date when the handwriting test at the Home Office took place. Inspector Black was quite certain that when on holiday at Cromer in 1953 he had been unexpectedly called to London to carry out the test, and had rejoined his family at Cromer the same day. Inspector Black said that he thought his stay in Cromer would be for a fortnight, Saturday to Saturday, and that his period of leave might be a little longer. Inspector Black was then at Scotland Yard. There are no leave lists available which cover Inspector Black's leave. On 21st August 1953, Chief Inspector Jennings reported to Chief Superintendent Barratt on the question of the time sheets which had then been raised. In that report he mentioned a meeting attended by Inspector Black on 18th August. In a report dated 1st September 1953, Chief Inspector Jennings wrote that the Inspector was then at Cromer on holiday and due to report back for duty on 6th September when the inquiry would be completed. The 6th September was a Sunday, and if the information in the report is correct it would suggest that Inspector Black would be coming back from Cromer on Saturday 5th September. If he did, it would appear that he went to Cromer on 22nd August. Since the handwriting test at the Home Office was on the 9th September and on the assumption that the reports are accurate, Inspector Black is wrong when he said that it was for the purpose of the test that he was brought back from his leave. I have no reason to doubt Inspector Black's recollection of the disturbance to his holiday plans which the summons to London caused. Inspector Black's recollection was shown to be faulty when he tried to relate this incident to another case, for the date he gave was wrong. He may well have come to London on a day visit for some purpose at this time, but it would not appear to be for the handwriting test which undoubtedly took place on 9th September.

∞⚬⟨⟩⚬∞

On the 13th January 1950 Evans was convicted. On the 20th February 1950 his appeal was heard by the Court of Criminal Appeal. The judgement of the court was delivered by Lord Goddard, Lord Chief Justice. There were many grounds of appeal. The Court although not confining its judgement to the consideration of this matter held that there was really only one point in the case which had any substance and which required to be dealt with at length. That was the point of law, whether Mr. Justice Lewis was right in holding that statements and an admission in respect of the death of Beryl Evans were admissible against Evans on a count alleging the murder of Geraldine. The Court of Criminal Appeal held that the evidence of the one was relevant in respect of the other, and decided the point of law accordingly. The appeal was dismissed, and in this Inquiry no one has sought to develop any point on this aspect of the case.

On arrival at Pentonville Prison Evans was seen by Doctor P.J.G. Quinn, M.R.C.P.I., L.R.C.S.I., D.P.M., then a medical officer of some three months experience in the prison service. Doctor Quinn is now the Consultant Psychiatrist and Physician Superintendent at Clifton Hospital, York. Prior to joining the prison service he had no mental hospital experience. He interviewed Evans, and his notes have been produced. Evans denied that he was guilty of the offence and repeated his defence at the trial, saying that Christie had said that he would dispose of Beryl Evans' body down the drain. Doctor Quinn described Evans as talkative and cheerful but somewhat fidgety on being questioned about the charge. He went on to say of Evans that he related his story without any deep emotion and "one gets the impression that it has been well rehearsed. He shows no suspicion or antagonism and there is none of the anger and indignation that one might expect if his story were true." On 16th January, when asked by Doctor Quinn why he had confessed to the murder, Evans answered that he did not know, saying that was his mistake. Doctor Quinn said in evidence that Evans could have been deceiving him about this but that he does not think that he was. Doctor Quinn said that Evans became more apprehensive about his position after his appeal failed.

Looking back now, Doctor Quinn said that Evans could not have been certified as a feeble minded person because of his reasonably good social and occupational history, but Doctor Quinn thought that a person such as

Evans might well make a wrong confession when flustered, under conditions of anxiety, in order to get away from the immediate discomfort of the situation of questioning, without giving the ultimate consequences any consideration at all. In that way Doctor Quinn now explains Evans' confession to Doctor Matheson made on 3rd December, saying that Evans' emotional state was still continuing. He went on to say that if such a young man had learned for the first time that his baby was dead and had been strangled, he might, under the stress of that emotional shock, make a confession which was not based on reality. If he had made such a confession Doctor Quinn did not think that Evans would be able to give an explanation for it. He agreed that Evans would not have the ability to reflect upon or analyse his motives. In the years since 1950 Doctor Quinn has not had a great deal of experience in the type of case about which he was speaking (where people make false confessions). When asked to quote examples he mentioned first husbands with paranoid ideas including paranoid schizophrenic husbands who constantly question their wives about their fidelity until in the end the wives wrongly admit their infidelity. The second example was that of children, innocent of theft, who being closely questioned by their parents about stealing eventually confess to stealing of which they are not guilty. Doctor Quinn's only other experiences of false confessions were by insane persons. There seems to be little or no comparison between the examples quoted above and the case of a man who, as I find on the evidence, when first accused of murder immediately admits it—for such was the situation when Evans made his first statement. Doctor Quinn stated that he has never heard of a person admitting to the murder of his wife, thereby exculpating the true murderer whose identity is known to the husband when making his false confession of guilt.

The Senior Medical Officer at Pentonville Prison was Doctor P.M. Coats, M.D., now the Principal Medical Officer at Wormwood Scrubs. He first saw Evans on 17th February 1950 and every day thereafter until his execution on the 9th March. He interviewed Evans at length, shortly after 17th February. Evans told Doctor Coats that Christie had committed the murders. Doctor Coats carried out certain tests in an attempt to assess Evans' mental age and those tests revealed in his view a mental age of 10½ years. Doctor Coats explained that this meant the standard that Evans had reached at school, and he put his intelligence quotient in the region of 75. With such a mental age, Doctor Coats had to decide whether Evans should be considered as a mental defective. His conclusion was that Evans was not a mental defective because there were other things to consider beside his mental age, namely the work that he did and the life that he led. The mental age of 10½ years was, according to Doctor Coats, based upon Evans' illiteracy and his standard in such things as mental arithmetic. Doctor Coats agreed that a man of Evans' age with a mental age of 10½ could be under a serious handicap in coping with some practical situations in life. He also said that there are workmen of the same intelligence quotient and mental age as Evans who cannot sign for their pay at the end of the week but do a perfectly good job.

A number of prison officers and others in the prison service who saw Evans in prison gave evidence. There is little in the written documents to support their recollections apart from notes made by Professor Curran referred to later in this chapter. To some, in one way or another, Evans protested his innocence. One officer said that Evans, on his return to Brixton prison from Court, said that Christie had "shopped" him. Another remembered that Evans said either that he came home and found his wife dead and put her in the wash house, or that he came home and found her in the wash house. Another, who was not a good witness, claimed that Evans had admitted more than once that he had murdered his wife and child. Another, who was a better witness, remembered when in Brixton giving Evans some tea and something to eat during the night, and being told by Evans, when explaining about the baby, that he had no one with whom to leave her and that she was crying and that he did her in. There is no contemporaneous record of these admissions or denials and I do not think that anything arising from this evidence can do more than support in some cases the findings based upon other, more reliable evidence.

In the days before his trial when Evans talked to Inspector Black on his journeys to and from Brixton prison, it was with a mixture of apparent admiration and dislike that he spoke of one of his fellow prisoners, Hume. When men are awaiting trial in the hospital ward they have many opportunities to share their experiences and obtain such help as they can from their fellows. The experienced may guide the beginners. Hume is a notorious criminal. Having been found not guilty of the murder of Setty, he pleaded guilty to being an accessory after the fact to the murder. He was sentenced to 12 years imprisonment. Hume is now in prison in Switzerland serving a sentence for murder.

On the 28th August 1965, Hume wrote a letter to the Deputy Controller at Scotland Yard, claiming that he could give, as he said, valuable information about Evans. He gave an account of how, according to Evans, Geraldine had been killed. On the 26th June 1953, Hume had given this account to the Assistant Governor of Wakefield Prison, who recommended Hume to see the Prison Governor. There is no record that he did. In a newspaper article based upon Hume's information and dated the 7th February 1958 after Hume's release from prison, Hume varied his account. He said that when told in 1953 that he should give evidence before the Scott Henderson Inquiry he had refused to do so. He also claimed that in 1949 Evans had betrayed details of some escape from Brixton planned by Hume and that confirmation of what he said would be found in the Hospital Ward Day Book. There is no confirmation in that book. There was evidence from a prison officer that one day he separated Evans from Hume when the latter hit Evans at the meal table. Hume apologised and the two were friendly again afterwards. The officer described Hume as the most egotistical person he had ever met. I place no reliance on what Hume has written. He has already received the publicity that he doubtless sought, and I draw no conclusions from his untested information.

On the 4th and 5th of March 1950, a Statutory Inquiry heard evidence and interviewed Evans. The Statutory Inquiry was one appointed by the Home Office to examine the mental state of a person convicted and condemned to death to see whether there was any reason why the execution should not take place. The members of the Inquiry were Sir Norwood East, Doctor Hopwood, and Professor Curran. Sir Norwood East was the Director of Prison Mental Services and had been concerned with some 250 of these Inquiries. He died in 1953. Doctor Hopwood is now 80 years of age. He is now retired after spending some years as Medical Superintendent at Broadmoor Hospital, and he has neither notes nor a recollection of the details of the Statutory Inquiry made in respect of Evans. This was one of over 100 such Inquiries which Doctor Hopwood attended. Professor Curran, C.B.E., F.R.C.P., D.P.M., said that Doctor Hopwood must have seen thousands of people charged with killing in one form or another.

Doctor Hopwood was unable to give evidence before me. Professor Curran, who is Professor of Psychiatry at St. George's Hospital Medical School, gave evidence and supplied copies of the notes which he made at the time of that Inquiry. The notes made by the other members have not been seen. Each member made his own notes. One has but to read the notes exhibited to be made aware of the care and detail with which the Statutory Inquiry was conducted. Naturally after all these years, Professor Curran cannot explain every word in the notes which he wrote in 1950.

The procedure which was followed at the Statutory Inquiry was the normal one of seeing witnesses on the first day, and interviewing Evans, then seeing Evans again the following day after he had had a night's sleep. Those making the Inquiry were supplied with the Home Office report on the case, the statements taken by the police from various witnesses, the depositions, the medical reports and the transcript of the trial. The Inquiry therefore was supplied with all available relevant information. When investigating the matter the three members although not concerned with guilt or innocence, treated the verdict of the Jury as correct. Therefore in this case when examining Evans they assumed that he had committed the offence for which he had been convicted. Anything that he said which contradicted this would be treated as a lying statement, and anything which was tantamount to a denial of guilt, he having been convicted, would be considered to be a purposeful lie.

Of the witnesses seen, the Governor of the prison and his deputy, and the Roman Catholic Chaplain, considered that Evans was below average intelligence but not a mental defective or insane. Certain disciplinary officers gave their estimates of Evans' intelligence, varying from on the lower side "is of very low intelligence" to "average intelligence". None of the officers thought that Evans was a mental defective or insane, and one who put Evans at below average intelligence added that, except for education, he was quite bright. Doctor Coats, having reported on Evans' mental age as being 10½ years, said that he was unusually well informed for a man of his class, and although a dullard seemed an extremely stable dullard. Doctor Quinn had reported that he thought Evans was feeble-minded, but went on to say that Evans was socially capable and adaptable, that his work record seemed quite good, that he seemed to have got on quite well with people, and that Evans was not certifiable as a mental defective. Doctor Matheson gave evidence that in his view Evans' mental age was 11 years and that he was of average intelligence with educational defects. Doctor Matheson again reported upon him as an inadequate psychopath because he had led an inadequate life, saying that he put the term "inadequate psychopath" at its highest; he could not say that it would affect Evans' responsibility in any way. He also told the Statutory Inquiry that Evans' had made his confession to him in a matter-of-fact way. Professor Curran made a note that Evans was a "decent" behaved boy. He thought that he became upset and restless when recounting the events of the 8th November and denying that he had anything to do with his wife's death, and Professor Curran said that that could be consistent with innocence. Professor Curran's recollection was that Evans appeared cheerful most of the time he was being interviewed.

Evans explained his confession as being due to shock on hearing of his daughter's death and thereafter not caring what had happened, and that, he said, was how he came to make his long statement. He said that he gave the account about putting the body down the drain because that was where Christie had said that he put the body. He insisted that he last saw Geraldine alive on the Thursday morning. There is no record that Evans told the Statutory Inquiry that he made his statements because the police had put the words into his mouth. A question relating to his admission of guilt was asked by someone in the form "Why tell the police you did it?", but no answer appears to have been recorded. Evans also denied the account given by Lucy that he was tripped up by her and said that he only slapped his wife once after she had thrown a bottle at him. Evans' examination ended with his saying, presumably in answer to a question: "The only thing that sticks in my mind is that I am in for something I have not done. The police caught me for a statement when I was upset. I say Christie done it." The last words were said with emotion and anger.

Professor Curran said that Evans' intelligence was measured at 10–11 years because of his lack of education, but that he had a vocabulary of a person of 14 years. These were the Professor's own assessments and the basis of them appears in his notes, although he would have known from the documents and the evidence the opinion which others had formed on this matter. Professor Curran said that he would describe Evans as a primitive individual, but in spite of his lack of education he had an ability to manage and get on in life. Taking also his work record, the way in which he lived, and his vocabulary test into account, he described Evans as being of average intelligence, putting him at the lower end of the average scale. He pointed out that although the scores which were given to him on intelligence tests would be compatible with his being a feeble minded person, this is only one of the items of information upon which a diagnosis is based, and none of the other members of the Statutory Inquiry considered Evans to be feeble minded. Professor Curran said that in

assessing intelligence it is much more important to consider the person's general behaviour in life than to put an
adult through a rather arbitrary test. Professor Curran says
that the first interview with Evans lasted over an hour. He
found Evans quick in answer and a fast and fluent talker.

As a result of their investigations a report dated 5th
March 1950 was submitted by the members of the
Statutory Inquiry to the Under Secretary of State, Home
Office. Having dealt shortly with the nature of the evi-
dence the report continues:

"Evans at both interviews was consistently well behaved
and we were informed that this has been so throughout his
detention at Brixton and Pentonville. He has had full control over himself and has shown no impulsiveness. He was
alert, attentive and co-operative except when questions
involved his guilt. He adheres to his statement that
Christie committed the crimes. When on the defensive his
untruths are purposeful and as far as practicable, acute. He
is not a pathological liar. His memory, perception, judgment and reasoning are good. He is not an epileptic and
we do not associate the crime with alcoholic intoxication.
We have no reason to believe his habits have deteriorated.
His work record is satisfactory. His education is faulty
owing to absences from school, the result of physical ill-
ness. But he is of average intelligence in spite of this. He is
well informed on matters of ordinary interest and common knowledge, and there are no grounds to regard him
as a mentally defective person. He is not insane and we
have no reason to consider that he is suffering from any
minor form of mental abnormality. We have no grounds to
justify us in making any medical recommendation."

The word 'acute' is used in the sense of answers quickly
given and to the point. It will be realised that where the

report refers to questions involving Evans' guilt and that where, for example, it says that when on the defensive his untruths are purposeful, such comments include the occasions when Evans would be denying his guilt.

When Evans was in Pentonville he was seen by the Roman Catholic chaplain. After Evans had been executed, two representatives employed by the Daily Mirror having heard that Evans had made a sacramental confession, saw the chaplain to try to persuade him to tell them something about that confession. According to a letter dated 11th December 1959 from Mr. Goodman of the Daily Mirror to Mr. Kennedy, Mrs. Evans had in April 1953 made a statement in which she said that her son went to his death protesting his innocence even during his last minute confession to the priest. Mr. Baker was one of the Daily Mirror reporters who saw the chaplain. In their publication "The case of Timothy Evans", by Lord Altrincham and Ian Gilmour, it was stated on page 20, 'It should also be mentioned that Evans who was a Roman Catholic, did not confess to either murder when making a full confession of his sins before execution.' Mr. Baker made a note to this effect when he interviewed the priest in question. If the authors were working from Mr. Baker's notes and accepting them as a factual record of events, it might explain why they wrote this, for Mr. Baker's note reads 'Evans died a good catholic, saying rosary as he hanged. He confessed but did not confess to murder. Priest has never believed he was a murderer. He was not type. Very patient and uncomplaining in prison. Was given last sacrament. Told priest he was not murderer. Visited often by priest.'

The words: 'Did not confess to murder' and the later sentence 'Told priest he was not murderer' were not matters told to Mr. Baker, but were his own comments included with what he says was the factual information given to him by the chaplain. Mr. Baker said that having declared that he was a reporter, he spoke to the chaplain telling him that he was looking into the Evans murders and his execution. He said that he asked the chaplain certain questions, and the answers to those questions are recorded in his notes. In answer to a question which sought to obtain information about Evans' last confession, the chaplain told Mr. Baker that he could not disclose what had been said in confession. Mr. Baker said that he understood that. At some time, according to Mr. Baker, the chaplain was asked whether it was worth Mr. Baker's while continuing with the inquiries. He was told that it was. Mr. Baker thought that by that answer the chaplain had said what he had in fact earlier declared that he could not disclose. On that assumption as the chaplain had said that he did not believe that Evans was a murderer, Mr. Baker included his comments as part of his note.

Mr. Goodman, in the letter to which I have referred, and speaking of the strong impression which the reporters had that the chaplain thought that Evans was innocent, said that he did not think that the priest ever expressed this in words, and he doubted the statements of Mrs. Evans and Mrs. Westlake about what they claimed the chaplain had said to them. The writer of the letter continued by saying that in a note made by Mr. Cyril Morton, who had spoken to the chaplain on the telephone after Mr. Baker's interview, the chaplain had said that he had given Evans the last sacraments, but that in no circumstances could he break the seal of the confession and that this would be his attitude if called to give evidence before the Scott Henderson Inquiry. In addition, according to the note, the chaplain said that he should not have expressed any opinion at all to Evans' sister, that it was only an opinion, and that he was greatly troubled.

Nearly two years later, on the 13th February 1955, an

article appeared in The People under the heading NEW SENSATION IN EVANS CASE; PRIEST SPEAKS. The article announced that there was a dramatic development on the previous day in the moves to secure a public inquiry into the case of Timothy Evans. It went on:

"His mother went to see the priest who comforted him during his last moments. And Father Joseph Francis said to the dead man's mother 'I have always believed your son was innocent. He was not a murderer.' "

There was nothing new in the article. The chaplain answered it by a letter to The People which read:

"My name has appeared in your column against my express wish. In regard to the guilt or innocence of the condemned man Evans I have never made any public statement. I have consistently refused to see all reporters. When the grief-stricken mother came to see me for consolation I did say to her that I always felt that her son was not the sort of person to be a murderer. This was purely my own feeling and did not rest on anything that Evans said."

The chaplain sent a statement to the Inquiry, but acting upon the recommendation of the Vicar General of his diocese he decided not to attend. As far as he recollected he accepted that the letter from Mr. Goodman was accurate when quoting what he had said at that time. He went on to say that the reason why he was greatly troubled was because he felt that his words to Mrs. Evans were being twisted to mean something which he did not intend. He said that he had never agreed that he heard the confession of Timothy John Evans, that he certainly would never disclose anything said to him in confession, and that he had never heard that a Roman Catholic priest would be prepared to give evidence of matters disclosed to him under the seal of the confessional for any reason whatsoever.

This matter was not taken any further in this Inquiry, and neither Mrs. Evans nor Mrs. Westlake had anything to say about it. The only evidence given was that of Mr. Baker to which I have referred. I do not think that this matter can be taken any further. To some it might seem both surprising and disturbing that people should attempt to deny, even to a man convicted of murder, the secrecy of the confessional which he has sought. I have dealt with the matter because it figured in the documents and in what has been written about this case. I do not think that anything can or should be deduced from it.

Evans was executed in Pentonville Prison on 9th March 1950.

In November 1949 Reginald Christie was 51 years of age. He was of above average intelligence and was employed as a ledger clerk at the Post Office Savings Bank at Kew. He had served in the army for part of the 1914–1918 war. From September 1939 until December 1943 Christie had served as a War Reserve Police Officer attached to Harrow Road Police Station. He had lived with his wife at 10 Rillington Place since about 1937. It was not known in the neighbourhood that between 1921 and 1933 Christie had served four terms of imprisonment and had once been put on probation. His offences were of larceny, false pretences and malicious wounding. After his last term of 3 months hard labour in 1933 Christie and his wife, who had lived apart for about ten years, were reunited. But it was known to Christie alone that during his wife's absences from home in 1943 and 1944 he had murdered two women by strangulation and buried their bodies in the garden at the back of 10 Rillington Place.

The events of the next three years need not be examined for the purposes of this report. Christie and his wife lived on at 10 Rillington Place. Mrs. Christie was last seen alive on 12th December 1952. On 13th March 1953, Christie saw a Mrs. Reilly studying an advertisement board in Ladbroke Grove. She was a stranger to him. At this time accommodation was hard to find. Christie announced that he had a sixteen year lease on a flat; that he had been transferred to Birmingham where his wife had been for some three months in a new flat, and that he was prepared to sublet his flat for three months rent in advance, plus £1 for odds and ends which he was to leave behind. Christie, who had no right to sublet or assign his flat in respect of which his own rent was in arrears, was paid £8 13s. 0d. by Mr. Reilly. On 20th March, when the Reillys arrived, Christie borrowed a suitcase from them and left.

When the landlord found Mr. and Mrs. Reilly on the premises he ejected them and arranged for a Mr. Beresford Brown to take over the premises. On 24th March 1953, when fixing a bracket for a wireless set in the kitchen, Mr. Brown pulled away a piece of wallpaper which was hiding a cupboard and then saw within it the bare back of a human body. The police were called, and Professor Camps came to the premises. There were three bodies in the cupboard. This cupboard which Christie referred to so often as the alcove, lay behind the back wall of the wash house.

The furthest body was stacked feet up with its head on cinders on the ground. It was wrapped in a blanket secured at the feet by plastic-covered wire tied in a reef knot. This body was that of Rita Nelson. The next body which was that of Kathleen Maloney, was also stacked feet up, resting on the head of Rita Nelson. It too was wrapped in a blanket, secured round the ankles by a sock tied in a reef knot. The body nearest to the cupboard door was that of Hectorina MacLennan. It was in a sitting position, facing inwards and sitting upon the head of Kathleen Maloney. The head and body were bending forward and into the cupboard, and were held in position by the corner of the blanket around the feet of Kathleen Maloney being tied to the back of Hectorina MacLennan's brassiere. The wrists of this body were tied together.

The bodies were removed to Kensington Mortuary. Later that night Inspector Griffin lifted the floorboards in the front room and found buried in earth and rubble beneath them a fourth body, which was that of Mrs. Christie, rolled in a blanket, secured by means of a safety pin at the top, with a nightdress wrapped round the body and a cotton dress beneath it. The heads of Kathleen Maloney, Rita Nelson and Mrs. Christie were covered. Hectorina MacLennan's was not. Professor Camps said that it is not uncommon for a murderer to cover the face of his victim to avoid looking at it and also because fluid may be coming from the mouth. In the case of Kathleen Maloney, there was a piece of material under the head covering and across the mouth. Between the legs of Kathleen Maloney, Rita Nelson and Mrs. Christie there had been placed an improvised diaper, but not in the case of Hectorina MacLennan. The diaper would be there as a protection against the expulsion of fluids from the body which is almost diagnostic of strangling when, with the relaxing of the system, such expulsions occur at the moment of death. None of the four women wore knickers.

In all but the body of Mrs. Christie, semen was discovered. In the bodies of Rita Nelson, Kathleen Maloney and Hectorina MacLennan carbon monoxide was found to be present in the blood to a saturation of 34 per cent, 40 per cent and 36 per cent respectively. Professor Camps said that even in artificial light the pink colouration which is found in bodies containing carbon monoxide was clearly perceptible. Only in the case of Kathleen Maloney was alcohol in any quantity found. Her blood contained 0.24 per cent alcohol. There was no obvious sign of pubic hair missing from any of the bodies. In the case of each, death was due to asphyxia associated with carbon monoxide poisoning.

On Hectorina MacLennan there was the mark of a ligature surrounding the neck which was a single mark at the back and double in the front. Professor Camps estimated that she had been dead for about four weeks. Due to decomposition on Kathleen Maloney, all that could be seen on the neck was the mark of a groove caused by a stocking which secured a cloth over the face and head. This body had been dead about eight weeks, possibly up to twelve. On Rita Nelson the nature of any pressure which had been applied to the body was obscured by post mortem changes. This body had also been dead about eight weeks, possibly up to twelve. At the time of death she was six months pregnant. Mrs. Christie had been dead about fifteen weeks.

Investigations showed that the three women concerned were prostitutes and among the most forlorn of their company. Their history was briefly as follows. On the 12th January 1953 Rita Nelson was working as a counter hand employed by a company in London, whose medical officer, finding her six months pregnant, gave her the necessary introduction to the Samaritan Hospital for Women

expecting her to go there. On 19th January 1953 her land-
lady reported Rita Nelson missing. Kathleen Maloney was
the mother of five illegitimate children and she usually
solicited in Southampton. In September 1952 she told a
friend that she was six weeks pregnant and that the police
were making life troublesome for her and she intended to
hitch hike to London. Christie was identified as being in
her company in October 1952 in a public house in Praed
Street. This information was supplied by another prostitute
who, in about early December 1952, claimed that she was
with her friend Kathleen Maloney when Christie took
them to a studio and Kathleen Maloney watched whilst
Christie took nude photographs of the other prostitute.
Early in 1953 a Mrs. Shields, an attendant in the Ladies
Lavatory in Edgware Road, knew Kathleen Maloney and
others who spent much of their time in the washroom,
often sleeping there. On one occasion in 1953 when
Kathleen Maloney came to the premises she told Mrs.
Shields that she had been to 10 Rillington Place in
Notting Hill and mentioned a man named Christie whose
wife had just died. Kathleen Maloney said she was sorry
for Christie who had promised to give her his wife's
clothes. She also said that when she was at 10 Rillington
Place the landlord arrived and ordered Christie to get rid
of her. About a week later, according to Mrs. Shields,
Kathleen Maloney came back with a case full of women's
and baby's clothes. The clothes were either sold or given
away by Kathleen Maloney. Mrs. Shields said that Kathleen
Maloney was pregnant, but there was no sign of pregnancy
when Professor Camps performed the post-mortem.
About a fortnight after Christmas 1952 Kathleen Maloney
told the postman in a public house in Praed Street that
although she had nowhere to sleep she had met a nice
man that afternoon who had promised to put her up in
Ladbroke Grove. During the evening, Christie was seen

drinking in the public house with Kathleen Maloney and a friend of hers known as Kitty Foley. At 10 p.m. Christie gave 2/- to Kitty Foley to buy a drink, and left with Kathleen Maloney who was never again seen alive.

Hectorina MacLennan was 27 years of age and the mother of two illegitimate children. She had been living with a man named Colyer. When this man was awaiting trial in Brixton Prison she renewed an association with a man named Baker. On 2nd March 1953, she called upon a minister of religion who had earlier befriended Colyer. She saw the minister's wife and claimed that she was pregnant by Colyer and according to the minister's wife appeared to be so. As Baker was round the corner whilst Hectorina MacLennan paid her call, it may well be that this was a ruse to obtain money. From enquiries made and the evidence given by Baker at Christie's trial, Baker and Hectorina MacLennan stayed with Christie from 3rd to 5th March inclusive. On the 3rd March all three sat up in the kitchen. On the 4th and 5th, Baker slept on a mattress in the back room. Christie would and Hectorina MacLennan sat up all night in the kitchen, for Christie would not permit the unmarried pair to sleep together. Eventually Christie told them to go, but they were to be allowed to come back on the Friday night if they were still homeless. On 6th March, Hectorina MacLennan left Baker at 11.40 a.m. saying that she was to meet Christie at his flat at 12, and she arranged to meet Baker again at 3 p.m. Baker, after waiting until 5 p.m., went to 10 Rillington Place and saw Christie, who declared that he had not seen the woman and later went to Shepherds Bush with Baker to try to find her. Her body was by now hidden in Christie's cupboard.

On the 27th March 1953, the police examined the garden at 10 Rillington Place. Part of a broken dustbin was found half buried under a heap of earth. In it or in the soil beneath it were found a number of pieces of bone. A large quantity of animal and human bones were found at depths varying from a few inches to 2 feet. Below that level clay was encountered, and this had not been disturbed. Two parts of a human femur were found supporting a post against the garden wall. With great skill and care the bones, teeth and other remains from different parts of the garden were assembled to create two female skeletons, with a skull and a pelvic bone being the only major deficiencies. The skull of one skeleton was reconstituted from many small fragments of bone, some of which, with the first, second and third cervical vertebrae which had been found in the bin, showed signs of burning. The broken dustbin was one in which Christie, according to his statement of 5th June 1953, burned his garden refuse. Christie said in the same statement that when digging in the garden he had come upon a skull and put it in the bin.

More than three years earlier, on the 6th December 1949, and four days after the discovery of the bodies in the wash house, a skull had been found in the basement of a bombed house at 131 St. Marks Road. It was then examined by a pathologist who was of the opinion that it was the skull of a female aged between 32 and 34 years. According to Christie's statement of the 8th June 1953, his dog had dug up a skull in his garden about the time of Beryl Evans' death. In 1949 the police had seen no sign of recently disturbed earth in the garden. It seems likely that the skull was dug up before the police came to the premises. Christie said that when it was dark, he took the skull to a bombed house in St. Marks Road, and dropped it inside through a window imperfectly covered with corrugated iron. This was undoubtedly the skull of the second skeleton. To complete the examination of the garden it was decided to sieve the soil to a depth of 2 feet. Amongst other discoveries a dental crown was recovered from the soil. It could be seen that it belonged to a molar tooth. Crowns of this type made, as this was, of silver palladium alloy are not commonly found in this country but are frequently used in dentistry in Central Europe. This limited the field for identification, and following a disclosure made on behalf of Christie by his advisers that one of the skeletons belonged to an Austrian, it was identified as being the skeleton of Margarete Fuerst. A further indication led the police to a more limited field of enquiry, and it was established that the second skeleton was that of Muriel Eady. It was her femur which was supporting the garden post and her skull that was found in the bomb-damaged house.

The history of these two women can be briefly stated. Margarete Christine Fuerst was a refugee, born in Germany, who had arrived in England on 8th June 1939. She had an Austrian passport. In 1953 she was employed as a capstan operator in premises in Davies Street, W.1, and at the end of June left her employment. Around the works it was rumoured at the time that she was pregnant. She lived at Notting Hill and was last seen at her home address on 21st August 1943. She was notified as missing on 1st September 1943. In his statement made on 5th June 1953, Christie said that he remembered the name Fuerst but did not recognise her photograph. He claimed that in 1943 when his wife was away, this woman, who was in the house, undressed and wanted to have intercourse with him. A telegram arrived saying that Mrs. Christie was coming home. The woman then suggested that the two of them should go away together. Christie refused, had intercourse with her, then strangled her with a piece of rope. This strangulation taught him the need for the use of a diaper. He said that he took her body into the front room and put it under the floorboards. The next day, when his wife was at work, he took the body to the wash house. He dug a hole in the garden, and when it was dark he buried the body.

Muriel Amelia Eady was aged about 30 at the time of death. She worked with Christie at the premises of Ultra Radio, Park Royal. She was a respectable young woman who had on occasions, with a man friend, visited the Christies in their home. Early in October 1944 she left her home in Putney at about 4 p.m., saying that she would not be late. She was later reported missing. Christie's description of her is contained in his statement of 5th June 1953, saying that she came to the house alone on one occasion. He believed that she suffered from catarrh, and came by appointment when his wife was on holiday. Christie maintained that he prepared an inhalant of Friars Balsam in a square glass jar with a metal screw top lid. There were, he said, two holes in the lid and through one by means of a rubber tube he fed gas into the liquid, and the unsuspecting Muriel Eady inhaled the gas, the smell of which was overpowered by that of the Friars Balsam. Christie then said that the had a vague recollection of getting a stocking and tying it round her neck. He believed that he had intercourse with her at the time of strangulation, and he thought that he put her body in the wash house and then buried it in the garden. In the same statement Christie said that he had become confused as to which of the two women he had gassed in this way.

The finding of the bodies at 10 Rillington Place led to a search for Christie which ended when on 31st March 1953, he was picked up by the police, unkempt and penniless, on Putney embankment. There was found upon him a newspaper cutting relating to Evans' committal proceedings in 1949. On the same day, Christie made a statement to Chief Inspector Griffin and Detective Inspector Kelly concerning Mrs. Christie and the three women found in the alcove of his kitchen. He sought to explain the strangulation of his wife as a mercy killing. He was to maintain this lie to the end. He said that on 14th

December he had awakened to find her convulsive and choking. Despite his attempts he could not restore her breathing and it was too late to call for assistance; therefore, in a situation that was hopeless and when he was unable to see her suffering further, he tied a stocking round her neck and put her to sleep. He then saw that she had taken twenty three pheno-barbitone tablets. After two or three days he put the body under the floorboards, saying that he thought it was the best place in which to lay her to rest. He explained that he sold the furniture and other bits and pieces. He was paid £1 17s. 0d. for his wife's wedding ring.

Christie then purported to describe his association with the other three women. Christie's first accounts have only to be read for their absurdity to be apparent. He said first that a drunken woman—this would be Kathleen Maloney—accosted him as he returned from a fish and chip shop and followed him home. She demanded 30s., threatening to scream and say that he had interfered with her if he did not pay. Being well known in the district he walked away but was followed by the woman who forced her way into his house and into the kitchen. The woman, who had started to undress, picked up a frying pan to strike him. Christie said that he closed with her. She fell into a deckchair upon which a piece of rope was hanging. The next thing he remembered was that she was lying still with the rope round her neck. He left her in the chair all night, and went to bed. The following morning he remembered opening the cupboard and realised that he must have put her into the alcove but he did not remember doing so.

He next dealt with Rita Nelson. He said that she came to 10 Rillington Place to see the flat which was soon to be vacant. She suggested that she should visit him for a few days and offered herself to Christie so that he might use his influence with the landlord to grant her the tenancy. Christie reproached her for making the offer which he told her did not interest him. She answered his refusal with threats, and started fighting. Although Christie sought to avoid fighting, the next thing she was on the floor. He said he must have put her in the alcove straight away.

He then went on to say that he met a man and a woman, who being homeless accepted his offer to permit them to stay with him for a few days. Christie then asked them to go. The next night, the woman returned alone, and although Christie wanted her to go she insisted on staying saying that she would wait for her man friend whom Christie said he was expecting. There was a struggle. As Christie tried to lead her out he thought that some of her clothes must have got caught round her neck. She fell. Christie pulled her to a chair, found that her pulse was not beating, so he said he must have put her in the cupboard. He lived on in the flat for about three weeks after this. Then he went out and wandered about as his mind was blank.

Christie's defence was paid for by the proprietors of the Sunday Pictorial. Messrs. Cliftons were the solicitors acting for the defence, the conduct of which was in the hands of Mr. Roy Arthur, the managing clerk employed by that firm at that time. At an early stage, leading counsel Mr. Curtis Bennett, Q.C., was briefed, and it was realised that the only possible defence open to Christie was that of insanity. On 4th April 1953, this decision was made, and on the following day Christie was told of it. On more than one occasion about this time, when Mr. Crump happened to meet Mr. Curtis Bennett socially, he was told that it had been made known to Christie that if he did kill Beryl Evans, he should admit it, and that he should admit to all the murders which he had committed. That Christie had been told this and realised it is confirmed by Constable Hammond who knew Christie before his arrest and saw him either in the police car or in the cells at the Magistrates Court. Christie told Constable Hammond that Mr. Curtis Bennett had said that he should admit to all the murders for which he was responsible. Mr. Arthur quickly realised that Christie did not tell a consistent story but would say whatever he thought was convenient. Mr. Arthur said that Christie would say 'yes' to any suggestion. It was also Mr. Arthur's view that if Christie could convince the jury that he was more involved in the Evans case than he had yet admitted, the jury would be more willing to look upon him as guilty of the act of killing his wife, but insane at the time of so doing. Mr Arthur said that he did not tell Christie this, but in his view Christie was no fool and he thought that Christie realised it. It is not known whether Christie shared this view or whether he thought that a jury might react more unfavourably to one who by such an admission was declaring that he had done so much to send an innocent man to his death.

The newspaper which was paying for Christie's defence wanted a story about Christie in return for its money. Mr. Arthur was not present when the agreement was made between Christie and the newspaper but he said that the newspaper's representative was understandably insistent in asking him questions. He told the representative that it was not part of his duty to supply the newspaper with material about Christie, which he was obtaining by way of instructions, pointing out that Christie was his client. Mr. Arthur said that he refused to disclose the information which he obtained from Christie. Eventually Mr. Arthur arranged that Christie should write out such information as he could about his life and general background. Christie welcomed this suggestion, being pleased to write his own story. Mr. Arthur read what

Christie had written and when he thought it opportune he passed on Christie's writings to the newspaper. It was a long and unreliable story. At a later date, after editing, certain parts of it were published in the Sunday Pictorial.

The Sunday Mirror kindly supplied the Inquiry with prints made from the photographic negatives of Christie's written statement, as supplied to the Sunday Pictorial. It is not possible to put an accurate date when each page was written, but the dates can be fixed with sufficient accuracy because the prison authorities put the date on each sheet of paper when they issued it to Christie. Thus it can be said that the writings would be on or after the date appearing on the paper. It was at this time that Doctor Hobson had been retained on behalf of the defence, and therefore Christie had three outlets for his information— Mr. Arthur, Doctor Hobson and the newspaper.

Christie's general attitude was one which to him, no doubt, sounded reasonable, for when asked or challenged about any matter which he thought was to his detriment, he would say "If you can prove it, I'll admit it." It was an admission which conceded nothing. On a date between 6th and 13th April 1953, Christie was writing that he could have had no connection with the Evans case and that it was physically impossible for him to have done so, as he was just crawling about at the time. He was of the same mind on 20th April when seen by Doctor Hobson in a four hour interview. Christie then denounced Mr. Malcolm Morris for suggesting at the Evans trial that he was responsible for Beryl Evans' death. Christie called it a monstrous suggestion and strongly denied that he was in any way involved. It would seem to be after this interview on 21st April that Christie was writing for the newspaper under the date of 20th April 1953, for there he prefaces his remarks about Beryl Evans with the phrase "as Doctor

(Psychiatrist) spoke yesterday . . ." Whether it was because of what was said by Doctor Hobson or not Christie went on to write that if he was mentally ill he could possibly have killed Beryl Evans, using force that came to him without his feeling the pain in his back. And later he wrote that he did not attack the baby. Had he written the truth he would have known that he did not have any pain in his back at the time. On 22nd April, at the Clerkenwell Court, Doctor Hobson saw Christie for a short time, and on 23rd April, had a lengthy interview with Christie at Brixton prison. Mr. Arthur was also present. Christie enjoyed being interviewed, and he liked talking and would try to keep the interview going as long as possible. Doctor Hobson said that in order to do this Christie had a habit of saying something provocative at the end of an interview, to tempt the interviewer to prolong it, and that other interview had ended on such a note.

According to Doctor Hobson, the interview on this day was not concerned with Beryl Evans. It was dealing in the main with the human bones which had been found in the garden at 10 Rillington Place, and Christie was now admitting that he had killed the two women, Margarete Fuerst and Muriel Eady. At the end of the discussion. Christie tempted his interviewer by saying "There is something about Mrs. Evans which I can't quite remember." It was a typical remark permitting him either to advance or retreat and committing him to nothing. But as Doctor Hobson and Mr. Arthur had had enough of Christie for the day the interview ended.

Under the date of the 22nd April 1953, which entry may well have been written after the 23rd, Christie wrote that it kept coming through his mind that he could have had some connection with the Evans case but he did not feel so emphatic about the possibility of it. He kept asking himself how he could have had anything to do with it, having pain or having painful after-effects the following day. He wrote that these thoughts ran through his mind when he was in court. On 24th April, Mr. Arthur saw Christie and told him that his explanation of the killing of Mrs. Christie did not accord with the prosecution's evidence and with other things that he had said and was not satisfactory. No doubt by now it was learned that there was no trace of barbiturates in Mrs. Christie's intestines despite the fact that Christie claimed that she had swallowed 23 pheno-barbitone tablets. Mr. Arthur said he wanted to know everything, and he told Christie to spend the weekend thinking it over, saying that he wanted to know exactly how Christie had killed the six women, namely, his wife, the two whose skeletons were in the garden, and the three in the alcove. Mr. Arthur went on to say that a good deal of public opinion connected Christie with the Evans case, and although up to now he had said he had had nothing to do with it, he was to think it over.

On Monday 27th April, Christie was seen first by Mr. Arthur and later by Doctor Hobson. As appears from Mr. Arthur's evidence given on 10th July 1953 at the Scott Henderson Inquiry, Christie broke down and he now told Mr. Arthur that he had killed Beryl Evans. His account was that he and his wife had tried to dissuade Beryl Evans from taking pills, that they knew of her domestic trouble related to the events of August, and that he visited Beryl Evans at her request and she told him of her desire to commit suicide. Christie sought to dissuade her, and arranged to see her next day. When he paid the second visit he found Beryl Evans in front of the fireplace, the room was full of gas, and she was almost unconscious. Christie rushed and opened a window and tried to revive her with water and then tea. Beryl Evans was disappointed that her suicide attempt had failed. On the following day Christie said that he went upstairs again, found Beryl Evans doped, and instead of trying to revive her he strangled her and had intercourse with her. Hearing this, Mr. Arthur asked Christie the question "Are you saying this on the basis of the more the madder?" At Doctor Hobson's interview which followed immediately after Mr. Arthur's, Christie explained that he went upstairs, saw Beryl Evans on a quilt having made a clumsy attempt to commit suicide because she had left the windows open. Christie then claimed that he strangled her and could not be sure whether he had had intercourse before or after death. On the same day in successive interviews Christie was telling Mr. Arthur of the two visits and killing Beryl Evans on the second and having intercourse. Immediately afterwards he was telling Doctor Hobson of the one visit when he killed Beryl Evans and was not sure about the time of intercourse. Doctor Hobson did not hear that Beryl Evans was supposed to have been gassed on two successive days until Christie made a statement to that effect on 8th June 1953.

On 18th May 1953 Beryl Evans' body was exhumed and a second post mortem took place. On 20th May, Doctor Hobson and Professor Curran saw Christie. In their two hour interview, Christie said that he gassed Beryl Evans because he felt sorry for her but he did not mention the two visits when she was gassed. Professor Curran described Christie as the complete liar who possibly at times partially believed his own lies. On 28th May, Christie's story was taking a different turn. He was writing that he had revived Beryl Evans on the first occasion, when he had come upon her semi-conscious on the floor and had feared an explosion. On the following day Beryl Evans had said that she wanted to go through with her suicide and would do anything if only Christie would help her. Christie said that he felt that she knew he wanted to make love to her. He had intercourse with her on the quilt on the floor, and then, whilst talking to her, he kept on giving her gas. She became unconscious and convulsive and he strangled her. He believed that he had intercourse with her a second time. He then removed the stocking from her neck and put it on the fire. But on 30th May, far from admitting intercourse with Beryl Evans, Christie was writing that intimacy did not actually take place, that he made two attempts, but owing to the fibrositis and enteritis he was physically incapable of doing anything. On 4th June, Christie was seen by Doctor Hobson and he took with him a piece of paper dated 30th May, on which was written, in somewhat similar language, his reasons why intimacy did not take place with Beryl Evans. Whilst being interviewed Christie changed his mind and he crossed out his written denial of having intercourse saying that it did take place. At the next interview he decided that the original entry was correct and that intimacy had not taken place.

On 5th June, at the request of his legal advisers, Christie was seen by Chief Inspector Griffin and Inspector Kelly. The purpose of this visit was so that Christie might admit his responsibility for the murders of Margarete Fuerst, Muriel Eady and Beryl Evans. Christie dealt with the first two but dried up when it came to Beryl Evans. Chief Inspector Griffin was asked by Mr. Arthur for the interview to be continued at a later date because Christie had become confused. The Chief Inspector agreed to this, and on the 8th June 1953, he took a further statement from Christie dealing with Beryl Evans. These statements were offered so that they could be put before the jury in cross-examination at Christie's trial and no doubt Christie knew this. In this statement, having dealt with the Evans' matrimonial trouble in August, Christie gave an account of two visits to Beryl Evans. He said that he strangled her on the second, he thought, with a stocking. Christie went on to deal with the arrival of the police, and said that when Evans came home on Tuesday he did not know that his wife had been strangled but thought that she had committed suicide. He said that the timber in the wash house had been placed there by Evans at Christie's request, and that he strangled Beryl Evans to help her commit suicide. He insisted that he knew nothing about what had happened to the baby. He then went on to explain how he had gassed the three women in the alcove, saying how they sat in the deck chair between the table and the door, that he permitted a piece of rubber tubing to hang nearly to the floor, that the gas fumes rose when he removed the clip from the tube and the victim was then overcome. He also said that pubic hair which had been found in a tin at 10 Rillington Place, came from the three women in the alcove and from his wife.

Whilst Christie was changing his story, it was necessary for Mr. Arthur to draft fresh instructions for counsel to keep pace with the changing statements. The dates when the instructions were drawn and delivered are not known, but in the first proof to counsel Christie's account of his association with Beryl Evans was similar to that of his general account, given in 1949–1950. In a second proof, which mentioned only one visit, Christie said that he had intercourse with Beryl Evans before strangling her. In the third and final proof, which mentioned two visits, he said that he strangled Beryl Evans but that his attempts at intercourse were frustrated by his fibrositis. In his first proof of evidence Christie's account of the murders of Kathleen Maloney, Rita Nelson and Hectorina MacLennan was of killings after rejection by him of either express or implied offers of intercourse. There is no mention of intercourse and no mention of gassing. In a second proof Christie denied intercourse with Kathleen Maloney calling her a repulsive type. In a final proof he admitted intercourse with her and that he gassed and strangled her.

In the second proof he remembered intercourse with and the strangling of Rita Nelson. In the final proof he said that she was gassed as they sat talking together and then he strangled her. In the second proof he remembered having intercourse with Hectorina MacLennan after she was dead. There was no mention of gassing. In the final proof he thought that she must have noticed the gas after he had put it on because she got up to go and he got hold of her. She went limp and he was afterwards intimate with her. He said that he put her in the cupboard quickly because he knew that her man friend would be coming back.

Although Christie was now at times admitting intercourse with Beryl Evans at the time of her death, it will be remembered that at the post-mortem on her body in 1949 no traces of semen had been discovered. Doctor Hobson in evidence said that this did not surprise him. He had considered as a hypothesis that Christie did not or may not have had sexual intercourse. In his statement dated 16th December 1965 he put it as probable that Christie never had intercourse with any woman, living, dying or dead. It was Doctor Hobson's suggestion that the discovery of semen in the bodies found in the alcove was not surprising as all three women were prostitutes and therefore such a finding could be expected. This is quite contrary to the opinion of Mr. Nickolls who saw the bodies. He said that the quantity of semen found in the body of each woman showed that there had been no drainage from the body, and this demonstrated that after intercourse the women had not had any time to walk or otherwise move, to permit drainage to occur. Mr. Nickolls said that he could not depart from the opinion that intercourse took place with each of these women at or about the time of death. Therefore only Christie could have had intercourse with each. In evidence Doctor Hobson said that, although not very sure about it, he thought that the likelihood was that Christie did have intercourse with the three women. I prefer Mr. Nickolls' opinion on the facts as proved which in my view show that Christie did have sexual intercourse with each of the three women found in the alcove, such intercourse taking place at about the time of death.

Although there came a time when Christie admitted to Doctor Hobson that he had killed Beryl Evans, Doctor Hobson did not hear from Christie any admission that he had killed Geraldine. On the one occasion when it seemed that Christie was about to make some sort of admission about this, Doctor Hobson broke off the interview. The reasons for this were, he said, first that Professor Curran was waiting to interview Christie, and secondly (and I think this was the real reason) that Doctor Hobson wished to see Mr. Curtis Bennett before receiving any such admission from Christie. He did this to find out whether there was any chance of Christie being charged with the murder of Geraldine. If there were, Doctor Hobson said that he would have found it impossible to support an opinion that Christie was insane in law if he strangled Geraldine on the 10th November, although such an admission would not have prevented his supporting the opinion that Christie was insane when he strangled Beryl Evans two days earlier. To avoid further disclosure Doctor Hobson did not see Christie after the 12th June save for brief periods and when accompanied by someone else. He did not hear nor did he ask any more about Geraldine. Doctor Hobson thought that Christie was intelligent enough to realise that the killing of Beryl Evans and Geraldine would be more likely to prejudice a jury against him even if Christie wanted to be found insane, which in Doctor Hobson's opinion was not Christie's wish.

I find it difficult to understand how Doctor Hobson could think that Christie did not want to be found insane, since he was there, as Christie well knew, to help if he could in establishing Christie's insanity. Christie disapproved of capital punishment, and he must have known that there were only two verdicts open to the jury, either guilty of murder or guilty but insane. Any doubts about which of the two Christie wanted were resolved by other evidence. On the 20th May, Professor Curran saw Christie in the presence of Doctor Hobson. Professor Curran's full notes of this and other interviews with Christie have been exhibited. Under the heading Prospects, there appeared the three words, Hanging, Broadmoor, Dartmoor. Against the entry Broadmoor, Professor Curran has written an abbreviation of Christie's exact words as he spoke them: "I have heard people very happy there. Good treatment and that is what I want." Professor Curran said that he has no doubt whatsoever that Christie wanted to be found insane. This is also borne out by the evidence of Constable Hammond who was told by Christie he was quite convinced that he had a good chance of going to Broadmoor.

∾∘⋈∘∾

At his trial Christie admitted that he had killed Beryl
Evans. He denied killing Geraldine. He gave evidence of
two visits to the flat, the first when he revived Beryl Evans
and the second when he strangled her and failed to have
intercourse with her. His account of later events was that
when Evans returned home he was told by Christie that,
in view of the quarrel in August and of the fact that he had
struck his wife in the street, no-one would believe that this
was suicide. Christie claimed that Evans dealt with his
wife's body and that Christie knew nothing about it, save
that Evans talked of bringing his van to remove the body.

He was asked to explain, if he now said that he killed Beryl Evans, how it was that when standing in the same witness box in the same Court in 1950, he had denied this when Evans was on trial. Christie gave as his first explanation for this contradiction in his evidence that at the Evans trial he had been accused of two murders, but he went on to say that when arrested on 31st March 1953, it had all gone out of his mind. Thus, by the time he came to give evidence at his trial Christie was saying everything and anything.

Whether Christie killed Beryl Evans or not was not considered in much further detail at the trial. It was raised as part of the defence but the Prosecution did not depart from the issue that was before the jury. Christie was being tried for the murder of his wife. He sought, with the assistance of the evidence of Doctor Hobson, to establish that he was insane at the time when he admitted killing his wife by strangulation. In order to establish that Christie was insane, it was necessary for the defence to satisfy the jury that Christie was labouring under such a defect of reason, due to disease of the mind, as not to know the nature or the quality of the act he was doing, or if he did know it, that he did not know he was doing what was wrong. In an effort to support this contention, Christie admitted six other killings, including Beryl Evans but excluding Geraldine. The general purpose of this was no doubt to show, in the words of his Counsel, that when Christie killed people he was as mad as a March hare. Doctor Hobson's evidence was that Christie was suffering from hysteria. He said that Christie knew what he was doing when he killed Mrs. Christie but that on the balance of probability his opinion was that Christie did not know that he was doing wrong.

The Attorney General, Sir Lionel Heald, Q.C., M.P., who led for the Crown, confined his questioning of Christie to showing that Christie did know that he was doing wrong when he killed his wife. Christie was driven to make admissions and proffer manifestly absurd answers to explain his conduct before and after his wife's death on 14th December 1952; to explain how, for example on 6th December Christie had given up what he considered to be a good job, saying that he was moving to Sheffield to a better one which was to start at the beginning of March; how he had altered the date from the 10th to the 15th on a letter written by his wife to her sister and added a few words of his own, and posted the letter after he had killed his wife, thereby giving the impression that she was still alive; to explain his later letter telling how his wife had rheumatism in her fingers but that the doctor had said that she would be O.K. in two or three days; and to explain the Christmas cards and presents which he sent or gave from Ethel and Reg, and how by forging a letter and the necessary cheque form and receipt he had obtained £10 15 s. 2 d. from his wife's bank and closed her account. Finally he was asked why, if he did not think that he was doing wrong in strangling his wife, he had buried her under the floorboards? His answer was "I said I did not want to be separated from her, I did not like to lose her and that is why I put her there. She was still in the house."

The jury convicted Christie of murder: he had doubtless convicted himself. The trial of Christie is not helpful in deciding where the truth lies in respect of the death of Beryl Evans.

The only acceptable evidence of an admission by Christie that he had murdered Geraldine was made just after his conviction and sentence at the Old Bailey on 25th June 1953. The conversation was recorded in a report made by Hospital Officer J. A. Roberts who was alone with Christie at the time. After congratulating himself and expressing his pleasure in the manner in which he had received the verdict and sentence, Christie said that if the police only knew they could charge him with the murder of Evans' baby girl. Mr. Roberts asked if this was true, whereupon Christie, introducing his customary reservations, said that it was, more or less, as far as he could remember, and added "They cannot do anything about it now." He went on to say of Beryl Evans that he had been asked by Evans to do her in because she was in the way. He claimed that he was having intercourse with her and then she was dead. The reason that he gave for killing Geraldine was that she was crying, so he had to do her in as well, both murders being done whilst Evans was at work. When he was told by Mr. Roberts that the conversation would be reported to Doctor Matheson, Christie asked Mr. Roberts why he did not tell the newspapers and make some money out of it. Christie's admission that he killed Geraldine was not maintained for long, because on the 1st July 1953, doubtless as a result of it, he was visited by Mr. Arthur. A record of their conversation exists in reports made of it by Mr. Innes and Mr. Williams, then Prison Officers at Pentonville. Mr. Arthur told Christie that the main reason for his attendance that day was because he had heard that Christie had made a statement with respect to the death of Geraldine. Christie vigorously denied having done so, remarking that it was a pity that Mr. Arthur could not find out from where this information came. Christie's account of the killing of Beryl and Geraldine Evans ended where it began. A few days after the trial he was to say that he did not kill the child and he did not remember anything about Beryl Evans, but he did not believe that he killed her. He said that he had become confused because his solicitor pressed him to confess to the murders and he got the impression that it was necessary for him to confess to them.

At the request of the defence and before Christie's trial the body of Beryl Evans was exhumed. There were two reasons for this request. In the garden of 10 Rillington Place a tobacco tin containing four clumps of pubic hair had been found. These had been teased out, forming ringlets each occupying a corner of the tin and all interlocking so that they were held in position. They were obviously sexual trophies carefully arranged. Christie had stated wrongly that three of these specimens were taken from the three women found in the alcove. The first reason for the exhumation of Beryl Evans was to see whether one of the four specimens could have come from her. The second reason was to find out whether there was any trace of carbon monoxide in Beryl Evans' body. The body was exhumed on 18th May 1953. Professor Camps was nominated by the Attorney General to carry out this second post-mortem. Various people were present, including Doctor Teare, Professor Keith Simpson and Doctor Hobson.

Only one of the four specimens could possibly have come from Beryl Evans. This was one of mid brown colour and of a very common type. The same specimen could also have come from some 15 per cent to 20 per cent of the population. At the second post-mortem all the hair on the abdomen and pubis was removed for examination and comparison. It was the opinion of Mr. Nickolls that on visual examination alone it could be seen that the specimen had not come from Beryl Evans, but all necessary tests were made. Examination of the specimen by Mr. Nickolls showed that the hairs had been cut at the proximal or root end. Therefore if the hairs had been taken at or about the time of death, the area from which they had been cut should have been visible on the body. No such area could be seen. Mr. Nickolls also found that the distal or free ends of the specimen hairs were frayed. This fraying showed that the free ends of the specimen had been cut in the past, whereas the free ends of the hairs on the body were generally uncut. Mr. Nickolls stated at Christie's trial that even if the specimen hairs had come from Beryl Evans, they must have been taken at least six months before death, for only in such a space of time could hairs be cut, grown and cut again—at which stage the specimen would have been taken—and grown again to leave no trace of removal from the body.

Professor Keith Simpson the pathologist who examined the pubic hairs was not called as a witness for the defence at Christie's trial. Doctor Hobson, who gave evidence for the defence, dealt with this matter in addition to the question of Christie's insanity. He expressed the view that the specimen hairs from the tin were probably vulval hairs commonly cut by women, including those with unwanted pregnancies and unsympathetic husbands. Doctor Hobson also thought that the vulval area would be more likely to attract a collector such as Christie, and as some of the vulval hairs on the body had been cut the specimen could be of vulval hairs and could well have come from Beryl Evans' body. Mr. Nickolls, however, said that the specimen hairs were not in his view vulval but abdominal as judged by their length. Mr. Nickolls is firmly of the opinion that the specimen hairs did not come from Beryl Evans' body. He agreed with the suggestion that if the specimen hairs had not been cut but had been plucked in very small quantities from the body and from various areas of growth, thereby leaving no trace of their removal, and if the root ends of those hairs had been afterwards cut, such a procedure could produce a sample similar to the specimen. Mr. Nickolls considered however, that the specimen which he saw had been taken as a single trophy. Professor Keith Simpson gave evidence at the Inquiry. He estimated that there were scores of hairs in the specimen. He considered that it would have been difficult to have plucked a single trophy of this size in life without tearing the skin. There was no sign of mutilation of the skin or hair and no visible place of removal. Doctor Teare had demonstrated to Professor Simpson the size of specimen which had been removed by him as routine at the first post-mortem in 1949; no sign of its site could be seen at the second post-mortem. This meant that a sample could be taken leaving no trace. Doctor Teare had taken his sample several weeks after death, but Professor Simpson said that the situation would have been different if a sample as large as the specimen had been taken by Doctor Teare.

Although accepting as possible the suggestion that the specimen might have been obtained by small separately plucked collections followed by the cutting of the root ends, Professor Simpson pointed out that when making his examination in 1953 he had considered this possibility but had rejected it. All the samples of hair taken from the body and seen by Professor Simpson had perfectly normal terminations. He was of the opinion that the specimen hairs were trimmed in life and that he could not possibly say that the specimen came from the body of Beryl Evans. His conclusion supported that of Mr. Nickolls. The only contrary opinion was that expressed by Doctor Hobson in 1953. In evidence Doctor Hobson said that he was not propounding a theory that the specimen did come from Beryl Evans, but he was not convinced that they were not hers. If they were not, he said that it was most likely that there is another body for he does not think that Christie would have collected them from a live body. But Doctor Hobson did not wish to labour the point, and I think that the evidence of both Mr. Nickolls and Professor Simpson is right, and that the specimen was not one taken from Beryl Evans.

The second reason for the request for the exhumation of Beryl Evans' body was to discover whether it contained any carbon monoxide. Such a discovery would have gone far to support Christie's claim that he gassed Beryl Evans.

Geraldine was buried with and on top of her mother. When the child's body was removed, the skin of Beryl Evans had a pink appearance. Certain organs placed into jars showed pinkness when pressed against the glass, although the pinkness disappeared when the organ was exposed to the air. The pinkness might have been significant but was not, for the following reasons. The haemoglobin, which is the red part of the blood, ordinarily combines with oxygen and carries the oxygen to the tissues. The haemoglobin will combine with carbon monoxide to exclude the oxygen in the circulating blood and when the necessary percentage saturation is reached the person dies of asphyxia. The percentage saturation to kill will vary greatly with the individual. When the haemoglobin combines with carbon monoxide it produces a pink colouration called carboxyhaemoglobin. This can be identified on a spectroscopic examination. If carboxyhaemoglobin is found it indicates the presence of carbon monoxide. In 1953 Mr. Nickolls could not find any haemoglobin present and therefore did not find any carboxyhaemoglobin, and he confined his scientific opinion to saying that at the time of the second post-mortem there was no evidence of carbon monoxide in the body. Experiments on the tissue which showed a pink colour proved negative, and spectroscopic examination showed that the pink colour was a haem compound and not carboxyhaemoglobin.

Having excluded the presence of carbon monoxide at the time of the second post-mortem the next stage was to determine whether it could be said in 1953 that there had not been any carbon monoxide in the body at the time of death. Mr. Nickolls found residues related to the original blood which had not been removed as a result of decomposition. He thought that since the residues were still identifiable it ought to have been possible to identify carbon monoxide if it had been there in any appreciable quantity at the time of death. Mr. Nickolls had done a considerable amount of work to discover what happens when blood decomposes. His findings were that in the first stages the carbon monoxide content, being more stable than oxyhaemoglobin, rose, and then they both fell together. Mr. Nickolls felt that if there had been any carbon monoxide he would have detected it. It is Mr. Nickolls' opinion that there was no carbon monoxide in the blood at the time of death. He agreed that his further experiments could not achieve conditions comparable to the situation where decomposition had continued over a period of three and half years. The period of decomposition which he used for comparison was over about as many months in laboratory conditions. Nonetheless Mr. Nickolls found that the oxyhaemoglobin decomposed more rapidly than the carboxyhaemoglobin, so that there should have come a time when there would have been only a residue, however small, of carboxyhaemoglobin in the body. None was found. Professor Camps was also of the opinion that the reasonable probability was that if there had ever been carbon monoxide in the body it would have been discovered. When carbon monoxide is present it can be expected to be found in the teeth. A pink colour was found in the teeth. This resembled the cherry red pigmentation of the tissues found in carbon monoxide poisoning. The teeth were examined by a dental pathologist. Spectroscopic examination of the tooth pigment showed that this was a haem compound and was not attributable to carbon monoxide poisoning. This also means that experiments in different areas independently conducted produced similar results. Professor Simpson examined the muscle as an alternative to blood to see whether it might or might not show a residue of carbon monoxide. He found no evidence of it. It was as a result of

his examination and his experiments after the second
post-mortem that Professor Simpson's report to the solicitors instructing him and dated 27th May 1953 ended as
follows:

"I am obliged to say that not only has exhumation proved
unrewarding but to some extent (in the failure to match
hair samples) provided evidence which goes to dissociate
any sample of hair found in the possession of Christie
from the body of Mrs. Evans. I hope Counsel will appre-
ciate that under the circumstances I can offer no useful
assistance to the defence if this were to contemplate
autopsy or scientific reference to the deaths of Beryl or
Geraldine Evans."

This report no doubt explains why Professor Simpson was
not called as a witness at Christie's trial.

The only contrary evidence on this is that given by
Doctor Hobson. Although Professor Simpson had pointed
out that a person of Doctor Teare's experience could not
have missed the presence of carbon monoxide at the time
of the first post-mortem, Doctor Hobson was of the opinion that Doctor Teare could have missed it. He suggested
this in 1953 at the Scott Henderson Inquiry, and is still of
the same mind, for he thought that the detection of carbon monoxide by Professor Camps in 1953 was due to the
latter's brilliance. Secondly he pointed out that if the
inhalation of carbon monoxide had been for a very short
period, as Christie had written on the 11th June 1953,
namely from 1–1½ minutes, the struggle which followed
would result in deep breathing which itself would wash
out all traces of carbon monoxide from Beryl Evans' body.
I think it is right that if Beryl Evans had only received a
very small dose of gas it would not have been possible to
detect the carbon monoxide in the blood, but the only

evidence that she received any gas comes from Christie when he said that she was dopey and unconscious. If that be right, it follows that the gas must have been present in a concentration sufficient to produce that result; and if it was present, I accept the opinion of the pathologists that Doctor Teare would have found it at the first post-mortem. If gas was present in anything approaching the concentration necessary to produce this result, the effect of a struggle would not have been the washing out of gas from Beryl Evans, but the inhaling by her and by Christie of more gas. For with deeper breathing the intake of gas is greater. It was under the date of 11th June 1953 and after he had been to court that Christie wrote, elaborating on his statement of 8th June:

"There is the possibility that as the gas was only used for a very short time (1–1½ minutes) that after a month (app.) there may not have been signs in the body. There was no hesitation on my part to use it."

By the time Christie was sounding this possibility he doubtless knew that on 5th June 1953, Professor Keith Simpson had reported to Christie's solicitors that there was no evidence of coal gas in the body. The results of the second post-mortem and other experiments were that Beryl Evans could not be associated with any of the specimens of pubic hair found in Christie's tin, and no trace of carbon monoxide could be found in her body.

Although it is established beyond doubt that Christie gassed the three women found in the alcove, his descriptions of his methods of gassing them are rejected by those competent to give an opinion about them. Subject to variations in the individuals concerned it can be said that with 20 per cent saturation of carbon monoxide a person exercising himself shows symptoms of dyspnoea and giddiness and with a 30 per cent saturation the symptoms will be noticeable even when resting. A 50 per cent saturation would produce loss of consciousness on exertion. Christie had maintained that the three women in the alcove were gassed in the kitchen whilst he was present. The kitchen was a room 9 ft. × 7 ft. × 8 ft. 6 in. The women were hardened prostitutes and could have been expected in time of trouble to take some care of themselves, by force if necessary. If, as Christie claims, by means of a bulldog clip attached to a rubber tube led from a gas source he filled the room with gas, it is difficult to understand how the victims failed to notice either of the two tell-tale warnings of gas, namely the smell it would produce and the hissing sound that it would make. If one excludes Kathleen Maloney who had obviously had a great deal to drink and may have been drunk, there is nothing to indicate that the other two women were caused by alcohol to lose their senses. Even if the smell and sound of gas had gone unnoticed, it is equally hard to understand how Christie, sitting each time with the victim in the same small room and breathing the same air, was not himself overpowered by the gas. He sought to say that he avoided its effects by sitting near the windows. This explanation is itself difficult to accept, for if by chance he had succeeded in placing himself in an air current so that he was immune whilst his victim was overcome, the idea that he could successfully so place himself on three occasions is unlikely. It is not surprising therefore that Professor Camps writing in 1953 considered that the explanation given by Christie of the method of gassing these women was improbable. This opinion was shared by Mr. F. C. Smith, F.C.S., M.Inst. Gas E., who made his contribution to Professor Camps' book 'Medical and Scientific Investigation of the Christie Case', approaching the problem on a mathematical basis.

Similarly, Professor Camps questioned the method

supposedly used by Christie to gas Beryl Evans. If, as Christie said, Beryl Evans was unconscious in a room full of gas, so that Christie was obliged to open the window, the saturation in Beryl Evans' blood must have been at least 50 per cent. Nor could she in such circumstances have recovered as quickly as Christie described. Equally, if Christie had the feelings of discomfort that he claims to have experienced as a result of the gas, the saturation in him would have been of the order of 30 per cent. Christie's description of himself holding the tube in position to gas Beryl Evans and either having sexual intercourse or exerting himself in an attempt to have sexual intercourse, but not being himself overpowered by the gas, indicates still further the improbability of his story. In 1953 Professor Camps described Christie's account of what he claimed happened as being improbable, if not impossible. At the Inquiry Professor Camps treated Christie's explanations with derision. One possibility is that Christie was not in the room when the women whose bodies were found in his alcove were gassed. They were the type of women who, unless they were tied up or asleep, would have fought their way out, if necessary by breaking the window. Another possibility is that they were gassed as a result of some form of sexual deviation to which they were willing parties, perhaps with the head covered. Professor Camps draws attention to the similarity in the concentration of carbon monoxide found in the three bodies. He suggests that this indicates the possibility of a standard dose of gas rather than a coincidence in the findings. That Christie could not have gassed the women in the manner he claimed is perhaps supported by the story of a woman who was traced by Doctor Hobson and Mr. Arthur, as a result of information from Christie. She told them that one day when visiting Christie she had noticed the smell of gas, and suspecting that there was something wrong she left the house and never went back there again. Christie himself told Doctor Hobson that he had given this woman Irish whisky whilst he drank tea, and when she smelt gas he had allowed her to go.

When the Christie murders became public knowledge, Mr. G. H. R. Rogers, C.B.E., was then, as now, the Member of Parliament for North Kensington, and he interested himself on behalf of the Evans family. He also saw Mr. Baker. On 30th June 1953, Mr. Rogers had a meeting with the Home Secretary when he mentioned certain matters relating to the Evans/Christie controversy which he thought were important. Mr. Rogers' information was that shortly before Geraldine's death, Evans had bought for her a yellow suit, the coat of which was missing. Mr. Rogers had received a telephone call from an anonymous caller, who said that just before Beryl Evans' death, Geraldine had been sent to a neighbour. Mr. Rogers told the Home Secretary that he thought that he knew the identity of this caller and he also thought that if this woman could be found, the missing coat would also be found with her. Mr. Rogers felt that if he were permitted to question Christie about this, he might discover the answer to the whereabouts of the coat and the identity of the unnamed neighbour. Mr. Rogers also mentioned other matters which he thought were important, namely: (*a*) the workmen's evidence, (*b*) the admission by Beryl Evans to Lucy that Christie was to perform an abortion, and (*c*) that insufficient care had been taken in the preparation of Evans' defence in particular because of the age of Mr. Saunders.

On 1st July 1953, Mr. Rogers wrote to the Home Secretary enclosing, as promised, a brief summary of the new facts relating to the Evans case which had been supplied to him. They can be summarised as: (i) The evidence of Joan Vincent's calls at 10 Rillington Place; (ii) Mrs. Barnett's evidence of her granddaughter's failure to turn up for tea on 8th November; (iii) Beryl Evans' admission to Lucy that Christie was to perform the operation; and (iv) evidence from the workmen that they had worked in the wash house between 4th and 11th November, and seen no bodies there. The information on these four matters had been supplied to Mr. Rogers by Mr. Baker.

Mr. Rogers gave evidence at the Scott Henderson Inquiry and explained that when he received the anonymous telephone call, the woman caller rang off when pressed to give her name. She had told him that she knew that the Evans baby was out of the house during the day of Beryl Evans' death and that an elderly neighbour had charge of the baby. The anonymous caller had told Mr. Rogers that if he could find the person who brought the baby back to 10 Rillington Place, he would then know who was being sought. Put another way, if he could find the person who had the yellow coat, he would find the woman who had looked after Geraldine on the day of her mother's death. Mr. Rogers said that he had a suspicion who this woman might be, but now he cannot remember the name of the person he then suspected. In 1953 Mr. Rogers sent his then agent to make enquiries in Lancaster Road, where Mr. Rogers thought the suspect lived. But she no longer lived there. Apart from this telephone conversation, Mr. Rogers did not speak to the woman caller, and he has never seen her. The name of the suspect had been given to Mr. Rogers by one of the many persons who at that time were passing on to him information and rumours indiscriminately.

On 8th July 1953, Mr. Rogers was permitted to see Christie in Pentonville prison, to ask him about the yellow coat. He was accompanied by Mr. Peacock, the Secretary to the Scott Henderson Inquiry. In the presence of the

Governor, the Chief Officer of the prison, and two warders, Mr. Rogers asked Christie about the yellow coat. Christie denied ever seeing the coat. In evidence at this Inquiry Mr. Rogers said that he was under the impression that Evans had bought the yellow coat in Wales, and that Evans would not be buying clothing for a child already dead, and therefore the purchase of the yellow coat supported Evans' contention that he had not killed his child. I think that Mr. Rogers' recollection has failed him for two reasons: first, because Mrs. Evans, in her proof of evidence, said that Evans had bought a yellow woolen suit for Geraldine on about 8th October 1949 and that Geraldine was wearing it on the 5th November when they went shopping to Hammersmith on the last time that Mrs. Evans saw her granddaughter. The yellow coat must, as far as Mr. Rogers knew, have been bought before Evans went to Wales, for the caller was saying that Geraldine was wearing it on the 8th November.

Mr. Rogers explained that at this time he was receiving information from various sources and he was prepared to follow up any lead which he thought might help him in his enquiries. He was listening to all kinds of suggestions but in the end they led nowhere. If the anonymous caller had first hand information which was reliable it meant that she had remained silent during the Evans trial and waited until 1953 to disclose her information without being ready to disclose her own identity. That sort of evidence helps no one. It may not be evidence at all.

When in 1953 Mr. Scott Henderson was appointed to hold an Inquiry, Mr. George Blackburn, Assistant Chief Constable of the West Riding, was appointed to assist in the investigation. Mr. Blackburn, who has now retired from the police force, gave evidence. In 1953 when notified of his appointment and anticipating that he would be called upon to make investigations necessitating perhaps the interrogation of Metropolitan Police Officers, Mr. Blackburn brought with him to London three officers from the West Riding Constabulary. They included Chief Inspector Woolcott who has now retired from the police force with the rank of Detective Superintendent. On 8th July 1953, at the request of Mr. Scott Henderson, Mr. Blackburn went to Pentonville Prison taking Chief Inspector Woolcott with him. According to Mr. Scott Henderson's supplementary report, his purposes in sending Mr. Blackburn to see Christie, then awaiting execution, were to find out whether Christie was willing to be seen by Mr. Scott Henderson and to tell Christie that he was not obliged to be seen. In addition, as Mr. Blackburn could not take a proof of evidence from Christie, he was told to have a general conversation with Christie and to make a report of it to Mr. Scott Henderson. Mr. Blackburn said that he was asked by Mr. Scott Henderson when seeing Christie to probe a little and try to find out whether Christie's admission of guilt in respect of Beryl Evans' death had been made because he had been affected by the defence which was being offered. Mr. Scott Henderson wanted Mr. Blackburn to find out, if he could, whether Christie's admission was genuine, or whether, as a result of interviews with his legal advisors, he had come to the conclusion that his defence would be better served if he admitted this murder.

At Pentonville Mr. Blackburn was kept waiting for half an hour for his appointment because Mr. Rogers was then interviewing Christie. At Mr. Blackburn's request the warders who were then present were dismissed and the interview took place in the presence of the Prison Governor, the Chief Officer of the prison and Chief Inspector Woolcott. Mr. Blackburn asked the questions and Chief Inspector Woolcott recorded what was said at

the interview. Mr. Blackburn was not asking questions
from a prepared list of questions, but said that he was careful in what he said, for it was an important interview
which took the form of a conversation over the table and
he was probing aspects of Christie's story. Chief Inspector
Woolcott had great experience in taking statements, for he
had some 30 years service to his credit. He recorded what
was said at the interview in his own handwriting, which
record covered some six pages of foolscap and has been
produced in evidence. The record shows that the interview
started by Mr. Blackburn introducing himself, and is written as follows:—

"Mr. Blackburn opened the interview by telling Christie
that he was enquiring into the Evans case and gave him
clearly to understand that no matter what he might reply
to any question, he could offer no hope whatever of any
favour being shown to him in any way or suggest anything
whatever to interfere with the course of justice."

The rest of the note is made under the heading 'Replies'.
Chief Inspector Woolcott said that sometimes his record
would be of Christie's exact words, sometimes it would be
a combination of questions and answers—it would no
doubt depend on how Christie was answering. After the
interview the two police officers went to a hotel room and
typed a copy of the document with slight and unimportant alterations, when the recollection of the officers was
fresh. A copy of the typed document was also produced in
evidence.

The next day Christie appeared before the Inquiry at
Pentonville prison where he was questioned by Mr. Scott
Henderson. During the course of the questioning he was
being asked whether he could remember having anything
to do with the death of Beryl Evans. He replied that if

there was definite proof of either death he would accept it as being right that he must have done it. The following question was then put:

Q. Short of your being satisfied that there is definite proof that you must have done it, are you prepared to say that you did it?

A. I was only informed yesterday that there is no such proof.

On 29th July 1953, in the House of Commons, Mr. Michael Foot, M.P., having referred to this question and answer said:

"So Christie was told on the day before the public interview between Christie and Mr. Scott Henderson and in a private interview, that there was no proof that he had committed the murder. Therefore his mind had already been conditioned by an interview that took place to which no reference is made and in connection with which I go so far as to claim that it has been sought to deliberately suppress the evidence that it did take place. It is only because of hasty and bad editing that they did not cut out that incriminating evidence from this document."

Mr. Kennedy described this interview in his book, saying that Mr. Blackburn had gone along to Pentonville on his own to ask Christie if such an interview would be agreeable to him. While he was there he "warned Christie that he was going to be asked questions about the death of Geraldine Evans and then added, for Christie's benefit as it were, that there was no proof that Christie had done it". By the time the matter was raised in the House of Commons Mr. Blackburn had returned to Wakefield, and Mr. Scott Henderson telephoned him to ask whether Mr. Blackburn had said that which was alleged. Mr. Blackburn said that he told Mr. Scott Henderson that he did not for one moment think that he had said this, but that he would check with Chief Inspector Woolcott and see what his recollection was. Mr. Blackburn says that he rang Chief Inspector Woolcott at Doncaster, whose recollection agreed with his own, and he then passed this information to Mr. Scott Henderson. Mr. Blackburn says that he never did think and does not now think that he was the one who told Christie this. He also said that Chief Inspector Woolcott was accustomed to interviewing and making notes of interviews, and that he could not imagine that he would have missed making a note of this if it had been said. Chief Inspector Woolcott gave evidence in which he made it clear to me that if Mr. Blackburn had said these words to Christie, Chief Inspector Woolcott would have recorded them. He does not now remember receiving a telephone call from Mr. Blackburn.

It will be observed that Christie did not say that Mr. Blackburn was the one who had told him that there was no proof against him. Christie had also been interviewed by Mr. Rogers, and I am equally sure that he is right when he says that he did not tell Christie this. In dealing with Christie's evidence, the first question that has to be answered is "Did anyone tell Christie this or has he made it up?", for much of what he said to Mr. Scott Henderson has only to be read for its unreliability to be obvious. Mr. Blackburn and Mr. Rogers were not the only people who spoke to Christie on this day. If anyone did say to Christie that there was no proof that he had killed Beryl Evans or Geraldine, I accept that Mr. Blackburn was not the person who said this. On the one hand there is the statement made by Christie, not related to any individual, which Mr. Kennedy still suggests does not seem to be a thing which Christie was likely to have lied about. On the other hand, there is the evidence of two men with honourable careers behind them whose evidence contradicts Christie's and is supported by a full and contemporaneous document. It is true that a statement made by Christie may have gone unrecorded, but I think that it is much more likely that such a remark would have been noted by Chief Inspector Woolcott: it is the sort of remark that he could hardly have missed.

For my part I accept the evidence of the two witnesses and reject Christie's remark in so far as it has been attributed to Mr. Blackburn. I would require corroboration of it before I would accept that it was said to Christie by anyone. In my view the relevance of this matter is limited to deciding whether or not anything was said, and by whom, which prevented or deterred Christie from giving reliable evidence which he would otherwise have given. At the time Christie gave evidence it was of no value. The mere fact that Christie admitted a killing or denied a killing does not help me in deciding whether he did or did not kill. If Christie thought that a denial of a killing would help him, he would deny it. If he thought that an admission of the killing would help him, he would admit it.

During the search of 10 Rillington Place in 1953 two articles of clothing were found. These have been thought by some to be relevant to the 1949 murders. Amongst the rubbish in the alcove a tie was found. Although Inspector Kelly remembered it the best record of its condition when found is the written description made by Mr. Nickolls at the Metropolitan Police Laboratory at the time. He said that it was cut obliquely in two along the thinner region at the back and that the ends were knotted in a reef knot. It had obviously been lying on the floor of a very dirty place for some considerable time. It was of a dirty grey background with thin red and dark blue stripes. Mr. Nickolls did not assume that it was a neck ligature; his rec-

ollection is that it was not. He said that it might have been
a ligature for some other purpose, but it did not strike him
as something significant as it would have done if he had
thought that it was a neck ligature. Underneath the floorboards at 10 Rillington Place the remains of a man's suit
were found. In the pocket of it there was a receipt dated
1911. Inspector Kelly said that such things are commonly
found by the police when searching in old houses and it
was his recollection that the suit was found under a part of
the floorboards which had not been renewed in 1949.
Inspector Kelly thought that the suit appeared to have lain
where it was found for many years. It was examined by
Mr. Nickolls who said that his examination of it did not
reveal anything significant. He described it as being full of
moth holes and more or less in rags. In 1955 Mr. Eddowes
thought that this suit had been left under the floorboards
by Christie after he had worn it when murdering Beryl
Evans and that thereafter he had ripped it up and put an
old receipt in the pocket, so that when found it would not
arouse suspicion in the mind of the casual finder. The
point was not pressed at the Inquiry, and on the evidence
the suit plays no part in the case. It had been in position
long before 1949.

A further enquiry at this time concerned a witness who
gave evidence before me and whose name was referred to
in 1955 by Mr. Rogers. This man said that he saw Mr.
Rogers at the House of Commons in 1953, for he maintains that Christie made an admission to him about killing
Geraldine. The witness had been a signaller in the Army
with Christie during the 1914–1918 war. Thirty-five years
had elapsed between their separation and their next and
last meeting in Pentonville two days before Christie's execution. He asked Christie whether he had killed the baby.
Christie replied that he could not remember as his mind

was a blank. But then he gave what the witness described as a sly look and blinked. The next day the witness said that he realised that Christie had been sending him a message in morse code by means of his eyelids, and despite his lengthy lay off from signalling, he accepted the message the day after it was sent and read it as "yes". I only mention this evidence because it was being specifically put forward in 1955 as relevant to the Evans/Christie matter. It ranks with other evidence which has been given before me and to which, because of its quality, I do not find it necessary to refer.

On Sunday 12th February 1956, in the Empire News there appeared an article under the heading FRIGHT-ENED WOMAN IN HANGING DRAMA. The article went on to say that there was sensational fresh evidence believed by an M.P. (this was Mr. Rogers) to be in the possession of a woman too frightened to come forward, and that this evidence would prove conclusively the innocence of Evans. The article was written in the present tense. It had to be, to coincide with the announcement that the sensational evidence was fresh. It announced that the name of the woman was known to Mr. Rogers and that he had seen her and questioned her and was trying to persuade her to make a legal statement. A quotation from Mr. Rogers then appeared, setting out how he was trying to help this reluctant woman to come forward and overcome her fears of giving evidence. The article purported to quote what Mr. Rogers was saying about the yellow coat and how he had found this woman when making enquiries in the neighbourhood. The article further stated that the evidence might prove that Evans' confessions were made because, being illiterate and of low mentality, he was dominated by the stronger personality of Christie. It is clear that this 1956 article was declaring as present fact the information about the anonymous telephone call which

Mr. Rogers had received in 1953, and which had led nowhere then or thereafter. Mr. Rogers had not met the woman as the article reported. At the Inquiry he explained the article as being the exaggeration of the reporter, but he also suggested that it might have arisen as a result or in pursuance of one of the attempts to secure a further inquiry into the Evans case. He agreed that when the article was written the matter to which it referred was dead and had been since 1953. The article was, as Mr. Rogers said, merely a sensational rehash of ideas which he had at the time of the Christie trial. The reporter's name does not appear and I have not heard his evidence, and the newspaper is no longer printed. The article was misleading and factually valueless.

Three different theories have been advanced to explain why Evans when making the admissions of guilt which he undoubtedly made was on each occasion making a false confession. All three theories have much in common when describing how the false confessions came to be made. They part company when reasons are advanced to explain why Evans said what he did and what he meant by the words he used. In considering any submission explaining why Evans behaved as he did it is necessary to determine what sort of person Evans was.

This has been stressed particularly by Mr. Kennedy

who has used many expressions to describe Evans. One is indicative of all, when he wrote that Evans had the body of a man and the mind of a child. Mr. Kennedy urged that this was the key to Evans' behaviour and one of the keys to the case. He has also said that this was the most single important thing about Evans and that whenever he does something which seems inexplicable or odd one has to say to oneself "Well what would a boy of 10 or 11 have done?" Assertions of this kind have considerable emotional appeal, but they are not supported by the evidence.

The medical evidence has made it clear that to say that Evans had the mentality of a child of 10 or 11 years shows a misunderstanding of the position. Today Professor Curran, Doctor Coats and Doctor Matheson are still in agreement with the opinion given by the Statutory Inquiry in 1950. The only contrary medical opinion in 1950 was that of Doctor Quinn. I consider that the medical evidence which is important on this matter shows that Evans was of average intelligence, and I accept Professor Curran's limitation of that when he placed Evans at the lower end of the average scale. These witnesses have the qualifications and the experience entitling them to give a trained medical opinion. Further they all saw Evans and when they interviewed him each in his own way was concerned with Evans' mind and intelligence. In addition the Statutory Inquiry was directing its attention to the same matter. It is I think improbable that the three members of that Inquiry individually or collectively would have failed to realise that Evans was a child in the body of a man and thereby failed to make the recommendation which such a situation would demand of them.

In addition to the medical evidence there is the general evidence of Evans' personality and behaviour. According to Mrs. Evans her son as a child would kick and scream if he did not get his own way and would not go to school if he did not want to. Evans was aware that he had had these tantrums for he told Doctor Matheson about them. As a small boy his mother described him as being pretty rough at times. She said that he used to wander, in that on two or three occasions he came home after staying out for two or three nights and could not remember where he had been. Evans was very backward at school. He had missed a good deal of it because of an injury to his foot which required frequent hospital treatment. His educational defect was not helped by his dislike of school which was no doubt due to the disadvantage he was under in being unable to read or write or do any school work to the standard of his age group. According to an account given by himself and others he played games on occasions, presumably when his leg permitted it. He started work at the age of 15 as a van boy. At about 16 he worked in the mines for twelve months or more until the work became too much for his foot and he returned to hospital. Thereafter he worked as a labourer and lorry driver with some periods of unemployment. He acted as a civil defence messenger. He was unfit for military service but he joined the Home Guard. His premarital associations with girl friends and pick ups were no different from those of many. He courted his wife in dance halls and cinemas. After marriage his recreations were the public house and the cinema. On occasions he would go to a football match or the dog track. When in funds he said that he would drink up to 6 or 7 pints of beer. He also said that he drank 2 or 3 pints each evening on the way home and often got drunk at weekends. There might be an element of boastfulness in these accounts. Evans was a hard worker, driving for long hours and covering a considerable daily mileage, often working overtime. He was described as an excellent driver. He was, despite his difficulties, in many ways living an ordinary life doing an ordinary job. Although Evans was a person with educational and physical defects, on the evidence it is wrong to describe him as a 10 or 11 year old child in the body of a man. He was a 25 year old man at the lower end of the average intelligence scale and as such a person his actions should be judged.

Doctor Hobson who has interviewed some forty or fifty prisoners accused of murder gave evidence to explain why in his opinion Evans made his various confessions of guilt and in particular the two ststements at Notting Hill police station. Doctor Hobson never saw Evans. He attributes the making of these confessions to three causes: guilt, tension and emotional shock. He said that people are more likely to make false confessions when they have a feeling of guilt or feel depressed. Doctor Hobson said that there were many reasons why Evans should have a feeling of guilt. There was the knowledge that his wife had died and that he had concealed her death over a period of weeks. There was the belief that she died as a result of an abortion which Evans had either condoned or not prevented, or to which he had in some way become an accessory. Added to this was his awareness that he was running away, knowing that the faults in the marriage had been on his part, that he had left the child to the care of others, sold the furniture, given up his job and sold his wife's wedding ring. Doctor Hobson said that all these matters would have inculcated a feeling of guilt in Evans. In addition there would be the feeling of tension which had eventually taken him to the police. There would be the feeling that he had neglected Geraldine, and there would be anxiety and depression caused by his unawareness of his future, by being brought to London and by being mystified by events. When he arrived at Notting Hill Police Station he was under the impression that his wife had died in an abortion and that his child was still alive. Thinking this, he was suddenly made aware that both the wife and child had been strangled, and the emotional shock caused to him resulted in his making a confession of guilt when he was in fact not guilty.

Doctor Hobson is of the opinion that when he made the confession Evans believed that what he was saying was the truth: that he thought that he had strangled his wife with a rope, possibly thinking that he had done so after hitting her in the face, and that he believed that he had killed the child by strangling her with a tie. Doctor Hobson does not think that Evans did immediately guess or conclude that Christie was the man who had done these acts. Doctor Hobson says that, in his view, with no suggestion of brain washing, Evans would assume that the police thought that he had strangled his wife and child, and that he would, or might, think that what the police thought had happened had in fact happened. His confession would be accountable as his expiation for his guilt. In Doctor Hobson's opinion all this was happening with the police officers acting with propriety. Doctor Hobson considers that by their very personalities, Chief Inspector Jennings and Inspector Black were, unknown to themselves, likely to produce this false confession, in that Evans would on the one hand be awed and innately fearful of Chief Inspector Jennings his accuser, while being dependent on the other hand upon the friendliness of Inspector Black, so that the combination of apparent hostility and friendliness would help to produce a false confession.

With the making of the confession, said Doctor Hobson, tension and shock would have slipped away, for the shock ends when the confession is made; but the belief in the false confession may last for two or three days and later on, with the realisation that the confession was false, the tension would return. Therefore, when later saying what he had done to Sergeant Trevallian, Inspector Black and Doctor Matheson, Evans was still thinking that what he was saying was true. On the 4th December says Doctor Hobson, his first true statement, after his return to London, was made when he told his mother that Christie had done it. Doctor Hobson was asked to explain why, if Evans was aware of this on the 4th December, did he not make a similar disclosure to Doctor Matheson on the 4th January 1950 when he was asked why he had told different stories to the police and gave the answer 'I do not know'. For he had by then had a month during which the true position was known to him. Doctor Hobson says the reason for that apparent evasion was that Doctor Matheson did not ask the direct question, and as Evans was unintelligent he did not volunteer the reasons, although probably aware that he had previously made an admission of guilt.

Doctor Hobson gave examples in his experience which were the nearest he could recall to illustrate how false confessions had been made. The first is related to four or five similar experiences, when on each occasion a person who at some time had been guilty of acts of homosexuality confessed to committing such an act when charged, which act the person later denied. In those particular cases, there being no other evidence, Doctor Hobson was entirely dependent on the word of the person speaking when deciding whether the confession or the retraction of it was the truth.

The second example concerned X, a youth aged 19, who called upon his girl friend to take her out, only to find that she was not feeling well. It became apparent, although X was until then not aware of it, that she was pregnant and in labour. A child was born when both present were ignorant of the basic elements of midwifery. X, when washing the blood off the baby, left it whilst he rushed to give further help to the mother. The child died and its body was hidden on waste ground, where it was later found. X was traced and he said that he had deliberately drowned the baby. In fact, the child had died probably from haemorrhage before X had started to wash it. It is said that if this youth had not been emotionally disturbed he would have known this.

Doctor Hobson does not suggest that this particular case bears great similarity to the Evans case. It will be remembered that when Evans admitted to being responsible for the death of his wife on the 8th November, he was not, if his evidence of events on that day is true, in the same room or in the same house. His wife was in Notting Hill; he was in Kent. On the 10th November, when Geraldine is said to have been killed at Notting Hill, Evans was in Brighton.

Doctor Hobson, while maintaining his opinion that Evans' confessions of guilt were false, also agreed that it might be that the confessions to the police were true and the denial of those confessions to his mother was false. I have to judge Doctor Hobson's evidence as he gave it before me in the witness box, and to compare it with the other material evidence which I have heard, including that of Professor Curran who said that he could not point to anything in the case that was psychiatrically helpful.

I found Doctor Hobson's evidence unimpressive and too facile. As presented it seemed to be the kind of theory which started from a conclusion and was sustained by moving backwards through the evidence, making the facts fit the conclusion. His evidence may explain a theory which in certain circumstances is medically acceptable but on the facts and as presented it was unconvincing.

A second reason given to explain why Evans' admissions of guilt were false was that when making his statements Evans had been what is called brainwashed. This view was advanced in Ludovie. Kennedy's book based on the writings of Doctor William Sargant and a study made by Doctors L.E. Hinkle and H. G. Wolff of the techniques used by the Chinese in brainwashing their American prisoners. Professor Curran thinks that he referred Mr. Kennedy to the paper by these two Doctors. It deals with Communist interrogation and indoctrination and was described by Professor Curran as an elaborate investigation by the American authorities into the methods used in various countries to break down prisoners. The victim, he said, would be completely isolated, usually for weeks, often for months. Mr. Kennedy had described that which happened to Evans as being in the classic Communist pattern save that with Communists the emotions were induced by the interrogators, whereas in Evans' case they were largely self-induced through misunderstanding and force of circumstances.

The theory is based upon experiments carried out upon dogs by the famous Russian physiologist Pavlov. As I understand that theory, it is that not only dogs but human beings may by various influences or stimuli become what is called transmarginally inhibited, when the nervous system has been so stimulated that it passes the stage when it will respond in the normal manner. Therefore, when a person is transmarginally inhibited he does not act normally and may act with increasing abnormality, according to the stage which is reached in this transmarginal inhibition. There are three such stages called phases: the equivalent phase, the paradoxical phase, and the ultra-paradoxical phase. The time taken to bring about a particular result will depend on constitutional factors and environmental circumstances. Doctor Sargant suggests that the Russians may have used physiological research to perfect the techniques used by the Inquisition and in a different way by the evangelical preachers. To obtain a confession of guilt in this way there must be present in the subject a feeling of anxiety and guilt, and if these do not exist they must be created so that the normal functioning of the brain will be disturbed and the subject's judgment impaired. The feeling of a preference for punishment rather than a continuation of the existing mental tension must if possible be induced, coupled with hopes of eventual advantage. In his book Doctor Sargant gives examples of the methods employed in Stalinist Russia to obtain confessions. These methods are however, ruled out by Doctor Sargant from any consideration of Evans' experiences.

At one time it was not certain whether Doctor Sargant would attend the Inquiry to give evidence. But on the 7th January 1966 he wrote to the Treasury Solicitor saying that he did not wish to do so, and pointed out that he had said all that he had to say on this subject in his book Battle for the Mind. Doctor Sargant also sent a paper which he had given before the British Academy of Forensic Sciences in 1964, and from him came the last copy to be received at the Inquiry of photograph A. Doctor Sargant mounted this against a photograph of Evans taken when smiling and happy. It would seem that Doctor Sargant, unlike Doctor Hobson, still attaches great importance to photograph A because in a letter dated 25th November 1959 from him to Mr. Kennedy, he wrote that the photograph that he had shown to Mr. Kennedy suggested the deplorable state Evans was in when he finally made his third and fourth confessions. I have assumed that the reference is to photograph A for no other is suggested and Mr. Kennedy draws attention to it more than once in his book. In his letter to the Treasury Solicitor Doctor Sargant, writing of photograph A, said: "But you can see from the contrasting photographs just what mental stress can do to people in his position and to people under interrogation, with no need at all to beat them up or to bully them mentally". Doctor Sargant's comments on photograph A would have been more helpful had he been comparing it with photograph B, and for the reasons which I have given earlier I think that photograph A merely shows what a flash bulb can do to a person photographed unexpectedly. By the end of the Inquiry photograph A was not being urged as an important piece of evidence.

Since he did not attend the Inquiry I can only consider what Doctor Sargant has written in his book and in correspondence. At page 195 of the 1957 edition of his book, Doctor Sargant describes how Evans being backward and illiterate had been in the hands of the police for 48 hours without any legal aid before he made his third and fourth confessions. Thereafter he speaks of Evans' panic and anxiety and his flight to Wales, and the subsequent events. He goes on: "If Evans' long fourth statement is read it will be seen how possible it is that at least some of the details describing how he murdered his wife and child could have included matters inadvertently and even quite unknowingly suggested and implanted in his mind by his police examination and questioning. It does seem possible that some of their own beliefs were given back to him again in the form of a confession, once fatigue and an increase of suggestibility had occurred in Evans".

The author's emphasis is on the possibility that Evans gave back something suggested to him. This matter is also referred to in Doctor Sargant's letter to the Treasury Solicitor when he wrote: "I hope I made it quite clear that if Evans' confession was false it was not done from fear of the police or threats by the police. This type of false confession so often happened in Stalinist Russian Trials. I have no doubt that it also occurs inadvertently in M.I.5 interrogations. These false confessions are also fully documented in all the old witchcraft trials when the suspected witch gave back to the interrogator all the current beliefs on witchcraft and also often started to believe them himself".

The witchcraft trials are hardly relevant, for the author explains how old women were subjected to treatment described as being as bad as most tortures for twenty four hours. To avoid further ill treatment they made admissions of guilt. As Doctor Sargant rules out any suggestion that Evans made a statement because he was in fear of the police, I read his letter to mean that Evans had reached such a state of suggestibility that he could be giving back to the police officer the suggestions made to him by the officer. For he goes on to point out that normally the point of exhaustion can be reached by the individual concerned after a long period of mental effort and great tension in which quite unknowingly he takes on the opinion of those around him at the time, and he could hold these opinions for a considerable length of time and only later on realise what a peculiar state of mind he has been in for perhaps a week or more. Evans' state of mind when he made the two statements in Notting Hill Police Station, if one of suggestibility, had certainly passed 40 hours later since by then he was giving his mother a very different account of events.

Doctor Sargant further suggests that I might obtain help from M.I.5 interrogators about their techniques. I do not see what help they can give, since the evidence in my view negatives the suggestion that Evans at Notting Hill was subjected to anything which could be called an interrogation. Having referred to photograph A Doctor Sargant continues "One only has to keep up alternating states of tension, hope and despair long enough to get changes in brain function . . . in the majority of people especially emotionally unstable, frightened and feeble-minded persons such as Evans".

On the evidence that I have heard, there was no situation which could be described as keeping up alternating states of tension, hope and despair. It is worth while considering the timetable of Evans' interviews prior to the making of his first statement at Notting Hill. On 30th November Evans made two statements at Merthyr Tydfil, neither preceded by interrogation. On 1st December he was interviewed from 11 a.m. to 12.30 p.m. about his mother's letter, the removal of the body from the flat and the tearing up of the clothing and effects. From 3.50 p.m. to 4.55 p.m. he was interviewed and made a statement about the stolen briefcase found in his flat. On 2nd December Evans was interviewed between 11.45 a.m. and 12.20 p.m. by Inspector Black about his wife and child. Thereafter until 9.45 p.m. over nine hours later, nothing was said to Evans about his wife and child. I can understand that Evans was under tension the extent of which would depend upon what he had done or not done, what he knew or did not know. Doctor Sargant does not say who was said to be keeping up the alternating states of tension, hope and despair. Presumably it can only have been Constable Evans in Wales or Inspector Black in the train. It is not clear whether alternatively it is being suggested that these two men unwittingly produced these alternating emotions in Evans.

Doctor Sargant refers to Evans as emotionally unstable, frightened and feeble minded. I do not know, as he does not say, on what grounds Doctor Sargant bases this opinion. The only doctor who ever said that Evans was feeble minded was Doctor Quinn in 1950, but he also at the Inquiry said that on the evidence of Evans' reasonably good social and occupational history Evans could not have been certified as a feeble minded person. If Doctor Sargant is stating a fact, then I do not know upon what he bases it; if he is giving an opinion he does not give his reasons. The evidence satisfies me that Evans was not feeble minded. And I prefer the evidence of Professor Curran who gave his opinion that he had not heard any evidence to show that Evans was not in what could reasonably be regarded as a normal mental state when he made his statements.

Professor Curran was also asked to consider the question of brain washing. He said that he had not come across a person reacting to a sudden shock and making a statement of the kind Evans made. He agreed that a person may make a false confession. When asked whether he agreed with the contents of the book Battle for the Mind, he answered that he did not entirely agree with the primary opinions put forward; that some years had passed since he read the book; that when he had read it he had thought that some of it was rather far-fetched, but he cannot say now which part. He agreed that the author had brought to public attention that there were certain necessary conditions to bring about a state of mind to obtain confessions of guilt voluntarily given, though untrue, as experience behind the Iron Curtain had shown.

Doctor Hobson said that he did not fully agree with the views expressed by Doctor Sargant in this book.

Professor Curran was also questioned at great length about a case in which he had come to the conclusion that a confession which had been made was not true. If Professor Curran's conclusion on that case is right, it establishes again that which is well known, that for various reasons a false confession may be made. The facts of that case were so far removed from those which call for decision in the case of Evans that they give me no help in deciding whether Evans' confessions are true or false.

I do not believe that the evidence comes anywhere near supporting the submission that Evans made his statements because he had become so suggestible that he was giving back to the officer what the officer had said to him.

Nowhere have the examples either in evidence or in the literature referred to pointed to a situation comparable to that of a person making such a series of confessions without there being anything that could be called an interrogation. I would need more convincing evidence than any which I have heard and read to accept the production of a state of suggestibility following upon the imprisonment in Merthyr Tydfil, the journey to London and the single challenge of Chief Inspector Jennings. The state of suggestibility on this argument was such that on two successive days Evans made an admission and two confessions of guilt to the police officers, another admission to Sergeant Trevallian, another to Inspector Black, and further admissions of the details of the killing of his wife to Doctor Matheson. The submission is not on the evidence even plausible.

A third view was urged on behalf of the Evans family to support the contention that despite his many admissions of guilt Evans was not in fact guilty of either murder. This view did not agree with that put forward by Doctor Hobson though in part it accepted what he had said. Nor does this view agree with the suggestion that Evans was in any way brainwashed in the sense in which that expression is generally understood. But it does agree with the alleged existence of the conditions which produce suggestibility. The argument is based on the assumption that Christie must have killed Beryl Evans. He was already a murderer of at least two women and had selected Beryl Evans as another victim. In two ways she presented him with an opportunity to satisfy his particular perversion which the permanent presence of Mrs. Christie otherwise prevented. Beryl Evans was living in the same house, whereas Christie's victims, both before and after her death, had to be brought there. Secondly it was common knowledge that Beryl Evans was determined to have an abortion.

Christie had in the past claimed proficiency as an abortionist as for example, when offering his unsolicited services to an acquaintance Mr. Spurling in 1947. Christie's future claims were to become even more boastful. In 1953 after the death of his wife Christie was offering his services as an abortionist to strangers and acquaintances alike, lying about his medical training, his surgeon father and, to some, his own medical qualifications. Therefore, it is said, Evans should be believed when he said that Christie offered to abort his wife. Christie's pose would make the necessary approach to Beryl Evans easy when she was desperate for any means to end a pregnancy then four months old. It is further said that Christie laid his plans well. He had deliberately told Evans of the one in ten risk of death because whereas others were talking and thinking of an abortion, Christie was intending to commit murder, and he required to make preparations to account for and explain away the death he intended to bring about. Hence his statement that one in ten would die. This is said to show Christie's devilish ingenuity providing him with an excuse to Evans when the so-called abortion failed, and a protection for himself in that Evans, thinking that the abortion had killed his wife, would know that he had been warned of the risk of death and done nothing to prevent it.

In addition, Christie was aware that the Evans were in debt; that their marriage was unhappy; that their quarrels were known to the family, probably to the neighbours and most fortunately of all, to the police. Christie knowing that he was to strangle also knew that the obvious suspect would be Evans. Christie therefore made his plans to kill, it is suggested, with the knowledge that he would be able to frighten Evans into doing anything that was required.

Christie having murdered Beryl Evans, had no difficulty in impressing upon Evans that he too was involved and that secrecy must be maintained. For had he not been told everything? Had he not brought the message that morning saying "Everything is all right" thereby at least permitting the abortion? Christie also knew that once Evans had told his mother and Mrs. Christie on the 9th November that his wife was in Brighton or Bristol he could not go back on the story. The theory continues that when on the 10th November, Evans found himself without a job, it was Christie who suggested that he should go away and who had put him in touch with Mr. Hookway to make this easy. It is said that this suggestion to leave, made to a weak character, would be a most attractive one. He would leave London feeling that all would blow over; that his wife's body was safely down the drain where Christie had said that he had put it; and that when Evans left London letting tomorrow take care of itself he did not realise that thereby Christie had put him into an impossible position for the obvious suspect had now fled.

On this theory it can be said that at this time Evans thought that his child was alive, and that since all the evidence shows that he loved Geraldine, the probability is that he would not strangle her. There is evidence that whereas he took the greatest care to tear up his wife's clothing to rags, Geraldine's clothing was left behind with Christie, and that he even refused to permit the rag man to take a rattle belonging to Geraldine. It can also be said that if, when Evans left for Wales the child was already dead and he knew it, the sensible action would have been to destroy the child's clothing and at some future date say that both his wife and child had left him. In Wales he frequently spoke of the child and when he returned there on the 23rd or 24th November to give his aunt his second false account, his story was not that his wife had walked out of the flat taking the child with her, but that she had walked out leaving the child behind. Evans, therefore, in both accounts that he gave to his relatives in Wales, was committing himself to the story that the child was alive and his wife had gone away. It seems odd if he had known that his child was also dead that he should pretend that the child was living elsewhere and not with her mother. No documents belonging to his wife were found, whereas amongst Evans' clothing brought from Wales were birth certificates, medical cards and National Registration cards for himself and Geraldine. It may be said that he had these documents because Geraldine died after he had disposed of his wife's documents, but if he had taken the trouble to destroy his wife's documents he would be more likely, if the child were dead, to destroy the documents relating to her also. When interviewed by Doctor Matheson on 3rd December, although Evans admitted killing his wife, all he said of the child was that she was disposed of on the Thursday.

When his mother's letter arrived in Wales this, it is said, precipitated Evans' visit to the police. Although he was properly held in custody, the lawfulness of arrest would not diminish its effect upon him, and when he learned that his wife's body was not down the drain as Christie had said it would be, he could not understand what had happened and was confused; the confusion remained as he made the journey to London, with conversation limited and without hearing any further information about his wife and child in whom the police officers had so suddenly and inexplicably lost interest.

It is urged that this confused state of mind built up the tension which Doctor Hobson says would be present, and with time available and little else to do on the journey but think, there grew within him the feeling of guilt for all that had happened to his wife, to his home and to his family. When accused by chief Inspector Jennings at the same time as he was told of the death of his child, he admitted that he was guilty with his first acknowledging "yes". He then made the first statement, saying that he strangled his wife because she was incurring one debt after another and went on to say without giving a reason that the child had been strangled by him.

The argument runs that he said that he used a rope to strangle his wife either because the officer said that a rope was used or because the rope was there to be seen, and for similar reasons he said that he used the tie to strangle his daughter. He was in effect repeating back the method of killing because the shock of his child's death had so unbalanced him that he saw only his own guilt for the death of both his wife and child. It was, it is said, Evans' first opportunity to expiate his guilt. He accepted the blame not because his wife died by his own hand, but because he knew that it was his conduct that had caused her death; that though not physically the strangler, he was morally responsible for her death—the reasons being that he had stood by whilst she had submitted herself to an abortionist who had previously declared that there was one chance in ten of death. Evans knew that his behaviour had brought unhappiness to the marriage and in every way he was responsible for the death. It is urged that this self analysis would be beyond Evans' mental capacity to put into words, and that if he had been called upon to explain it he could only have done so in some phrase such as "It's all my fault. I as good as killed her".

It will be seen that all three theories given to explain why Evans' admissions should be treated as false are based on the assumed facts that Evans was under tension, filled with feelings of guilt, was depressed and was anxious. The effect of seeing what he saw and hearing what he heard resulted in his giving a false statement because:

(*a*)   he said what he thought was true, or

(*b*)   he repeated back what was said to him, or

(*c*)   when he said that he strangled his wife and child he was seeking to expiate his feeling of guilt and was meaning that he was responsible for the deaths.

I have explained in this chapter why I find the first two theories unacceptable. The third theory is discussed in the course of the chapter that follows.

In considering the evidence which has been given it is now too late for all of it to fit together. It can only be expected that there will always be some apparent event or circumstance which calls for an explanation and for which none can be found. Despite this I have not felt that I could not make findings upon the main issues before the Inquiry.

For some months immediately before his wife's death Evans and his wife were living unhappily together. Evans had been unfaithful in August 1949 and for several months his wife who had spoken of the strained relationship with her husband had been unsuccessfully trying to end her pregnancy. Although receiving Evans' basic wage Beryl Evans had not paid any rent for about four months, the hire purchase arrears on the furniture stood at about £48, the outstanding liability being over £60. At this time, when his wages were being improvidently spent, his wife's limitations as a housewife would be even more noticeable. Early in November Evans was telling his salesman, and Beryl Evans was telling her brother, that she was taking Geraldine with her for a stay in Bristol. Evans was making it clear to the salesman that he wished he had not married his wife. That his domestic life was having its effect upon him is shown in a statement made by the same salesman in 1949. He worked with Evans during the last three weeks of his employment and described Evans as highly strung, unbalanced of character, very nervous and becoming more so. Evans' employer also found him more nervous and neglectful at this time. Evans was in this state at the time of the 'terrific row' on Sunday 6th November, of which he spoke. It was on the following morning that Beryl Evans refused to see Joan Vincent, and on that evening the row continued, for Evans having threatened to slap her face took from his wife the milk bottle that she intended to throw at him. Evans was later to tell Doctor Matheson that his wife kept at it until Tuesday.

With that background, when it is known that Evans had a violent temper and on earlier occasions had struck his wife, it would not be surprising if he did use force upon her on Tuesday 8th November. That someone used physical violence on Beryl Evans in addition to the strangulation is proved by Doctor Teare's finding of considerable swelling of the right eye and upper lip. That injury was caused by a blow or blows from hand or fist, about twenty minutes before death. Evans said at Merthyr that on his return home he saw that his wife had been bleeding from the mouth and nose. He said at his trial that the blood on the pillow slip appeared to come from the mouth and nose. I find it difficult to accept that Evans seeing his dead wife and noticing, as he thought, blood from her face would also miss seeing the swelling of the face. Seeing it or seeing only blood, he could not have failed to ask why the face should be swollen or bleeding or both. He would know that such a condition would not be caused in an abortion. It is in my view no explanation to say that his wife was lying on her side or that he only saw what he was looking for. Evans on his own story never asked Christie to account for this injury to his wife. Evans also said that there was blood at the top of his wife's legs. No sign of this was found at the first post-mortem. Either Christie smeared blood there and later removed all trace of it, or Evans is lying. The other reference to the condition of Beryl Evans' body is in Mr. Baker's note reporting that Evans found his wife 'with blood all over her'. Even allowing for the figure of speech, that cannot be an accurate description. This was either Evans' lie, or an exaggeration growing out of repetition by others.

Evans had other opportunities to see his wife's body. He did not disclose until asked about it on 1st December that he had helped to carry his wife's body to Mr. Kitchener's flat the night before. He only said so when Constable Evans asked about this. He did not say then that he had also removed his wife's wedding ring. The time when he did this has never been explained. The more often Evans in any way sees or handles his wife's body the more difficult it is to explain his failure to see or ask about the injury to his wife's face or the weal on her neck.

The injury to the face was caused on Doctor Teare's estimate about twenty minutes before death. This is only an estimate. None of Christie's known victims of lustful killing showed any signs of violence in addition to the strangulation. Doctor Hobson made the suggestion in a statement which he supplied that the bruising of Beryl Evans could have been caused by someone, presumably Christie, kneeling on Beryl Evans' thigh and butting his head against her face, thereby causing the bruise on the thigh and the swelling of the face. I find this suggestion difficult to accept, or to know why Christie was doing this. It would mean that in the house, whilst workmen were in the yard and moving through the premises, some twenty minutes elapsed after the infliction of the blows and before death, and nothing is heard from Beryl Evans. If Christie was using gas on Beryl Evans the time lag could well be used for his sexual acts. But there was no trace of gas in her, and no sign of sexual intercourse. If therefore Christie was to strangle for the sake of strangling, it would be likely that he would do so immediately after striking her and not wait for twenty minutes or five minutes when screams might be heard. Equally if, as is suggested, Christie struck Beryl Evans because as he mimicked the abortionist she became a frightened or unwilling patient, the time lag is not explained. Christie never said that he struck or butted Beryl Evans in the face. No one asked him because no doubt Doctor Teare had not been asked any questions about this at Evans' committal or trial.

Besides the unusual feature of violence additional to the strangulation in a Christie killing and the unlikelihood of the time lag, the pattern of Christie's killings cannot be ignored. It is true that Christie almost invariably lied about the killing of his victims. He was always changing his story. His sense of values was so distorted that, were the facts not established, they would be difficult to believe. He could admit to a killing done for no reason at all; he could not admit that he met a victim in a public house. Therefore I pay no attention to Christie's description, standing alone, of how he killed or why he did not kill Beryl Evans.

Christie's evidence always requires to be corroborated. In 1953 Christie undoubtedly had sexual intercourse with each of the three women found in the alcove and he gassed them. His own evidence that he gassed one and had sexual intercourse with both women killed in 1943 and 1944 is probably true. The earlier murders and those in 1953 bridge the events of 1949. If as Evans said Christie killed Beryl Evans as a result of arrangements for abortion, the killing would have been a sexual crime since Christie was not an abortionist. I think that it is significant that Beryl Evans was not gassed and that there were no traces of sexual intercourse found. It may also be true that Christie did not always achieve intercourse as the staining of his clothing at the time of arrest might indicate. But in addition there is Evans' own statement that he struck his wife with his flat hand. That came from Evans alone and it shows that he saw the injured face. I think that the evidence indicates that it is more likely that Evans struck his wife in the face in a violent argument some twenty minutes before death, than that Christie struck her at such time before strangulation.

The evidence further satisfies me that the only person who mentioned that Beryl Evans had been strangled with a rope was Evans himself. He said so at Notting Hill police station. He could only have known of this because he used a rope, or because he saw a rope used or saw one on his wife's neck, or because Christie told him that a rope had been used. Evans, within minutes of his arrival at Notting Hill Police Station, said that he had used a rope. If any of the other alternatives were known to him Evans would sooner or later have said so. He never did. He sought to say that the police mentioned the rope. I do not believe it. Evans also told Doctor Matheson that he strangled his wife after a row had started over debts. I do not know why Evans said that he moved the body into the wash house on the night of the 8th November if, as I think, the body went into the wash house on or after the 11th November. Evans undoubtedly helped to move the body that night of the 8th, and at some date to the wash house. I do not believe that Chief Inspector Jennings mentioned the 8th November or any date. It must always be remembered that Evans lied easily.

It is emphasised in the three theories accounting for the making of false confessions that Evans was afflicted with feelings of guilt, and that it is the basis of the third theory that in expiation he admitted the killings although he had not done them. This condition of mind is said to have existed until after his interview with Doctor Matheson on 3rd December. It is important to relate that submission to the factual evidence supplied by Doctor Matheson, to see whether Evans was burdened with feelings of guilt when making an admission of it. When Evans saw Doctor Matheson he did not accept all the blame for the trouble with his wife. He apportioned it between the two of them. He accepted that his infidelity and his drinking had given his wife cause to upbraid him. He said that it was his wife who kept up the rows which were about debts and that his wife could not account for the mounting debts. On 3rd December, he did not mention that his being party to an abortion, or his selling the furniture or fleeing to Wales, or his neglect of the child had any effect on him. He never mentioned them save to say that he went to Wales on Sunday to his relatives and he brightened up at the mention of Wales. Since he is giving Doctor Matheson the reason why he killed his wife, and if as submitted he did not kill her but was saying that he did in expiation for his matrimonial failures for which he felt to blame, he might have been expected to speak of them.

Evans has never admitted to having had anything to do with the abortion other than passing a message to

Christie. He said that when Christie spoke of his medical training and experience in abortion he told Christie that he was not interested in the subject. He claims that he at times forbade and always discouraged the abortion. I think that his statement at Merthyr is partly true and partly false, but that the account of this conversation with Christie is true. He did not mention the abortion to Doctor Matheson on 3rd December. The only matter which could be said to be in self condemnation and mentioned on that date was that he had been drinking quite often lately. I do not see why Doctor Matheson should have been wrong in considering that Evans' conduct at his first interview was more or less that of a normal man who appreciated what was happening at the interview and the position he was in. Whereas it is said that Evans was making expiation for his conduct he did not specifically admit the killing of the child to Doctor Matheson. I do not accept that Evans was falsely admitting that he had killed his wife because he felt that he was to blame for her death, knowing full well that if he were right he was nowhere near 10 Rillington Place when she was strangled there.

I think that when Evans said that he had killed his wife he had done so. If, as is suggested in all three theories, on arrival in London Evans had a sense of guilt it was one of true guilt because he had killed his wife. When he was brought to London the shock which he received was seeing that the police had the wrappings from his wife's body and the child's clothing which until then he did not know the police possessed. That, I think, was the factor which brought about the change in his story. To Evans it would seem that the police knew it all. When Evans said to Inspector Black that he removed the ring from his wife's finger after he killed his wife, that was true. It explains why Evans gave to his mother an account of his treatment in the police station which he gave to no one else, and which was given when he knew that he had already admitted his guilt. He explained his admission by lying. It was because as he later told Inspector Black, he could not tell the truth to his mother.

It is not possible to know how Christie became aware of the killing of Beryl Evans. Whether he discovered it after hearing yet another row, or whether Evans sought his help after he had killed his wife, cannot be known. In any event, with Beryl Evans dead, Christie, who was staying at home, would have become aware that Geraldine was alone in the flat and thereby would learn that the mother was at least missing and might well have discovered her death. Christie knew everything that went on in that small house. He was known to creep about the stairs and landings. It is argued that when Christie learned of Beryl Evans' death he would have brought in the police, and prevented the discovery of his own two murders. He might have done. I think that Christie at the time may well have not wanted the police upon the premises at all. He alone knew how shallow were the graves of his victims. In place their bones were lying just below the surface of the garden. He had inadvertently dug up a femur and a skull. He was to say in his statement of 8th June 1953,—and there is only his word for this—that it was at about the time of Beryl Evans' death that his dog dug up Muriel Eady's skull. I can well believe that if Beryl Evans' body could be removed Christie might prefer that it should be for he had not killed Evans' wife. I do not think that it should be ignored that the body was bundled and roped, and not wrapped as were the three bodies found in 1953. I think there is much to support the suggestion that it was intended to remove this body on Evans' van. The bundling of it was what Professor Camps called the norm for disposing of a body. It was not as one would expect it to be if prepared for burial. But Evans unexpectedly lost his job and different arrangements had to be made. I do not know why Beryl Evans' clothing was open, but if Christie bundled up the body he would at least have had an opportunity to indulge in some kind of sexual depravity with a dead body. It would seem that Christie may have supplied the blanket which enclosed the body inside Evans' tablecloth. The absence of the knickers might point to Christie; the absence of a diaper would suggest the contrary. Neither is more significant than the other.

In so far as Evans in his two statements at Notting Hill Police Station admitted his guilt for the killing of his wife, I think, subject to errors in detail for which he is responsible, his statements of what he did are true. In making the finding that I think it more probable than not that Evans killed Beryl Evans, I think the evidence is telling, subject always to the problem of coincidence to which I later refer.

I find the evidence in respect of the death of Geraldine more perplexing. I do not believe that he who killed Beryl Evans must necessarily have killed Geraldine. They were separate killings done I think for different reasons. Beryl Evans was killed in anger. Geraldine could have been killed because her crying drove Evans to distraction. She could have been killed because of despair or because she was in the way. I attach little weight to what Evans said when in Wales about his child being alive for he was at the same time talking of a living wife, and she was dead. It is also said that Evans went to the police because he was worried about his child, and that the visit was merely precipitated by the arrival of his mother's letter. Sergeant Gough has held this view for some years. I do not agree with it. The evidence of Constable Evans is to the contrary and I prefer it. He could not get any truthful information about the child out of Evans. For an hour after making his first statement Evans prevaricated before giving Christie's name. If anxious about the child, why not immediately give to the officer Christie's name? Why not tell of the couple in East Acton and of his own visit to London a week earlier when, according to Evans, he was not allowed to visit the child? The mention of Christie's name in the Telex message is not an indication of Evans' early disclosure about Christie; it shows more how the sending of the message was delayed for an hour after the writing of the first statement until Christie's name was given. East Acton was not mentioned until several hours later. The message to Mrs. Evans was only passed after more questioning about the child by Constable Evans after 11.50 p.m. Evans did not then mention his trip to London to see the child. He could hardly have forgotten it if he had gone to the police because he was worried about the child. On the contrary he said in the next statement that he had been in Merthyr Vale since 15th November. That was a lie.

I do not think that Evans went to the police because of Geraldine. He went because his mother's letter showed that something was known and more would soon be known in London. I think Evans went to the police on an impulse. He had no money. He left his aunt shortly beforehand saying he was going to London and he went to the police instead. His unpreparedness for the visit is shown by the stupid lies told in his first statement. For some reason Evans in Merthyr Tydfil Police Station was taking steps to protect Christie in respect of the child. With each disclosure so reluctantly made, something else was held back. I think that Evans on his return to Wales committed himself to the story that his wife had walked out on him, leaving the child behind, because Christie had told him to say so. A woman abandoning her child and husband in this way would leave behind the child's pram and clothes. Christie had the pram and the clothes and any story must fit that possession. He would tell Evans that he must say that the wife had deserted the baby, for otherwise Christie could not give an explanation for holding these articles once it had been decided to say that Beryl Evans had left for good.

Evans' admission that he killed the child without blaming the man who he must have known had done it is not in my view explained by any of the three theories put forward. In all three explanations Evans is said to have been in the same state of mind when he saw Doctor Matheson as he was at the police station the night before. Evans made the fullest confession of guilt to Doctor Matheson in respect of his wife, but not of the child. I think that his admissions relating to the child in the two statements he made at Notting Hill Police Station and to Sergeant Trevallian mean either that he killed the child or that he knew all about her death. His refusal to be frank about the child with Constable Evans indicates guilty knowledge. When he told Doctor Matheson that the child was disposed of on Thursday he did not mean handed over to the couple in East Acton, he never mentioned them. He meant that Geraldine was killed on that day. The last time he had spoken of a disposal was of his wife being put down a drain. It is not without significance that when interviewed by Doctor Matheson on 3rd December Evans admits that he killed his wife; he admits that he strangled her and gives the reason for doing so. At no time—according to Doctor Matheson's notes—did he say more to the doctor about Geraldine's death than 'Baby disposed of on Thursday'.

I think that this is all bound up with Evans' remarks "Get Christie" and "Christie is the only one who can save me now" which have been referred to earlier. These were not calls to bring Christie to justice but to obtain his help. At the time when Evans was speaking in this way no one asked Evans what he meant by these words or what help Christie could give.

Mrs. Evans is certain that this was said on 15th December 1949 and not on the 5th as recorded by Mr. Baker. She says that she went round to see Christie and shouted at him 'Tim wants to see you' but a policeman moved her on. Mr. Roberts the hospital officer, who remembered Evans coming back to Brixton Prison from Court carrying newspapers and in strong language saying that Christie had shopped him, cannot remember from which Court Evans returned. I think that it must have been from the Committal Court on 15th December. Christie gave evidence on that day about the events of 8th November 1949, the day when Beryl Evans was killed and when he and Evans were together concerned in moving the body and bundling it up, the latter probably being done by Christie though Evans in a statement in Notting Hill said he did it himself. In his statements to the police made on 1st and 5th December 1949 Christie had said that he saw Evans about 7 p.m. on 8th November, and was told by him that he was going to Bristol later to join his wife, who had already gone there. Evans knew nothing of Christie's statements but could expect Christie to agree that he had seen Evans at that time. When Christie gave evidence on 15th December, having first said that he saw Evans at 7 p.m., he changed his evidence and said that he had made a mistake and thought that he had not seen Evans on that day. He went on however to tell of the noise in the night which he heard from above. Evans, as he heard this evidence, must have realised that Christie was abandoning him and as it were leaving him with both the bodies. Hence Evans' remark "Christie has shopped me" and his plea to his mother on this day that only Christie can save him. Evans could not tell the full story for he had killed his wife.

As I find that Christie knew that Beryl Evans' body was on his premises, I am sure that he would not have permitted two bodies to remain there unless he was himself involved in the killing of one or both persons. If Christie killed Geraldine, Evans either knew this at the time, learned of it later, suspected it, or was unaware of it. When Evans lost his job, the body of Beryl Evans could not then be moved. On the same day Christie alone, or in the evening Christie and Evans together decided that Geraldine must die. If it was Christie who killed her, it was to his advantage to get Evans out of London. If Evans had not killed Beryl Evans he would never have left London, nor would he have admitted to killing her and the child. Evans left London because Christie told him to go, and having killed his wife he was glad to go. He fled from his crime. What is not clear is whether he then knew that the child was dead, or whether he later learned of it. I think that it is likely that Geraldine was killed because she was constantly crying and was in the way. Whether there ever was a couple in East Acton, or whether it was Christie lying to Evans, or whether it was the cover story of both, I do not know. It may be it started with Christie saying on 8th November, according to Evans at his trial, what he would do but later deciding that Geraldine must die. Although Evans in the normal way would never have been party to such an act, or stood idly by while it was done, or done nothing when he learned of it, this was not a normal Evans, for he already had a killing to hide.

Despite those two short sentences in the two statements at Notting Hill Police Station and his remarks to Sergeant Trevallian, all of which are admissions of guilt, I am not satisfied that Evans himself killed Geraldine. I think it is more probable than not that Christie did. It was a killing in cold blood which Christie would be more likely to do. The fact that Christie until the end of his own trial denied that he killed Geraldine was because he was clever enough to know that to admit killing her would have inflamed any jury against him—first, because Evans had been hanged for her death and secondly because it was the deliberate killing of a baby in cold blood.

It was suggested to Professor Curran that a man of low average intelligence of Evans' mental calibre and character, when in a state of anxiety, who had been detained in custody, brought back to London and shown the relics of his child's clothing, might make a false confession when told for the first time that his child had been strangled. Professor Curran said that he might but for such a man to make a confession of guilt implicating himself and not the man whom he knew had committed the murder was quite outside his experience or reading. I was impressed by Professor Curran's evidence and I think it most unlikely that in the light of all the evidence Evans' statement was attributable to shock on hearing of his daughter's death as was claimed. I think that Evans knew, either at the time or shortly afterwards, what had happened to Geraldine. In either event he was helpless, as Christie knew, to do anything about it. Somehow, and I cannot on the evidence explain the reason for it, I think that Christie succeeded in persuading Evans not to involve him in respect of the child. Whether Christie threatened Evans or convinced Evans that he would be able to deal with any situation to save them both, I do not know. Any possible explanations are on the evidence no more than conjecture. But Evans I find did tell Sergeant Trevallian that the constant crying of the baby got on his nerves. He said something similar to a member of the prison staff. It could be said that Evans' apparent reliance on Christie is explained by his remark to Mrs. Ashby that Christie said that if he confessed it would be all right. It would explain how Evans whose hand had not strangled the child, could convince his sister that he spoke the truth when he said at their parting, "I didn't touch her Eileen." I doubt if Evans was truthfully reporting to his sister what had been said by Christie. Untruthfulness is always liable to be runing through much of what he says and the truth remains elusive. Like so much that he said, it may have been partly true.

It is argued that when Evans referred to the body being put down the drain he must have been quoting Christie. I agree with that. Evans must have asked Christie where the bodies were going. Christie would not tell anyone least of all Evans, that the bodies would go into the garden. When Evans went to the Merthyr Tydfil police he did not know that the body of his wife was still in the wash house; he thought that it had disappeared down the drain. Whether one or both brought Beryl Evans' body down to the wash house cannot be known, but Evans said at Notting Hill that he blocked the front of the sink with pieces of wood. By 12th November Christie had injured his back and thereafter there is no doubt that he was in great pain. He was in no condition, if minded to do so, to dig graves. Just as Evans did not bargain for or know how to meet the change in the situation brought about by his mother's letter, when all his lies were spent, so Christie did not bargain for Evans going to the police; but Christie had made his plans, and provided nothing was discovered in his garden, everything would point to Evans' guilt, as it did.

Having come to a decision on the evidence as I see it, there still exists what to many may seem the strongest reason for saying that Evans cannot have been guilty of either killing. It is the coincidence which it is claimed cannot be accepted as a fact. In human affairs few things are surprising. But can one accept that to this small house in their turn there came two men, each to become a killer, each a strangler, each strangling women always by ligature, and until Beryl Evans' death, when Christie knew what Evans had done, neither aware that his housemate was like himself? Some claim that to suggest that this coincidence could come about is to stretch credulity too far. If that be right, then any kind of inquiry becomes unnecessary, for in the absence of the testimony of an eye witness this duplication of criminality cannot be accepted, no matter how often a man admits that he did strangle and kill. It is always the instant coincidence which is said to be beyond belief. The problem of this coincidence was in my mind before the Inquiry began, and it is still present. But I think it is no solution to the problem to ignore the evidence which points to the coincidence being a fact.

I think that it would be wrong to say that any finding which upholds the existence of this coincidence must be rejected. I feel that the doubts which it raises are such that on the state of the evidence no jury could overlook it so as to be satisfied of Evans' guilt beyond reasonable doubt. I am not called upon to be so satisfied and by my findings I say that the probability is that both these men killed and that both killed by strangulation using a ligature.

Between the 8th and 14th November 1949, there were never more than four adults living at 10 Rillington Place, Notting Hill, London: Timothy and Beryl Evans, Reginald and Ethel Christie. They, or some of them, are the only persons who know for certain what happened in that house between those dates. The two women have been murdered and the two men executed. Evans has admitted that he killed Beryl Evans. He has denied that he killed Beryl Evans. He has admitted and he has denied that he killed his child Geraldine. When admitting that he killed he said that he did so by strangulation, using a ligature. Christie has admitted that he killed Beryl Evans. He has denied that he killed Beryl Evans. He has admitted and he has denied that he killed Geraldine. Christie has admitted that when he killed he did so by strangulation, using a ligature. Christie has admitted that he killed his wife; she was strangled by a ligature. He has admitted that he killed five other women; certainly three, and probably all five, were killed by strangulation, a ligature being used. Either Christie or Evans killed Beryl Evans; either Christie or Evans killed Geraldine. One fact which is not in dispute and which has hampered all efforts to find the truth is that both Evans and Christie were liars. They lied about each other, they lied about themselves.

I have come to the conclusion that it is more probable than not that Evans killed Beryl Evans. I have come to the conclusion that it is more probable than not that Evans did not kill Geraldine.

DANIEL BRABIN
D. G. STORER
(Secretary)
10th August 1966.

Timothy Evans had been found guilty only of the murder of his daughter Geraldine. As a result of this enquiry he was granted a free pardon.

He had been hanged in 1950

Other titles in the series

John Profumo and Christine Keeler, 1963

"The story must start with Stephen Ward, aged fifty. The son of a clergymen, by profession he was an osteopath ... his skill was very considerable and he included among his patients many well-known people ... Yet at the same time he was utterly immoral."

The Backdrop

The beginning of the '60s saw the publication of 'Lady Chatterley's Lover' and the dawn of sexual and social liberation as traditional morals began to be questioned and in some instances swept away.

The Book

In spite of the spiralling spate of recent political falls from grace, The Profumo Affair remains the biggest scandal ever to hit British politics. The Minister of War was found to be having an affair with a call girl who had associations with a Russian Naval Officer at the height of the Cold War. There are questions of cover-up, lies told to Parliament, bribery and stories sold to the newspapers. Lord Denning's superbly written report into the scandal describes with astonishment and fascinated revulsion the extraordinary sexual behaviour of the ruling classes. Orgies, naked bathing, sado-masochistic gatherings of the great and good and ministers and judges cavorting in masks are all uncovered.

ISBN 0 11 702402 3

The Loss of the Titanic, 1912

"From 'Mesabe' to 'Titanic' and all east bound ships. Ice report in Latitude 42N to 41.25N; Longitude 49 to 50.30W. Saw much Heavy Pack Ice and a great number of Large Icebergs. Also Field Ice. Weather good. Clear."

The Backdrop

The watchwords were 'bigger, better, faster, more luxurious' as builders of ocean-going vessels strove to outdo each other as they raced to capitalise on a new golden age of travel.

The Book

The story of the sinking of the Titanic, as told by the official enquiry, reveals some remarkable facts which have been lost in popular re-tellings of the story. A ship of the same line, only a few miles away from the Titanic as she sank, should have been able to rescue passengers, so why did this not happen? Readers of this fascinating report will discover that many such questions remain unanswered and that the full story of a tragedy which has entered into popular mythology has by no means been told.

ISBN 0 11 702403 1

Tragedy at Bethnal Green, 1943

"Immediately the alert was sounded a large number of people left their houses in the utmost haste for shelter. A great many were running. Two cinemas at least in the near vicinity disgorged a large number of people and at least three omnibuses set down their passengers outside the shelter."

The Backdrop
The beleaguered East End of London had born much of the brunt of the Blitz but, in 1943, four years into WW2, it seemed that the worst of the bombing was over.

The Book
The new unfinished tube station at Bethnal Green was one of the largest air raid shelters in London. After a warning siren sounded on March 3, 1943, there was a rush to the shelter. By 8.20pm, a matter of minutes after the alarm had sounded, 174 people lay dead, crushed trying to get into the tube station's booking hall. At the official enquiry, questions were asked about the behaviour of certain officials and whether the accident could have been prevented.

ISBN 0 11 702404 X

The Judgement of Nuremberg, 1946

"Efficient and enduring intimidation can only be achieved either by Capital Punishment or by measures by which the relatives of the criminal and the population do not know the fate of the criminal. This aim is achieved when the criminal is transferred to Germany."

The Backdrop

WW2 is over, there is a climate of jubilation and optimism as the Allies look to rebuilding Europe for the future but the perpetrators of Nazi War Crimes have yet to be reckoned with, and the full extent of their atrocities is as yet widely unknown.

The Book

Today, we have lived with the full knowledge of the extent of Nazi atrocities for over half a century and yet they still retain their power to shock. Imagine what it was like as they were being revealed in the full extent of their horror for the first time. In this book the Judges at the Nuremberg Trials take it in turn to describe the indictments handed down to the defendants and their crimes. The entire history, purpose and method of the Nazi party since its foundation in 1918 is revealed and described in chilling detail.

ISBN 0 11 702406 6

The Boer War: Ladysmith and Mafeking, 1900

"4th February − From General Sir. Redfers Buller to Field-Marshall Lord Roberts … I have today received your letter of 26 January. White keeps a stiff upper lip, but some of those under him are desponding. He calculates he has now 7000 effectives. They are eating their horses and have very little else. He expects to be attacked in force this week … "

The Backdrop

The Boer War is often regarded as one of the first truly modern wars, as the British Army, using traditional tactics, came close to being defeated by a Boer force which deployed what was almost a guerrilla strategy in punishing terrain.

The Book

Within weeks of the outbreak of fighting in South Africa, two sections of the British Army were besieged at Ladysmith and Mafeking. Split into two parts, the book begins with despatches describing the losses at Spion Kop on the way to rescue the garrison at Ladysmith, followed by the army report as the siege was lifted. In the second part is Lord Baden Powell's account of the siege of Mafeking and how the soldiers and civilians coped with the hardship and waited for relief to arrive.

ISBN 0 11 702408 2

The British Invasion Tibet:
Colonel Younghusband, 1904

"On the 13th January I paid ceremonial visit to the Tibetans at Guru,
six miles further down the valley in order that by informal discussion
might assure myself of their real attitude. There were present at the inter-
view three monks and one general from Lhasa ... these monks were
low-bred persons, insolent, rude and intensely hostile; the generals, on the
other hand, were polite and well-bred."

The Backdrop
At the turn of the century, the British Empire was at its height,
with its army in the forefront of the mission to bring what it saw
as the tremendous civilising benefits of the British way of life to
what it regarded as nations still languishing in the dark ages.

The Book
In 1901, a British Missionary Force under the leadership of
Colonel Francis Younghusband crossed over the border from
British India and invaded Tibet. Younghusband insisted on the
presence of the Dalai Lama at meetings to give tribute to the
British and their empire. The Dalai Lama merely replied that he
must withdraw. Unable to tolerate such an insolent attitude,
Younghusband marched forward and inflicted considerable
defeats on the Tibetans in several onesided battles.

ISBN 0 11 702409 0